Solutions for Secretaries of Small NPO's

Solutions for Secretaries of Small NPO's

A guide for nonprofit corporate secretaries and administrative assistants. Learn how to build a first class image on a third rate budget.

Gene L Warner
www.solutionsforsecretaries.com

Published in the United States by

BoysMind Books
www.boysmindbooks.com

Book Description: A practical guide for volunteer secretaries of nonprofit organizations, with an emphasis on creating and maintaining a first class image, even with a third rate budget. Information includes how to form a nonprofit corporation and receive IRS recognition, governance and parliamentary best practices, fundraising, membership recruitment and retention, volunteer recruitment, and practical approaches to the development of low cost but highly effective desktop publishing and graphics arts capabilities.

Publishers Cataloging in Publication Data

    Warner, Gene L.
        Solutions for Secretaries of Small NPO's, A guide for nonprofit
            corporate secretaries and administrative assistants who want to
            build a first class image on a third rate budget – First Edition –
            Published August 2007
        p. cm.
        Includes index
        ISBN: 978-0-9797896-1-8
        1. Nonprofit Organizations – Management. 2. Directors of
    Corporation. 3. Philanthropy.   I. Warner, Gene L. II. Title

HD62.6.W36 2007
658.048 – dc22
                                   BISAC: BUS074000
                                   LCCN: 2007903960

Author Website address: www.solutionsforsecretaries.com

To you ...
A dedicated and tireless volunteer.

If we did all the things we are capable of
we would literally astound ourselves!
Thomas Alva Edison

Table of Contents

Section 5: Desktop Publishing

Section 6: Graphic Arts

Section 7: Fundraising Basics

Section 8: Mustering Manpower

Section 9: Doing I.T.

Section 10: Conclusion

Index

About the Author

—— ⚜ ——

Notes and Disclaimers

Examples and templates supporting this book are provided the *SfS* website; www.solutionsforsecretaries.com. You are invited to visit the site to make use of its content as instructed in this book. Anything found on the site may also be freely downloaded and employed for personal or nonprofit use. Access to this material is not contingent upon purchasing a copy of this book. The material available for download is provided without charge, as is, and with no warranties of any kind.

Comments regarding this book are invited, and may be sent by email to gwarner@solutionsforsecretaries.com. Please report errata using the link provided for that purpose at the *SfS* website. Technical support is not available for the *SfS Database* application, the *SfS Website Template* application, or any of the other solutions offered in this book. You are invited to share questions and answers and discuss problems and solutions with the reader community by participating in the *SfS* forum at the *SfS* website.

Allusions to commercial and nonprofit enterprises found in this book are provided for information purposes only, and should not be construed as endorsements by this book, or by those organizations for this book. The author has no proprietary or other commercial interest in any of the organizations mentioned.

To simplify and clarify illustrations and examples, this book invents an incorporated nonprofit organization named *Friends of the Manitous* with the URL *www.friendsofthemanitous.org*. *FotM* is purely fictional. Similarities with real organizations are unavoidable, but coincidental, and should be disregarded.

— ❧ —

Foreword

When asked to write a foreword for this new book, I thought, "Oh, my! Yet another book on nonprofit management." What could I say? It seemed to me that there is already a complete selection of books like this on the market; maybe even too many. I did, in fact, point to my library on the shelves that cover the back wall of my office, where many of them can be found.

But my curiosity got the best of me. I've been distantly acquainted with the author for several years, but wasn't aware he had any degree of interest or expertise in the area of philanthropy and nonprofit management. What a small world!

So I agreed to have a look at a draft copy of the book.

Surprise, surprise! This book *was* different. Books of this kind are usually written for established organizations of moderate size, else address one particular aspect of nonprofit management or governance. The few that do talk about starting and managing small nonprofits are usually so general in scope and simplified in content that they are really not very helpful.

This book, however, is tightly focused on very small, all-volunteer organizations, yet is comprehensive to the extent that it might better be thought of as a handbook, manual or desk reference. It doesn't devote much space to theory or philosophy; instead, it provides common sense solutions to the challenges little nonprofits have to cope with day in and day out. When it does occasionally wax philosophical, the discussion is light, sometimes comical, and the advice is always practicable.

The focus is refreshingly direct and sensible. Little nonprofits almost always have the same problem: not enough money to work with. Because money is tight, it's tough to develop an image that engenders the sort of confidence and enthusiasm that encourages generous financial and volunteer support. Thus, the lack of adequate funding and staffing therefore remains a problem, inhibiting programs, brand development and growth. It's a Gordian knot that's not easy to cut, but this book shows how to do just that.

I can confidently recommend this book to its intended audience; board members and other volunteers who are struggling to make their little nonprofit meaningful and viable. The book provides downloadable extras such as simple office systems, a relational membership database and an instant website; tools valuable enough to justify its purchase all by themselves.

With perhaps a little tongue in cheek, I can even recommend this book to those involved in larger organizations, many of whom will benefit from its very practical approach to the handling challenges common to organizations of all sizes. In large organizations we're often apt to forget the value of innovation and resourcefulness, and in those situations this book can serve as a very effective refresher course.

Congratulations on your decision to add this book to your bag of tricks. Within these pages you're going to find lots of valuable resources – and also a lot of fun!

> ❧ Invitation: Do you have standing in the world of philanthropy or nonprofit governance and management? Have you distinguished yourself in a way that might be relevant to readers of this book? Claim this foreword, or write your own.

— ❧ —

Preface

Most American nonprofit organizations are small. Unfortunately, most of the administrative functions necessary to success aren't scalable. To survive, achieve any meaningful success in accomplishing the mission, and to grow, a little NPO must ably grapple with the same issues as any other organization. Meanwhile, small NPO's are typically run by an all-volunteer executive board. Serving on the board of one of these small NPO's pays nothing, is usually a thankless job and doesn't do much to enhance one's resume. Thus, it's usually difficult to get anybody to serve, let alone people who, by virtue of their education and experience, are up to the task. New officers and directors very often come to the table having no real concept of what they need to know, but don't. Herein lies the reasons why small nonprofits often languish after the initial exuberance wanes.

What volunteers need to know is not secreted as privileged information. Books, seminars and conference sessions on relevant topics abound. If these tend to be rather expensive, there is a wealth of free information available to anyone interested in searching it out on the Internet. But then there is the problem of sorting through what is directly appropriate and useful, and what is mostly academic, irrelevant given the particular situations at hand, or just plain bad information – outdated, inaccurate, incorrect, or otherwise faulty. All this can consume more time than volunteers may be willing or able to invest, and not everyone is interested in or good at doing this sort of research.

This was exactly my situation as I entered upon my first adventure as a volunteer officer and director of a small, dying nonprofit. I hadn't volunteered; I *was volunteered*, being blind-sided in front of an annual meeting by my nomination for election as the corporate secretary. It was an awkward moment. I didn't want the job, yet there were no other takers. Although the surprise nomination was inappropriate, I was reluctant to decline after it was immediately seconded, and enthusiastically "thirded." I rationalized not having enough backbone by thinking perhaps I was just what the doctor ordered, since the organization really needed to be put out of its misery; meaning disbanding and dissolution. As an experienced businessman, I knew I would be able to handle that gracefully. When my colleagues on the executive board didn't agree, I decided that my *Plan B* would then be to figure out what had led the organization to failure, and see if we could turn it around. Four years later, the corporation had been completely reorganized, was engaged in meaningful and rewarding mission projects, its membership was expanding, and contributions had increased tenfold.

What I learned in the process has been put into this book. My purpose is to help you help your organization to succeed in a similar way, but without your having to re-invent the wheel. You can read this book from cover to cover in a day or two, and you'll then be in possession of everything I learned over my four-years of service as that organization's corporate secretary. After that, it will serve as a handy desktop reference until you develop a style of your own and a degree of expertise that will relegate it to irrelevance.

Introduction

What's this stuff all about, and who needs it?

This book is for the person doing the office work of a small nonprofit organization. That job has a variety of titles, such as Corporate Secretary, Administrative Assistant, Executive Secretary, or even just "Clerk."

In small organizations, the job is often held by an elected volunteer director, or a volunteer staff member. People who are skilled in this area, who have experience in administrative work, know how much time and effort is involved, so usually do not volunteer for these positions. Those who do are therefore often unpleasantly surprised when they find that out the hard way. They wind up investing much more in the job than they ever dreamed would be necessary, or if they're not willing to put that much into it, do a poor job, which makes the whole experience unpleasant and unrewarding.

On the other hand, a skilled and experienced person might take on the job, especially one who is retired and looking for something interesting and rewarding to do. But they are likely to experience culture shock when they discover that the norms of the familiar business setting do not fit the small nonprofit paradigm. In a commercial setting, it often makes sense to spend money to save labor costs. That rationale doesn't work in small nonprofits, which are usually served entirely by volunteers. Quite to the contrary; the goal is to maximize the amount of money spent on mission, and minimize what is spent on running the organization. Without much of a budget, it seems impossible to do the job right, so their personal goals are not met, and they're happy to leave the job when their term is up.

The operative phrase in the previous paragraph is "seems impossible." If you are in this position, you can in fact do a great job without spending much money.

If you've come into this job without much previous experience, what's in the following pages will show you everything you need to know. If you have previous experience in administrative work, this is a good time to change your mind about how things should be done. There are no secrets or slick schemes involved. You need only be willing to be innovative and resourceful, and to make use of the many resources available to nonprofits.

Not in a nonprofit situation? That's fine too. Many grant-funded services and commercial businesses get into the habit of rationalizing overhead spending on the basis of nebulous labor savings. This is especially easy when times are good, things are going great, and people feel too busy to worry about the small stuff. Waste, however, adds up, and when times aren't so great, it isn't as easy to justify continued spending on frills. The following pages provide simple ways to achieve the same things without special expenditures, so you are sure to find the book useful.

— ❦ —

1

Setting Up Shop

Okay, so what do I need, and
what do I need to know?

— 🍃 —

1
Setting Up Shop

Prerequisites

"... a first class image on a third rate budget?"
How could that be possible?

The components of the solution are (1) a desktop PC, (2) a connection to the Internet, (3) the proper software, and (4) your creativity and resourcefulness. If you're up to speed in the first two departments, you may skip the next two paragraphs.

Computer Literacy

According to the U.S. Census Bureau's 2003 data, 62% of U.S. households had one or more computers, and 88% of these were hooked up to the Internet. As far back as 1995, Newsweek reported that 89% of U.S. teens were routinely using computers, and more than two-thirds of them regularly used the Internet. There was little difference between economic classes, but some difference between genders, boys being somewhat more likely than girls to be engaged with computers and the Internet. Since computer prices and the cost of Internet access have plunged during the past several months, these percentages are without doubt, now much higher.

If for some reason you are not skilled in the use of computers and the Internet, you need to decide either to catch up to the culture, else decline the opportunity to handle your organization's administrative duties. Your interests might simply not compel you to get involved with technology. If this is the case, it is not likely that you'll find administrative work challenging and rewarding anyway. Age may explain why, thus far, you haven't had to become involved, but it is no excuse for not learning now, since people well into their golden years have taken up the challenge, and even become power users. Almost every senior center, library and school system offers free workshops especially designed for senior citizens. Feeling somewhat intimidated by your grandchild, who plays the PC keyboard like a fine-tuned piano? Turn that into an opportunity to spend some quality time together, as he or she teaches you how to use the computer, and surf the web.

The Desktop Computer System

The computer system should be a "Win/Tel" desktop type; in other words, a regular PC running the Windows operating system. An older Pentium type running Windows 98SE (Second Edition) is fine. Newer systems are nice because they're faster and have much more memory and storage space; they usually come with Windows XP.

Your system must also have a very good ink-jet printer. If buying a new printer, check the online reviews to find out about print quality and ink consumption. The conventional marketing strategy is to sell the printer for cheap, then soak users with high ink prices. As for print quality, good photo printers are not always the best text printers; choose a printer that does a good job on both text and images. In particular, see how the printer produces the color gray. Printers that produce gray by dithering black are often the better choice, as compared with those that attempt to produce the color gray by using the colored inks. Duplex printing (printing both sides of a page) should be as convenient as a selection in the "Print" dialog box properties, with the printer driver controlling the process (as opposed to you having to figure out how to re-feed the pages for the second pass). Be especially particular about the paper transport system, making sure it works reliably with various weights of paper, cover stock or card stock, and envelopes, always feeding the material squarely, never crookedly. The margins of full text pages should always be perfectly parallel to the left edge of the paper.

A flat bed scanner is also very handy. You'll be able to scan photographs for your newsletters, and can use the system as a copy machine. Scanners are now often integrated with printers, so often involve little extra cost.

The Internet Connection

Internet connections are either dial up or high-speed.

Dial-up service is provided by connecting any regular telephone line to a device in your computer called a "modem" (stands for "modulatedemodulate"). Regular telephone lines are designed to carry audible electrical signals, so modems are used to convert the computer's digital signals to audible signals which can travel over the telephone lines, and the signals it receives from the telephone line to digital signals for the computer. This system is called dial-up because when you wish to go online, your computer actually places a call to a service that will connect you to the Internet. The advantages of this approach include its easy setup, low monthly cost, and security. The main disadvantages are its relatively slow speed, and the fact that it ties up the telephone line. While connected in this way, you cannot place or receive calls with your telephone, since the line is busy.

A high-speed internet connection is nice to have, since your system is constantly connected, and the Internet is always immediately accessible. These connections are provided by your local telephone service, or your local cable system. The telephone service uses your existing ordinary telephone line, but through a special add-on service called "DSL" (stands for "digital subscriber line"). No special telephone wiring is required, and your telephone service is not affected in any way by your Internet connection; you can make and receive calls while simultaneously accessing information on the Internet. A high-speed connection can also be provided through the same cable system that is connected to your television, without affecting television reception in any way. The chief advantage of DSL and cable, other than the fact that you are permanently connected so the Internet and your email service is always instantly available to you, is the high speed at which data is transferred. Web pages and email attachments download quickly. The chief disadvantages are that these systems are somewhat more difficult to get up and running and the monthly cost is higher.

For our purposes, the difference in speed between the various DSL and cable choices probably isn't significant. At the time of this writing, the monthly prices are about the same, although they are changing rapidly because the market has become very competitive. If you use a cellular phone, you might not have a regular telephone line, so would probably find it cheaper to go with cable. In either case, with these connections your computer is permanently connected directly to the internet as an open station, and is readily available to any hacker who happens to discover your vulnerability. To prevent that, include a device called a "router," which will act as a firewall between your computer and the Internet connection, keeping snoops and intruders out.

The Software

Here are the programs you'll need:

- Microsoft Office Professional
  - Word
  - Excel
  - Access
  - PowerPoint
- Corel PaintShop Pro
  - Alternate: IrfanView (freeware)
- NoteTab Pro
  - Alternate: NoteTab Lite (freeware)
- CoreFTP Lite (freeware)

Optional:

- ClickToConvert
- Adobe Acrobat

Microsoft Word is the word processing application in Microsoft Office, and will be the workhorse of your office. Instructions for the many desktop publishing ideas presented in this handbook are based upon Word. Since Word also provides the best spelling and grammar checkers, you'll also prefer to use it even for the more mundane tasks, such as drafting newsletter articles, writing letters, composing long email messages, and so on. You probably already know how to use Word, but if not, it's not difficult to grasp a basic understanding of how it works. After that, you can learn about its many advanced capabilities over time, as you need them.

Microsoft Excel is the spreadsheet program. If you're the Secretary/Treasurer, Excel is a great way to keep track of the checkbook. Otherwise, you might use this program only to keep track of your reimbursable expenses. Excel can also be used as a simple flat file database, and if your membership is very small, might be your choice for managing your membership list and mailing lists. Templates for all these suggested applications are provided on the *SfS* website, with explanations and instructions that will show you how they can be used.

Microsoft Access is the relational database management system (RDBMS). The advantage of keeping your information in a relational database is that you then have the capability of compiling lists by selecting records on the basis of values in certain fields. For example, you probably will not want every name in the database to receive a newsletter, since a single copy will ordinarily suffice for households with two or more members. Or perhaps you'd like a list of those who made contributions during the last quarter. You can easily create lists of those whose "receives_newsletters" field is checked, or those whose "contribution" field contains a value ">0" (greater than zero) between a "starting_date" and an "ending_date."

Microsoft PowerPoint is called presentation software. PowerPoint has become the de facto standard for conducting meetings, seminars, workshops, and so on. If you have attended such events, you have probably already seen what PowerPoint slides look like, and how the material is organized and presented. That's the main purpose of PowerPoint – to help you organize your material, and present it effectively in any of these ways:

- Manual Electronic Slide Show
- Self-Running Electronic Slide Show
- Overhead Transparencies
- 35mm Slides
- Handouts
- Web Document
- Pack 'N Go (a PowerPoint player that works on any computer)

PowerPoint, run as a manual slide show, is a very effective way to engage groups in tasks such as evaluating and approving the corporate charter or bylaws. It's much easier to keep everyone interested and on-topic when their heads are up, with their attention focused on the matter at hand (as opposed to heads down, browsing and reading paper handouts on their own). If nothing else, you might choose to use PowerPoint as an easy way for the President to manage the agenda during your annual meetings.

Corel PaintShop Pro is an image editing tool. It can handle photographs and drawings in virtually any format, and is a very reasonably-priced alternative to the industry standard Adobe Photoshop. PaintShop Pro started out as a very simple little shareware program, and has developed over the years to a poor man's equivalent of Photoshop. You'll use this program to prepare pictures and illustrations for insertion in Word documents, PowerPoint presentations, and your web site. It'll permit you to do things like crop, sharpen, lighten or darken your pictures, and save them in a format appropriate for printing or use on a web page. But in addition to these mundane uses, PaintShop Pro has all sorts of other capabilities, such as the ability to easily create feathered edges, drop shadows or picture frames, to remove backgrounds and replace them with something else, to remove red-eye, fix damaged photos or restore old faded images, and lots more.

IrfanView is a freeware image viewer with basic editing capabilities. It's a quick and easy way to handle very basic operations such as crop, sharpen, resample, create transparent backgrounds and save in a different format. It's also a much more handy way to view collections of images. You can easily browse through a collection of photos, create contact sheets, and run slide shows manually or automatically. Even with PaintShop Pro installed, you'll find that IrfanView is handier as the default image viewer on your computer.

NoteTab Pro is a shareware text editor; a much more capable replacement for the NotePad program that comes with the Windows operating systems. NoteTab is handy for certain scratch-pad uses, but its real value arises from its usefulness as a web page HTML editor. Small organizations need simple, easily-maintained web sites, and the most direct way to achieve that is hand coding. Web publishing tools like Microsoft's FrontPage are great for large projects, but are not cheap, and typically involve steep learning curves. Furthermore, hand-coded content can be maintained on any standard UNIX (or LINUX) web server, using free web-based web site management clients or FTP programs. NoteTab Lite is the freeware version. Those on a very tight budget may choose this version, but it lacks some of the features that make the Pro version so useful; namely the powerful search and replace capabilities, and color-coded text, which visually separates plain text from HTML tags.

ClickToConvert is a marvelous print driver type application that automatically converts Microsoft Office documents to HTML-coded pages for your web site. For example, if you type up the minutes for a meeting in Word, a click of the ClickToConvert icon on Word's toolbar generates a HTML version that displays exactly like the ".doc" format file produced by your printer. You will otherwise spend hours converting such documents to HTML manually, and the results will not even be as good as what ClickToConvert produces in just a few seconds. Office applications themselves offer the capability of saving documents in HTML format, but the results are rarely acceptable. ClickToConvert can also convert Office files to Adobe PDF format.

Adobe Acrobat converts files of all kinds to PDF, which stands for "Portable Document Format." This preserves the visual integrity of documents so that they can be viewed and printed on a variety of platforms (WinTel, Mac or UNIX/LINUX) using Acrobat or the free Adobe Reader software. This is often the best way to make original documents available as e-mail attachments or for download from the Internet. Besides being universally compatible, PDF files are usually more trustworthy than native file formats; Word's ".doc" files, for example, being capable of carrying macro viruses. Many applications are now capable of converting documents to PDF. In fact, Adobe even provides this capability as a free online service. However Acrobat provides the additional capability of managing multi-page documents, creating fill-in forms, and more.

CoreFTP Lite is a utility program similar to Windows Explorer that will provide easy access to your files and folders on a remote web server. You'll use this handy utility to maintain your web site. With CoreFTP Lite you can easily upload, download, move, rename and delete content.

Where to Get the Software

Name brand software makers donate software products for nonprofit users through an organization called "TechSoup.Org – The Technology Place for Nonprofits." For Microsoft Office and Adobe applications, visit http://www.techsoup.org/ and click on "TechSoup Stock." A small, usually negligible, administration fee is usually charged for each product.

Corel sells PaintShop Pro online as a download. Nonprofits qualify for discounted education pricing. Go to http://www.corel.com and visit the Corel Education Store (or Google "Corel Education Store.")

Download IrfanView (say "EarfanView") from www.irfanview.com. It's free, and contains no advertising banners or other nuisances.

NoteTab Pro is available online from http://www.notetab.com for just US$19.95. You can download NoteTab Lite from the same site.

You'll find CoreFTP Lite at http://www.coreftp.com. The regular free version is "Core FTP LE 1.3c."

Click-To-Convert is offered direct from its New Zealand maker as a download from http://www.clicktoconvert.com. A discounted price is available to nonprofits upon application from the web site's ordering page.

If you're a registered 501(c)(3) charitable organization, as of this writing, the total cost for all of the above, procured from the sources listed, is less than US$130.00!

OpenOffice.org

OpenOffice.org 2.1, an open-source project sponsored by Sun Microsystems, is a multiplatform and multilingual office suite. Compatible with all other major office suites, the product is free to download, use, and distribute. It's *Writer, Calc, Base* and *Impress* components are alternatives to Microsoft's Word, Excel, Access and PowerPoint applications mentioned above. Although not exact replacements, the OpenOffice.org applications are very impressive in terms of capabilities, ease-of-use and document compatibility, and even offer a few handy features not provided by the Microsoft applications. For example, documents can be saved as PDF, the conversion being done perfectly and almost instantly with no special setup. Get it free from http://www.openoffice.org/.

Other Office Essentials

Here's a short list of tools, materials and supplies that will come in handy. Except for the paper cutter, these things are all inexpensive. Search Internet price comparison sites to find bargain sellers, and buy at the low price. The classic Ingento #1142 15" paper cutter retails for about $160, but sells new online for as low as $112 and is usually available on eBay for half of that. A low end home use imported 18" x 15" paper cutter sells for as low as $13.75 at the online wholesaler web site www.edmwi.com.

- 15" Paper Cutter
- Glue Stick
- 5" Snap-Blade Box Cutter
- Stapler (Palm Size "Flat Clinch" - MAX HD-10DF)
- 10" Scissors

Staple items include:

- 20# printer paper for general purpose use
- 24# paper for booklets and special projects
- #10 business size envelopes for letters
- 9" x 12" manila envelopes for documents you don't wish to fold
- 110# card stock premium (ink jet) grade
- 67# cover stock for booklet covers
- staples (MAX 10-5M: Mini Staples for Flat-Clinch Stapler)

Sections 5 and 6, which cover desktop publishing and Graphic Arts projects, call for these additional specialty materials, which you may purchase as needed:

- 9' x 12" self-adhesive laminating sheets (Avery 73603)
- clear 6" x 6" PVP shrink bags (papermart.com 3636066)
- glossy poster board (Staples)
- No. 5-3/4 remittance envelopes (actionenvelope.com 17889)

2

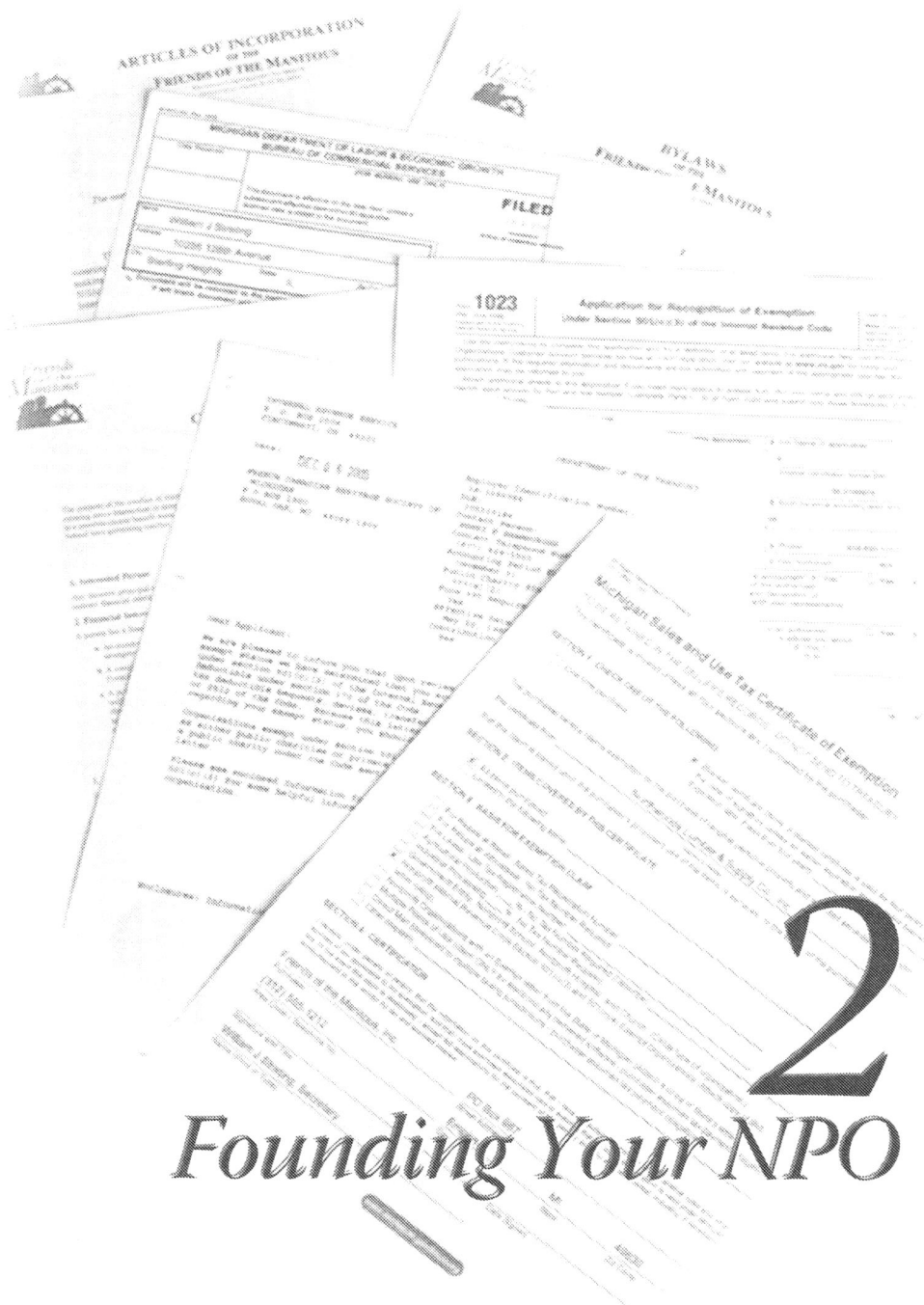

Founding Your NPO

The beginning is the most important part of any work ... for that is the time at which it's character is being framed. – Plato.

— ❧ —

2
Founding Your NPO

The Reality Check

Starting a nonprofit is the easy part –
keeping it going is the hard part!

This probably sounds somewhat less than credible if you've never had the experience of founding a corporation or serving on the board of an established organization. Other texts often suggest that you need to hire attorneys and spend a lot of money in order to do the founding job properly, but that isn't usually necessary. For new fledgling organizations, dismissing the bootstrap approach (a.k.a., the do it yourself approach) isn't very sensible.

If you are creating a small organization from scratch, you can do everything that needs to be done yourself, spending only a few hundred dollars on fees and materials. Before deciding to invest more than that, this is a good time to think about the future of your new organization. If this conversation is meaningful at this point, you're probably in the steering committee phase. How sure are you about its chances of success? How dedicated are the people on the committee. How dependable?

Your cause might be wonderful, your intentions admirable and your dedication laudable, but that's what they all thought – all the people who founded the thousands of little nonprofits that file their information updates year after year and pay the $20 fee (Michigan), but accomplish little else. Engineers are cliché for naiveté in this respect, often thinking that the product they created is so wonderful that it will sell itself. Founders of nonprofits sometimes mistakenly think the same thing; that their cause is so worthy that good people everywhere will flock to it.

You are actually founding a business, and all the same rules apply, for profit or not. You'll have to sell your agenda successfully to others, and probably in a very competitive environment. As a rule of thumb, nine out of every ten new businesses fail within ten years. The usual reason is sales. They either didn't have, or didn't acquire, the necessary marketing and sales skills, else misjudged the potential of their idea, finding that the market didn't share their exuberance about the product or service they brought to it.

This is the era of the X-Generation. "GenXers" are people who have little interest in the intangible rewards of altruism and delayed gratification, and evaluate opportunities by asking themselves, "What's in it for me, right now?" It's therefore easy to understand why civic engagement is on the wane. Whether this is good or bad is irrelevant. This is simply a fact of life; the environment your new organization will live in. Assuming that you will depend upon voluntary contributions of money and manpower, these are the people you'll have to sell your agenda to.

This hard sell situation is further complicated by competition. Everyone receives pitches similar to yours every week, and they're all worthy, perhaps even more deserving than yours!

The benchmark for a conventional business is earnings. If there are none, the business is obviously a failure. Failure is not fun. In most cases all of the original investment is lost, and a burden of debt remains even after the assets are liquidated.

Nonprofits, on the other hand, have no tangible benchmark. Nonprofits can continue to exist forever, whether they actually do anything or not. There is no law that says you have to accomplish anything, other than to keep your registration current with your state's corporate division. If your receipts are zero, you can trim your expenses to zero, or to whatever you're willing to pay out of pocket, and still go around proudly passing out your business cards. The fact is that many little nonprofits are doing little more than that; not because they want to, but because they're unsuccessful, and nobody has the courage to face that reality, nor the heart to finally pull the plug.

Unless you're intentions involve the creation of a multi-million member global organization, spending a lot of money on start-up is most likely either an extravagance or an ego trip. If an extravagance, think about what that tells you about the probability of your being a good steward of other people's donated money. You should start thinking about cost-effectiveness (how much bang you can get for each buck) and your cost-mission ratio (maximizing the percent of revenue you spend on mission).

If an ego trip, maybe you should just forget the whole thing.

Having said all that, to get your corporation up and running, you'll need to call some official organizational meetings and do these five things:

- Create a mission statement.
- Draft your corporate charter and bylaws.
- File your Articles or Incorporation .
- Obtain an EIN number (a.k.a FEIN; Federal Employer ID Number).
- File for recognition of exemption with the IRS.
- Apply for exemption from state sales tax.

A search of the Internet will turn up all sorts of helpful information in each one of these five areas, making it readily possible for you to fulfill these requirements for yourself, if that is your choice. You can spend as much time on these things as you wish, or you can treat them each as necessary start-up tasks that need to be gotten out of the way in the most efficient and expeditious manner. Towards accomplishing that, consider the following guidelines.

— ❧ —

Original Organizational Meetings

*Disciplined and businesslike organizational
meetings help build a solid foundation.*

The Founders

Ideas for new organizations do not usually just materialize out of the blue. They more often arise from existing activities which have grown to a point where those involved sense a need for a higher degree of organization. The original organizational meetings should ordinarily be open to everyone with an interest. Offer that opportunity by providing general announcements in appropriate places. People who have previously been involved and are enthusiastic about the project should be personally invited to participate. These are the people who are likely to become engaged as founders; people who are willing to volunteer their time and talents, and also contribute the money needed to cover the early expenses of the project.

Although there is no need at this point for rigid formality or close compliance with parliamentary procedure, a businesslike decorum is appropriate, and will help ensure that things start off on the right foot. Founding meetings can be conducted as follows.

The First Meeting

The first organizational meeting can be called to order by someone previously designated to play that role; usually the person primarily responsible for making the arrangements up to that point. The first order of business should be the election of a *chairman pro tem*. After the newly elected chairman takes the chair, a *secretary pro tem* should then be elected to record the minutes.

The chair can then call upon key individuals to make their case for the creation of the organization. Others can be called upon to ask questions or share comments and opinions. After a reasonable time for discussion, someone should offer a resolution proposing a definite action. For example: *"Resolved, That it is the sense of this meeting that (fill in the type and purpose of the proposed organization) now be formed."* This can then be debated, amended and ultimately voted up or down. This does not actually do anything more than serve as a formal statement of the group's intentions. It does not actually create the proposed organization.

If the resolution is adopted, a motion should be offered authorizing the chair to appoint a committee to draft a corporate charter and bylaws for the proposed organization. Another motion should authorize the committee on bylaws to provide copies of their proposed bylaws to all who will attend the second organization meeting. Expenses at this point will have to be covered by personal funds, so provisions like this should always be included to allow individuals to be reimbursed later on. At this point, a general discussion of the proposed organization's purposes, structure and other issues that might be helpful to the bylaws committee is appropriate. This is a good time to draft a mission statement for the organization, or to assign that additional task to the committee.

If it is not already established as a *res ipsa loquitur* matter, the names of those who will be listed as incorporators (or founders) on the Articles of Incorporation should be determined at this time. Most states require only one incorporator, but provide space to list others, all of whom must usually sign the state form before it is submitted. Being listed as an incorporator is mostly an honorary thing, since the title involves no real legal or fiduciary obligations beyond the point where the organization is operating with its own duly elected or appointed board of directors.

Prior to adjournment, a motion to set the date, time and place for the second organizational meeting should be offered and adopted. Because of the uncertainties likely to exist at this point, it is appropriate to simply vote to meet again *"at the call of the chair,"* or *"at such time and place as the chair deems appropriate."*

The Second Meeting

The second organizational meeting is a very business-intensive and exciting event, which results in the actual creation of the organization.

The first order of business is the reading, revision if necessary, and approval of the minutes of the first meeting.

The second order of business is to receive the report of the committee on bylaws, which involves the consideration and adoption of the proposed bylaws. This will be a lengthy process, since the articles must be considered one-by-one. The corporate charter must be considered first, then the bylaws. Each article is individually read, discussed and amended, if needed, then the document is voted up or down as a whole. (If, during this process, it becomes clear that the documents need much more work, a motion to recommit is in order, and the meeting can adjourn with a motion for a third organization meeting.)

Having adopted the corporate charter and bylaws, the enrollment of *charter members* comes next. Those wishing to join the organization at this point may register with the secretary pro tem, providing their signature as a commitment to abide by the bylaws and for the payment of dues, if any. This roster will be filed as part of the organization's original records.

The new membership roll is then read, and the chairman pro tem then calls for the election of permanent officers, as provided for in the bylaws. After the election, the newly elected officers take charge, dismissing the temporary ones.

Motions should now be offered directing the chief executive officer to file for incorporation with the state, obtain an FEIN number for the organization, and to file for recognition of exemption with the IRS.

The final organizational meeting will usually be adjourned to the next regular meeting, as now provided for in the bylaws.

—— ❧ ——

The Mission Statement

The fewest words can achieve the greatest impact.

So much has already been said about the importance of having a good mission statement that there are actually people who specialize in this field. A good mission statement is said to be essential to keeping everyone on the same page, and is often credited will all sort of other magical and mystical qualities.

Be that as it may, what will you say to someone who asks, "What does your organization do?" How many times have you asked that, eliciting a rambling, incoherent response that never seemed to answer the question? It's nice to have a brief, concise response readily available. Besides saving a lot of time and hot air, it creates the impression that you really know your stuff.

Even if your organization actually does lots of things and engages in lots of seemingly different activities, you'll find it possible to come up with a brief statement that says it all if you think about it long enough. How long should that be? Here's the goal: plan on printing your mission statement on the back side of your business cards in eight point text. That

> The *Friends of the Manitous* helps preserve the history and cultural traditions of Michigan's Manitou Islands. We assist in the collection and preservation of knowledge about the Islands, develop and distribute educational and interpretive materials and programs, promote the proper care and maintenance of historic and cultural assets, and serve as volunteers assisting the Sleeping Bear Dunes National Lakeshore in the delivery of rich visitor experiences.

will limit you to about sixty-five words. Here's an example:

This is actually a rather lengthy statement. However, although the organization chose to mention several related, but different, activities, they were all included in a single paragraph. Never use line breaks and never, ever use bulleted or numbered lists.

Once you have a concise, compact mission statement, you'll find all sorts of places to use it. Besides the backs of your business cards, other possibilities are on letterheads and envelopes, contribution envelopes, contribution acknowledgements, newsletter address panels, and even on certain legal forms, such as your Articles of Incorporation and IRS Application for Recognition of Exemption. Long, messy statements are unsuitable for such uses, and should therefore be rejected.

— ⚜ —

Branding Tools: Logos & Tag Lines

The practical application of image

A mission statement serves as a verbal snapshot of what an organization stands for, or what it does. But what is the organization really like? How earnest and effective is it? Can it be trusted to use donated funds and gifts responsibly? Is it open and inclusive?

What's "Brand"?

"Brand" refers to a distinctive image that identifies an organization and the goods and services it produces and distributes. The word is current Madison Avenue vernacular for what used to be called corporate image.

Until recently, the word was used much more narrowly to differentiate products, and would usually bring to mind specific trademarks or slogans. It is now used in a much broader context, referring to all the characteristics, tangible and intangible, that make an organization and the products and services it offers, unique. That aspect is discussed at length in the *Fundraising Fundamentals* section, which comes later.

Logos and tag lines (or trademarks and slogans) are fundamental components of any brand, which serve as identity-building tools. Because you'll want to begin building your brand recognition immediately, try to come up with these tools before you begin to design anything that will be disseminated outside your office.

Creating the Logo

Once you have a logo, you'll use it everywhere – on letterheads, memos, formal documents, envelopes of all sizes, shipping labels, brochures, certificates, newsletters, pamphlets, booklets, checks, web pages, monogram license plates, tee shirts, coffee cups, bookmarks, signs and whatever else you can think of. In fact, as a matter of policy, every item you generate and distribute, no matter what the purpose, should carry your logo.

With that in mind, two fundamental requirements become immediately apparent:

- It must be scalable.
- It must not depend upon color.

You'll need to shrink or enlarge your logo to suit many different applications. For example, from small enough to use on a monogrammed promotional pencil, to as large as you might use on a sign or banner, or the back of a tee shirt. Logos that contain a lot of text, light characters or intricate detail will not work well when scaled down. As the image shrinks, line widths also diminish, with the result that text becomes illegible and fine features disappear completely.

In many simple applications, your logo will be printed in black and white, or grayscale, or a single color, so designs that depend on color combinations can become a problem or add cost. Multi-color designs are acceptable only if they also work well when rendered monochromatically.

The May 15, 2003 35th Anniversary American Icon issue of *Rolling Stone Magazine* ranked the above as the eight best logos of the past thirty-five years. There are thousands of great trademarks and logos, but these are clearly representative of designs recognized around the world. Here's some of the thinking behind the development of these marks:

- The *Nike* logo swoosh design was actually intended to represent a wing of Nike, the Greek goddess of victory, thought to be an eminently appropriate motif for a marketer of athletic equipment. It was designed in 1971, netting its designer Carolyn Davidson the handsome fee of $35.

- Adapted by *Apple* Computer's founders from an originally much more complex design featuring Sir Isaac Newton sitting beneath an apple tree, the multicolored once-bitten apple was inspired by the biblical Adam and Eve story, the apple being the fruit of the Tree of Knowledge. The rainbow design was soon abandoned for a solid color version.

- The *Starbucks* logo was based on an old sixteenth-century Norse woodcut, the two-tailed (originally bare-breasted) mermaid, or siren, representing the seductiveness of the coffee itself.

- *McDonald's* golden arches evolved in the 1960's when the two separate arches that made the original hamburger stands a familiar landmark were merged together to form an "M."

- The *Coca-Cola* logo, carefully rendered in script according to the 1866 handbook *Spencerian Key to Practical Penmanship* by the new company's bookkeeper, became the company's official trademark in 1887. It originally included the words "Delicious and Refreshing" beneath. The classic curved coke bottle was added as a background in 1915 to form the most recognized and enduring trademark ever.

- Fred Smith started *Federal Express* in 1971 to provide overnight delivery of time-sensitive documents and freight. The name originated from his plan to guarantee the survival of this risky venture by contracting with the Federal Reserve System to carry checks and money orders to clearing centers to enable faster processing. That plan never worked out; however the name "Federal Express" became as synonymous with "guaranteed overnight delivery" as "Coke" is to soft drinks. The company was soon popularly referred to as "FedEx" by its customers. The corporate name was changed accordingly, and current logo was adopted to represent the many corporate units now operating under the FedEx banner, the purple "Fed" part followed by a different color "Ex" for each division of the company. Many fail to notice this logo's other distinctive feature; the forward-pointing arrow embedded in the "Ex."

- Hugh Hefner, the creator of *Playboy* magazine, once explained, "I selected a rabbit as the symbol for the magazine because of the humorous sexual connotation, and because he offered an image that was frisky and playful. I put him in a tuxedo to add the idea of sophistication. Since both *The New Yorker* and *Esquire* use men as their symbols, I felt the rabbit would be distinctive; and the notion of a rabbit dressed up in formal evening attire struck me as charming, amusing and right."

- *IBM* is the successor to the Bundy Manufacturing Company, begun in Auburn, New York in 1888. The company grew through several name changes, The International Time

Recording Company (ITR), The Computing-Tabulating-Recording Company, The International Business Machines Corporation, and finally, on New Year's day in 1947, "IBM," as the company was then popularly referred to anyway. The eight-bar logo first appeared on the company's System/370 mainframe computers in 1972. Designed by preeminent graphic designer Paul Rand, horizontal stripes replaced the formerly solid letters to suggest speed and dynamism. The logo is usually rendered in blue, reflecting the company's nickname, "Big Blue," which probably arose from the cabinet color of its large mainframe computer systems.

There are lots of resources available in literature and online that can help you design a *good* logo. But as you can see, *great* logos are more often the result of evolution and serendipity than intentional design. Your task is to come up with a distinctive, but simple, graphic that minds can readily learn to associate with your corporate image. This is a creative process, and as such cannot be engineered or scheduled. You might consider brainstorming sessions or design contests, but even with several heads working on the problem, it might take a while for the best idea to suddenly appear.

Stock Logos

The projects in Sections 5 and 6 require logos of various sizes. To simplify the projects, make them up in advance so they'll be immediately available. Ideally, the aspect ratio of your logo (ratio of width to height) will be 1:1; however values from 4:3 to 3:4 will work fine:

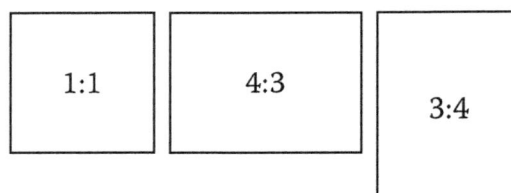

1:1	4:3	3:4

After designing your logo, scan it if it is not already in digital form and then, using IrfanView or PaintShop Pro, resize or resample your original to create these sizes:

width	resolution	used on
1.25 ins	300 dpi	brochures, booklets, newsletter, letterhead
1.0	300	newsletters, business cards, note cards
1.0	300	rotated 90-deg for regular envelopes
1.0	300	rotated 180-deg for card envelopes

.625	300	membership cards
180 pixels	72	your website

Saving these files in PNG or JPG format will ensure that their mechanical size will be preserved when inserting them into Word documents.

Tag Lines

We used to call them slogans. But that term took on a rather banal character, and was further stigmatized by criticisms of "empty slogans" during political campaigns. So we now call them "tag lines." Tag lines serve the same purpose as logos, but do it in words instead of pictures.

An eye-catching logo is intrinsically of little value, until observers are trained to associate lots of positive qualities with that particular image. In the absence of that visual trigger, a memorable and preferably catchy phrase can elicit the same positive response. For example:

> *Nike –"Just do it!"*
> *Apple – "Think different."*
> *Starbucks – "Romancing the bean."*
> *McDonald's – "I'm Lovin' It."*
> *Coca-Cola – "It's the real thing."*
> *FedEx – "The World On Time."*
> *Playboy – "Entertainment for men."*
> *IBM – "Solutions for a small planet."*

Our mental storage system arranges things according to frequency of use, and our minds talk to us in sentences. In writing tag lines, the challenge is to come up with something easily associated with a variety of common thoughts and/or concepts related to what you do, so that those general thoughts will bring your tag line to mind. That mental sentence will then elicit an image of your logo, and all the positive feelings associated with it. That's why logos and tag lines very often appear together.

Tag lines can be meaningful in their own right, but it's difficult to achieve that with the required economy of words. An example is Coke's slogan, *"It's the real thing,"* which disparaged Pepsi and other competitive colas as cheap and unequal imitations. That 1971 tag line, which ended the *"Things go better with Coke."* era, was integrated with a touching little song, *"I'd Like to Buy The World a Coke,"* to become one of the most popular ads ever created after the song became a top ten hit. At that point it was hard to think of cola without the little song playing back in the mind, which ended with the tag line, "It's the real thing – Coke."

A different kind of example is Nike's *"Just do it!,"* three little words appearing in 1988 which had very little meaning with respect to the company's products, but linked up quite well with the swoosh logo. Nike's market is youthful – energetic, full of dreams and aspirations, impatient and avidly sexual. The tag line merges images of grit and determination with suggestions of passion, and with a bit of tongue-in-cheek humor. The almost instant result was that Nike's image became "kewl," which is all it takes to dominate youthful markets.

> ❧ Note: Another example of serendipity, the Nike tag line was coined by Dan Wieden of the Wieden & Kennedy agency during a meeting in 1988 with his first and biggest client. At the time, Nike served only the top of the market – professional athletes and fitness aficionados – while Reebok was rapidly running off with all the rest of it. Full of admiration for the company's positive attitude after hearing the client's employees confidently explain their strategy for capturing a bigger share of the market, Dan said, *'You Nike guys, you just do it!'*. Quite without intention, he'd come up with one of the most successful tag lines of all time.

As you look at the above list of tag lines, you'll realize that some work, some really haven't. For example, if you had previously encountered *"Entertainment for Men,"* would you have immediately associated that with Playboy? It says exactly what the magazine is, of course, but it doesn't immediately bring the rabbit to mind. *"Solutions for a small planet."* sounds pretty cool, but does it suggest IBM – or AT&T?

As with logos, coming up with a great tag line is a creative process. The difference is that tag lines are verbal, so the words could come to you in a dream, during your commute, or otherwise out of the blue. The mind doesn't seem to like to be creative by decree, so the harder you think about it, the less likely it'll be that you'll come up with anything useful. The advice is: keep this in the back of your mind, and remain open to the power of suggestion.

> ❧ Note: AT&T's tag line, by the way is "Your world. Delivered." Another shoulder-shrugger. Hmm – 'My world, delivered?' Seems more suggestive of pizza. ("It's not delivery, it's DiGiorno!")

Articles of Incorporation

*A legal document registering the structure
and purpose for your organization with your state.*

Also called the "corporate charter" or "certificate of incorporation," this sounds like it should be a document printed on a piece of parchment with a fancy glided border. Actually, it's just a state form in most cases. Fill it out, vote its approval, and send it in with a $20 bill attached (or whatever the fee is in your state). The state will rubber-stamp it and, *viola*, you're a corporation! If you wish to transcribe the information from the form to your own formal document, that's fine too.

The Articles of Incorporation will be your document of highest authority. It supersedes all other rules, and no other rules you make may conflict with this document. Once filed by the state, you may not independently change anything in the Articles of Incorporation. If changes become necessary or desirable, you must file an amendment with the state. Therefore, it is generally unwise to include anything but the minimum of essentials in the Articles, leaving everything else bylaws, or policy and procedure manuals.

Corporate charters are often drafted by the same committee that writes the bylaws, and must be adopted in the same way as the bylaws, usually at the second founding meeting. After adoption, they can be submitted to the state for registration and filing. The state's corporate division will review your form to make sure it has been filled our correctly and completely. If so, it will be "filed." That does not infer anything about your organization other than the fact that you know how to fill in the form and had enough money to pay the filing fee. The state officials will not concern themselves with the merits of your organization, whether or not your purposes seem sensible or even useful, or whether or not you have a right to exist.

Here's an example of the information required on a typical state form (Michigan), and a brief explanation of what's being asked. The forms also include their own instructions, which clarify most issues.

Article I asks for the name of your organization as you wish it to appear on formal records. For example, you might enter "Volunteer NPO Secretaries Association." If the state accepts your application, "Incorporated" will be inferred, so you need not include that word.

For *Article II*, enter the mission statement you created above. For IRS purposes you might wish to attach a full statement of your organization's purposes.

The answers for questions asked under *Article III* are probably obvious. As a nonprofit, you will be organizing on a nonstock basis, so you can say that and enter "0" under item 2, if you wish. For item 3a, "real property" means real estate (i.e., land and buildings). For 3b, "personal property" is generally anything other than real estate, such a computers, machinery, and furniture and fixtures. For 3c, simply say where you intend to get the money needed to finance the agenda you entered in Article 2. This could include membership dues, voluntary contributions, and

Articles of Incorporation

ARTICLE I
The name of the corporation is:

ARTICLE II
The purpose or purposes for which the corporation is organized are:

ARTICLE III
1. The corporation is organized upon a (Stock or Nonstock) basis.
2. If organized on a stock basis, the total number of shares which the corporation has authority to issue is _____. If the shares are, or are to be, divided into classes, the designation of each class, the number of shares in each class, and the relative rights, preferences and limitations of the shares of each class are as follows:
3. a. If organized on a nonstock basis, the description and value of its real property assets are: (if none, insert "none")
   b. The description and value of its personal property assets are: (if none, insert "none")
   c. The corporation is to be financed under the following general plan:
   d. The corporation is organized on a (Membership or Directorship) basis.

ARTICLE IV
1. The address of the registered office is: (Street Address) (City) (ZIP Code), Michigan
2. The mailing address of the registered office, if different than above: (Street Address or P.O. Box) (City) (ZIP Code), Michigan
3. The name of the resident agent at the registered office is:

ARTICLE V
The name(s) and address(es) of the incorporator(s) is (are) as follows:
    Name Residence or Business Address

I, (We), the incorporator(s) sign my (our) name(s) this day of _____,

Name of person or organization remitting fees:
Preparer's name and business telephone number:

ADDITIONAL ARTICLES

CERTIFICATION

fundraising projects. Under 3d, a "membership organization" is one where the ultimate authority rests in the membership, who ordinarily exercises that authority by electing officers to serve on a board of directors. A "directorship organization" may have members, but all authority rests in a board of directors (or "board of governors," etc.) who are appointed by the founders, then by successive boards. Your corporation will probably be organized on a membership basis.

Article IV reflects the practical need for a responsible agent with a permanent physical address. Think of this in the context of legal matters. Suppose someone decided to sue your corporation. Who would be served with the summons and complaint? Or suppose you forget to file the required information updates; who would the state's corporate division contact? Board members change, post office box numbers change, etc. Boards of small corporations also seldom have a legal officer. So, the state would like to have a reliable name and address on file, and this will usually be your attorney and his office. If you are on good terms with a lawyer friend, ask if they would be willing to be listed as your resident agent and registered address. Since this seldom involves anything more than receiving and passing on an occasional piece of mail, your friend will very likely be willing to do this without charge, especially if you're willing to steer some business their way, should you ever have need for legal representation. Otherwise almost any law firm will be willing to provide this simple service for a small annual fee.

Under *Article V* you can put the names and address of your organization's founders or incorporators. This is simply a matter of record, and perhaps personal prestige. Persons listed here are under no obligation whatsoever. To get to this point, you have probably made use of a steering committee, formally or informally, so those who have participated in that most wholeheartedly might appropriately permit their names to be listed here for the record. On the other hand, only one name is usually required.

You can include additional articles as considered necessary or desirable. For example:

- Article II: Purpose or Purposes of Your Organization (Full Statement)
- Article V: Activities Not Consistent With Tax Exempt Status
- Article VI: Prohibition Against Political Activities
- Article VII: Indemnification Of Directors & Officers
- Article VIII: Limitation Of Personal Liability For Volunteer Directors
- Article IX: Assumption Of Liability For Acts Of Volunteers
- Article X: Conflicts In Governance Documents
- Article XI: Dissolution

In this list, Articles V, VI and XI are needed to support your application for tax exempt status. The language used should comply with the suggested language provided in IRS Publication 557, *Tax Exempt Status For Your Organization.*

Most states limit the liability of nonprofit corporate directors and officers. In general, the officers, directors and members of nonprofit corporations are not personally liable for the acts of the corporation or each other. Any liability is generally limited to the assets of the corporation. Some states allow nonprofit corporations to assume much of the personal liability of their directors and to indemnify their officers and directors for certain acts. Where available, this protection can be invoked by including declarations such as Articles VIII, IX and X in your corporation's articles of incorporation. The requirements can usually be found in various sections of your state's nonprofit corporation act. As a shortcut, search the Internet for organizations incorporated in your state that publish their corporate charter online, and extrapolate from the boilerplate provisions used in the several examples you are able to find.

The statement provided in Article XI simply clarifies that the corporate charter takes precedence over any and all other corporate documents, including bylaws, resolutions, policy and procedures manuals.

Most states provide this form online in an Adobe PDF fill-in format. Check your state's corporate division to see what's available (search example: Google "articles of incorporation" California form).

As mentioned above, you may, for your own purposes, type up your Articles of Incorporation as a more formal, or more readable, document. Examples of both a state fill-in form and a corresponding formal rendition are provided on the *SfS* website.

Information Updates

Having successfully filed your articles, you must keep your information up to date by filing some sort of information update form, usually each year. Your state will probably send this form to your registered agent when needed. Several states, including Michigan (see https://www6.dleg.state.mi.us/corpsfilings/), now make it possible for you to do such filings online, and prefer that you do so.

— ❧ —

Bylaws

*Rules for the conduct of your
corporation's business and affairs.*

Bylaws are simply the basic rules and game plan for your organization. Think of the U.S. Constitution as the bylaws of the United States of America. Your bylaws should define how your organization is structured and how it should generally operate. For example, the bylaws will define who can be accepted as a member and what each member's duties and responsibilities are. They will also define the makeup of your Board of Directors, and the process used to elect or appoint board members.

Writing the Bylaws

In the best of all possible worlds, a committee would be formed for the purpose of drafting your bylaws. In the real world, that job will probably fall to you. Forget about hiring a lawyer. Since bylaws are typically very organization-specific, attorneys who are not intimately associated with your project would not know what would be appropriate for your organization, and would have to get most of their information from you.

If you're interested enough to have read this far, you are probably quite capable of preparing the original draft. Begin with the proper mind-set, and you'll do just fine. What is the proper mind-set? Think about openness, inclusiveness and fairness.

Confidentiality within your organization should be limited to matters involving sensitive personal information. Secrets are otherwise almost always an attempt to conceal questionable practices or outright wrongdoing, to keep people from finding out about embarrassing mistakes, or to protect one's turf. Never engage in questionable practices or wrongdoing and you'll have no need to be secretive. Honest mistakes are forgivable; we all make mistakes, personally and corporately. Turf wars are poisonous games that never have any winners. For problems of this nature, therapy will work better than secrecy.

Every organization has some people who feel they are privileged insiders, or somehow more equal than others. That's just human nature. As you work on your bylaws, take care that what you craft will not inadvertently give any individual or faction an advantage over any other. One of the hallmarks of parliamentary law is the principle of protecting the interests and rights of minorities. The person who is elected President and

Chief Executive has a special role to play in service to the organization. Beyond that, they are no more important or essential to the organization than even the most newly recruited member. The unfortunate reality is that over time the same old people will make up a small cadre of the most active participants. That can easily develop into what appears to be a seniority system or insiders club. What is written into the bylaws should make it clear that everyone is equally valued, and eligible for the same opportunities.

Before you begin, you should consider these points:

1. The bylaws must conform to the Articles of Incorporation. They might contain provisions that seem to duplicate what is already stated in the Articles, but may contain nothing that conflicts. In the event of a conflict, the Articles always rule, since they have standing as a legally registered document.

2. The bylaws must ordinarily be approved by a vote of the general membership, and once that happens, things written into the bylaws can thereafter only be changed by a vote of the general membership. The bylaws should therefore only address matters that are important enough to justify that process. These would be matters involving the organizational integrity of the group and the protection of minorities within the organization. You should not include mundane operational details that are more appropriately defined in a policies and procedures manual.

3. The bylaws should not include what are generally referred to as "rules of order," except for details that might be needed to address something that is peculiar to your organization. Most of the decision-making for your organization will occur within the context of meetings, and it's always in everyone's interest that meetings be conducted in a manner that is efficient and fair to all who participate. By convention, this is accomplished by employing parliamentary procedure. Include a provision in your bylaws saying which manual of parliamentary law will be your organization's *parliamentary authority*. After doing that, you need only include *special rules of order* that might be needed to supplement or modify rules contained in that manual.

Robert's Rules

Of the several manuals in existence, Robert's Rules of Order is, by far, the accepted standard. While others attempt to simplify (e.g., the *Democratic Rules of Order*, published in Canada by Fred and Peg Francis), the detail in Robert's has developed over the 130-years since it was first published, from practical experience with real organizations. You might never have any occasion to refer to this manual, except when disputes arise. Then its detail is likely to be helpfully definitive.

Robert's is not necessarily as procedurally complicated as it looks. The manual advises, in fact, that strict procedural compliance isn't always necessary or appropriate. Quoting an opening paragraph in the book: *"In small boards and committees, parliamentary rules apply, but certain modifications permitting greater flexibility and informality are commonly allowed."* As your organization grows, you'll be able to grow with it as a parliamentarian under the authoritative guidance of Robert's Rules, which is clearly the definitive parliamentary manual for U.S. corporate organizations. Robert's is therefore recommended over other possible choices.

Robert's Rules of Order Newly Revised provides a very helpful chapter on writing bylaws, which includes an example that you will find useful as a template for your organization. An example is also provided on the *SfS* website.

Final Adoption

The proper adoption of your bylaws will be a high priority item on the agenda of the organization's second organizational meeting. The motion to adopt the bylaws is considered so important that the proposed bylaws must be considered on an item-by-item basis, and then a two-thirds majority is required to pass it.

This raises an interesting conundrum; a two-thirds vote by whom? The bylaws establish the criteria for membership, so until they are in force, how can there be any membership? The answer is simple. The bylaws are adopted by the meeting, with all in attendance who wish to do so being eligible to vote. Immediately thereafter, the meeting is recessed for the purpose of registering those who voted as "charter members." When the meeting is called back into session, it proceeds under the newly adopted bylaws, with participants then voting as members.

The Board, the Bylaws and the Rules of Order

Once the bylaws have been adopted, they might very well languish in the archives without anyone ever having any reason to study them again. The salient points, such as the schedule for regular meetings and board meetings, and matters related to elections, are usually well understood and easily remembered. Most people are also familiar enough with the rudiments of parliamentary procedure to be able to conduct and participate in orderly meetings. Members usually become interested in the bylaws and rules of order only when disputes arise.

Most small membership organizations are actually run by an executive board. The members exercise their power by voting for the officers who will make up the board of directors. Unfortunately, it is not usually easy to recruit board members who will take the job seriously and become engaged in the mission and management of the organization. Even if you are able to recruit willing nominees, the next challenge is to ensure that they take up their duties with the proper leadership perspective.

Board members should understand that they have been entrusted by the membership to perform a certain essential function, not elected as a reward for their seniority, participation or generosity. Elected officers must also know that their proper role involves loyalty and service to the organization and its membership, not to themselves, or any faction within the organization.

Lucky is the organization that has well briefed, high caliber people serving as its board of directors. In that environment, small organizations can operate quite comfortably, efficiently and effectively without rigid adherence to the documented rules and protocols, and people problems are likely to be few and far between.

EIN Registration

All business entities in the U.S. are identified for tax purposes by this serial number. The number is assigned by the Internal Revenue Service, but is now also used by many states in lieu of the sales tax licenses previously issued. Thus *EIN* has come to be a misnomer; it's neither an employer number nor a tax license number per se.

Why Register?

Your organization may never employ anybody, nor sell anything subject to the collection of sales tax. Moreover, all purchases by nonprofits are sales tax exempt in most states, so why would you need an *EIN* number? Some important reasons are:

- Your organization will need bank accounts, at least for deposits and checking. When opening such accounts on behalf of the corporation, your bank will require you to provide this ID number.

- If your annual receipts ever exceed $25,000, you will have to file a tax return with the IRS, and the number is required on such filings.

- In order to take advantage of your exemption from sales taxes, sellers will usually require that you provide them with a certification that you are indeed a legitimate nonprofit corporation. You will need an EIN number for such certifications.

- If your mailing list ever exceeds more than a few hundred people, you will want to take advantage of bulk nonprofit rates. Before issuing you a permit, the USPS will require proof that you are a registered nonprofit organization.

- If you decide to apply for grants, similar proof is also usually required.

How to Register

Register your organization using IRS Form SS-4. This is a simple form which you can fill in by hand, or fill in and submit online. There is no fee, and in most cases an EIN number will be returned immediately. Go to the IRS website *www.irs.gov/businesses* and click on *Employer ID Numbers*.

Using the online fill-in form is convenient, and will provide you with a nicely formatted and legible copy of the application for your records. Although the application is basically simple, as with most IRS forms, a few of the line items are somewhat less than intuitive. Therefore read the instructions prior to filling out and submitting the form, to ensure that it will be accepted on the first pass.

Some of the items which might remain somewhat vague even after reading the instructions are these:

Line 2: Type the legal name of your organization in box 1. Since you do not do business under any other assumed names, mark "N/A" in this box.

Line 3: Enter the name of your resident agent shown on your Articles of Incorporation. Do not enter the name of one of your officers, which is subject to change with every election.

Lines 5a and 5b: Enter the physical address of the registered office shown on your Articles of Incorporation.

Lines 7a and 7b: The principal officer at the time of filing will probably be your President. Enter that person's name and social security number, as it appears on their personal tax returns. Accuracy is important here, since these lines are automatically verified when using the online form to see if they correspond. If not, the application will be rejected.

Line 8: Check "Other nonprofit organization" and write in what kind (e.g., "educational organization," "amateur sports association," "boy scout troop," "historic preservation society," "friends of the ... organization," etc.)

Line 9: Usually check "Started new business" and enter "nonprofit corporation." Another reason, if your organization is such that there is never likely to be a tax liability (no employees; no significant income), might be "Banking purposes."

Line 10: Enter the filing date the state stamped on your Articles of Incorporation.

Line 11: Select "DEC" if your fiscal year is the same as the calendar year; otherwise enter the last month in your fiscal year.

Line 12: Unless you have paid staff, enter "N/A" on this line.

Line 13: If you entered "N/A" in line 12, enter "-0-" in each box on this line.

Line 14: Check "Other" and say what kind (e.g., "nonprofit fair housing advocate").

Third Party Designee: Leave this blank – this section is not applicable.

A filled-in example of this form is provided on the *SfS* website.

Application for Recognition of Exemption

Becoming a "real nonprofit" – a "501(c)3."

The full title for this section should be *"Application for Exemption Under Section 501(c)(3) of the Internal Revenue Code."* Section 501(c)3 describes *public charities* and *private foundations*. Examples include religious, educational, charitable, scientific, and literary societies or associations. Also included are nonprofit organizations whose purpose is testing materials or products for public safety, to foster national or international amateur sports, or the prevention of cruelty to children, the elderly or animals.

> ❧ Note: Most public benefit and religious corporations should apply for exemption under Section 501(c)3 of the Code. Other classes of organizations range from 501(c)1 through 501(c)28, and beyond, covering special cases such as cemetery associations, labor organizations, farmers co-ops, child care organizations, social clubs and fraternal organizations, and so on. This conversation is limited to conventional, publicly supported nonprofit organizations. If you think your corporation might be something other than that, you should read *IRS Publication 557, Tax-Exempt Status for Your Organization* before going any further.

The Value of Achieving 501(c)3 Status

As far as the IRS is concerned, this is about exemption from federal income tax for your corporation, and deductibility for certain contributions you may receive from others. As far as you are concerned, the application process would probably not be worth the bother were it only about those tax benefits. Under the current law, your organization will be tax exempt anyway so long as your average annual receipts do not exceed $25,000. Until your annual gross receipts exceed $5,000 your organization will be treated as described under Section 501(c)3 of the code anyway, without having obtained a *letter of recognition* from the government. You could therefore rightly claim that donations to your organization were deductible under Section 501(c)3 of the Code. But that won't mean much to most donors in any case, since most provide small amounts, and use the standard deduction rather than itemized deductions when filing their own income tax.

The real value of recognition is that you will generally not be perceived by others as a legitimate nonprofit organization unless you can produce a copy of a letter from the IRS to prove that you have been formally recognized as a 501(c)3 organization. In addition to enhanced credibility, recognition will provide these additional benefits:

- exemptions from state corporate, sales and use taxes
- price discounts when purchasing equipment, materials and supplies
- lower interest rates on borrowed money or financed purchases
- reduced postage rates for bulk mailing
- eligibility for grants from the government and other organizations

Conditions and Restrictions

The exemption for your corporation is considered by the government as a privilege, not a right. Furthermore, it is not something that is granted once, and then continues on in perpetuity. Accordingly, to achieve and maintain exemption under 501(c)3, your organization must initially meet certain requirements and comply with some explicit restrictions, then continue in that mode into the future. Because the Senate Finance and House Ways and Means Committees, in a cooperative effort, have recently moved to crack down on abuses, the IRS has become more discriminating in considering new applications and the validity of existing determinations.

In general, you will have to convince your *EOS* (Exempt Organization Specialist, the person at the IRS who will evaluate your application) that your corporation is (1) *organized and operated exclusively* for exempt purposes, (2) that it will not permit any earnings or any other financial benefit to inure to private individuals, (3) that it will not carry on *substantial* lobbying activities, and (4) that it will *absolutely* not participate in campaigns to elect candidates to public office.

The EOS will expect to find appropriate restrictions cited in your corporation's charter, including appropriate provisions for disposition of any assets in the event of its dissolution. You must therefore be sure that your Articles of Incorporation explicitly addresses these issues, and that any other exhibits you might include with your application contain nothing that might suggest a real or potential conflict with any of these basic restrictions.

The Application Process

Nonprofit public benefit corporations apply for recognition of exemption by filling out *IRS Form 1023*. This is a multi-page form, which collects a lot of information about your organization. You must also include:

- a conformed copy of your Articles of Incorporation
- a copy of your bylaws, if bylaws have been adopted prior to application
- a check in the amount of the applicable user fee

The IRS may also request additional attachments to clarify or substantiate details included on your application, such as:

- representative copies of your advertising
- copies of your publications
- copies of papers expressing your views on proposed legislation
- copies of leases, contracts or agreements

Your application will not be processed unless the required fee is attached. Incomplete applications are usually returned without being processed, along with a letter explaining why, and giving a deadline for resubmission. Your money will not be returned. If your revised or amended application is not returned prior to that deadline, the application will be treated as a new application, and dated accordingly. Naturally, the appropriate fee must also accompany the new application.

The Application Fee

"User fees," as the IRS calls them, have been increased with the June 2006 revision of the form. If your actual or estimated gross receipts are not expected to exceed $10,000, the fee is now $300; otherwise it's $750 (was $150 and $500). The non-refundable fee must be included when you mail your completed application.

Private Foundation or Public Charity?

By definition, a "foundation" is a kind of philanthropic organization, set up by either individuals or institutions as a legal entity, usually either a corporation or a trust, with the purpose of distributing grants to support causes in line with its expressed charitable interests. Foundation funds are usually derived from endowments. In popular use the term "charity" is often used as a synonym for voluntary, nonprofit organizations that raise funds to provide some public service or support to the disadvantaged in society. The distinction between what is popularly understood to be a foundation, and what is popularly referred to as a charity, is the source of the organization's funds. Foundations are formed to leverage existing money for charitable purposes, often money derived from estates of the wealthy. Charities are formed to raise new money for charitable purposes.

The IRS will presume that your organization is a *private foundation*, unless you give notice within 15-months after its original legal inception to the contrary; namely that you are a *public charity*. The main distinction between these two categories is that public charities must be able to show that they have broad public financial support. The IRS will otherwise assume that the money is coming from one, or a few, private sources.

The main difference between these two categories, as far as tax exempt status is concerned, is that private foundations are liable for certain taxes on investments, and subject to certain operating restrictions and income distribution requirements. Private foundations will not be exempt from taxes, nor will contributions to them be deductible, unless provisions recognizing these additional rules are included in their Articles of Incorporation. IRS Publication 557 gives examples of the appropriate provisions.

The significance of your filing date is that the IRS rules provide that organizations filing for recognition within 15-months of their legal inception can use financial support received within that early period to demonstrate that they are a publicly supported organization. If you can make your case in a timely manner, you may receive a *definitive ruling*. On the other hand, if you can convince your EOS that your organization can reasonably be expected to meet the support requirements, you will receive an *advance ruling* that you are a public charity, or publicly supported organization.

"Publicly supported" generally means that you receive at least a third of your total revenue from government or the general public. The IRS calls this its *one-third support test*. Alternatively, if you can show that you have (1) substantial government and public support (which is taken as at least 10% of your total revenue), (2) a program for attracting government or public support on an ongoing basis, and (3) favorably met at least some of an additional *five public support factors*, you may meet what the IRS calls its *facts and circumstances test*.

If you are, in fact, organizing what is essentially a foundation, then you would obviously seek recognition as such. If, as is more likely, the purpose of your organization is to promote or support particular interests and causes through volunteerism and fundraising, then you most certainly should seek recognition as a public charity.

If you are recognized as such under an advance ruling, the IRS will give you five tax years to accumulate experience that will show you are indeed publicly supported. This does not mean that your recognition is temporary, only that your status, private foundation or public charity, has not been settled. At the end of your advance ruling period, the IRS will send you a letter asking you to fill out and return a copy of IRS Form 8734, *Support Schedule for Advance Ruling Period.*

To ensure that you will be able to successfully make your case when that time comes, you will need to be a conscientious record keeper, recording individual contributions of all kinds, including membership dues, cash donations, receipts from the sale of fundraising items, in-kind donations and non-reimbursed expenses. Record the dates, the amounts, and the name and address of each donor.

Filling Out Form 1023

IRS Form 1023, *Application for Recognition of Exemption Under Section 501(c)3 of the Internal Revenue Code* – the title itself is enough to intimidate the uninitiated. The June 2006 revisions are current versions of the form and its instructions. The form itself is 27-pages long; the instructions are another 38-pages long. There isn't any question as to your qualifications and capabilities. There are thousands of little nonprofits, and someone like you has done this successfully time and time again. But there also isn't any question that the application process is labor intensive and time consuming. According to the *Paperwork Reduction Act Notice* included in the instructions, the estimated average hours involved are:

- Recordkeeping   89.4 hrs
- Learning about the law or the form   5.2 hrs
- Filling out the form   9.7 hrs
- Copying, assembling and mailing the form   0.5 hrs

That's a total of 104.8 hours. Were you to hire a tax attorney or accounting firm experienced in such applications, that time could probably be cut by more than half. But you would still have to provide them with a lot of information, and 40-hours of their professional services would probably cost you at least $5,000!

Obviously, the sensible approach is to bite the bullet, and resolve to do the application yourself, realizing that it's not going to be easy, and will take at least a week or two of concentrated effort.

Having decided that, the form and instructions can be downloaded from www.irs.gov, the IRS web site. Just enter "1023" in the box at the top of the opening page and click the Search button. Both are available in Adobe PDF format; the form is provided in the fillable PDF format, so you can fill it out neatly on your computer, and save it as you work.

Line-by-Line Help

Because of the difficulty of the process, and the importance of achieving 501(c)(3) status, the following detailed walk-through is provided as an example of the application task. The form that accompanies this example can be found at the *SfS* website. To see how this discussion relates to the finished product, you might choose to download and print the filled-in form.

Part I ~ Identification of the Applicant

- Enter the name of your organization as it appears on the Articles of Incorporation form you filed with the state. If you have obtained a post office box as a permanent mailing address for your organization, you may use that. Otherwise give the name and address of your resident agent *("c/o Name")* and registered office as also shown on your Articles of Incorporation.

- You must provide an employer identification number *(EIN)*. If you don't yet have one, refer to the previous discussion about *FEIN Registration* and obtain this number.

- The accounting period (or fiscal year) is often the regular calendar year, so the answer here would be *"12."* There are many reasons why some might choose differently however. For example, an organization that holds officer elections at their annual meeting might choose to have their fiscal year end on or about that date, terminating with the outgoing board. If your organization's accounting period is defined in your bylaws, what you enter here should agree with the bylaws.

- The *Primary contact* is a knowledgeable person in your organization the IRS can speak with regarding your application. That's probably you.

- Unless you've authorized a professional to negotiate for you, the answer to Question 7 is *"No."*

- Why would the IRS want to ask *Question 8?* This question, which is new to the 2006 edition, is designed to help the IRS detect paid preparer tax shelters and schemes, and excess private benefit transactions. The best answer is *"No."* If the truthful answer is *"Yes,"* your explanation will have to reflect a perfectly reasonable and legitimate purpose in contracting for such help.

- If you have a web site, provide your web address. Audit your web site to make sure there's nothing online that might raise any IRS eyebrows. If you have a web site at this early point in your organization's development, it was probably developed and is being maintained by a volunteer who might not be keenly tuned in to nonprofit political correctness, and might have taken a generous amount of creative license. Include an email address for the primary contact given in Question 6, if you wish to receive announcements and other mailings from the IRS.

- Certain types of church and government related organizations are not required to file annual tax returns, known as *Form 990*. If you're one of these, you'll probably know about it. If your annual gross receipts are not expected to exceed $25,000, you're also not required to file; however you might wish to file anyway:

- as a matter of good practice

- because it's an easy way to update the IRS, yourself and newly elected officers on your organization's status

- because your Form 990 will be available online to the prospective funders via GuideStar.org, and

- because it'll capture the kind of data you'll eventually need for your five-year advance ruling follow-up (assuming you'll receive an advance ruling).

  You can therefore check *"No,"* if you wish. If you check *"Yes,"* include a note for Part I-10 indicating simply *"Actual or projected gross receipts less than $25,000."*

- Answer Part I-11 by inserting the date that your state filed your Articles of Incorporation. That is usually stamped on the copy the state returned to you. Most states also make information about your corporation available online, since it is a matter of public record, and you'll find this date on that record.

- Answer Part I-12 as appropriate – probably *"No."*

Part II ~ Organizational Structure

This part of the form is intuitive, for the most part. Your answers will probably be:

Question 1: *"Yes"*
Question 2: *"No"*
Question 3: *"No"*
Question 4a: *"No"*

Question 4b: (blank – n/a)
Question 5:   *"Yes"*

With respect to Question 1, the IRS requires a copy of the document your state returned to you after you filed your Articles of Incorporation. They probably just sent you a copy of the form, stamped with the date it was filed. Attach a copy of that to your application.

For Question 5, include a copy of your bylaws that includes a certification of adoption by your membership. To see what that looks like, see the sample bylaws provided on the *SfS* website.

Part III ~ Required Provisions in Your Organizing Documents

"Organizing document" refers to your Articles of Incorporation. For the purposes of this section, make reference to the copy you attached in response to Part II-5. You must check the boxes on lines 1 and 2.

Regarding dissolution, rather than simply rely on state law, include appropriate provisions in your Articles of Incorporation. This will simplify things for your IRS EOS. But it will also make this particular issue clear to your members. Members otherwise sometimes have the idea that contributions and gifts can be returned in the event your organization fails, or that remaining assets can be spent down on pet projects, given to a favored but unrelated charity, or divided up between splinter groups. Generally, the state will determine what happens to any remaining assets. That usually means they'll go either to some nonprofit organization with a similar mission, else to the government.

Compare the example Articles of Incorporation (State form) provided on the *SfS* website to the citations entered for lines 1 and 2a.

Part IV ~ Narrative Description of Your Activities

This part of the form lets you explain in your own words, and in your own way, how your organization matches what is envisioned in United States Code: Title 26, Subtitle A, Chapter 1, Subchapter F, Part 1, Section 501, Subsection c, Paragraph 3. You should understand, however, that the word "narrative" is not used here in the literary sense. What you write should be concise, on topic and tastefully presented.

"Concise" means "expressing much in few words." Put yourself in your EOS's place when you proofread and edit what you have written. Most busy people don't read forms for enjoyment. Do your

EOS and yourself a favor by keeping things simple and to the point. Long, verbose narratives that include irrelevant material are not likely to engender an affirmative mood. Don't parrot material that is provided elsewhere in the application.

"On topic" means your conversation should stick to how your organization qualifies for tax exempt status under the Code. Limit your comments to the facts. Everyone knows you are great people with a worthy cause, but that's irrelevant here. So are goals and wishful thinking. For the purposes of this application all the EOS cares about is tangible evidence that what you're actually doing qualifies you as an exempt organization.

"Tastefully presented" means try to say what needs to be said on one to two pages, formatted to match the fill-in sections of the form (9pt blue Helvetica bold or Arial bold – see the examples on the *SfS* website). Organize your content logically and arrange it on the page effectively. Judicious use of white space can give a page an elegant, well organized appearance. A page crammed full of text appears busy, cluttered, and is typically difficult to read. Diligently honor the protocols for attachments and the assembly of your application specified on pages 3 and 4 of the *IRS Instructions for Form 1023*.

Before you begin, review the Code to see where you fit in. Here is what the Code looks like:

> **§ 501. Exemption from tax on corporations, certain trusts, etc.**
>
> **(c) List of exempt organizations**
>
> (3) Corporations, and any community chest, fund, or foundation, organized and operated exclusively for religious, charitable, scientific, testing for public safety, literary, or educational purposes, or to foster national or international amateur sports competition (but only if no part of its activities involve the provision of athletic facilities or equipment), or for the prevention of cruelty to children or animals, no part of the net earnings of which inures to the benefit of any private shareholder or individual, no substantial part of the activities of which is carrying on propaganda, or otherwise attempting, to influence legislation (except as otherwise provided in subsection (h)), and which does not participate in, or intervene in (including the publishing or distributing of statements), any political campaign on behalf of (or in opposition to) any candidate for public office.

The items that apply for our example, *Friends of the Manitous*, are highlighted.

- The *Friends* are incorporated.
- The board understands the restriction on lobbying and the prohibition on campaigning.

These matters are covered elsewhere in the form, so there's probably no need to restate these facts here. By process of elimination, the only "purposes" that might apply are these –

- charitable, and
- educational.

In the simplest perspective "charity" has Dickensonian connotations that do not describe what we do. But what exactly might the legislators have had in mind when they included this word? In its traditional legal meaning, the word "charity" encompasses religion, education, assistance to the government, promotion of health, relief of poverty or distress and other purposes that benefit the community. So evidently "charitable" is a broad category. Again, the operative phrases for this particular case are highlighted. Does the IRS have anything specifically to say about this? With a little research (Google this: "definition of charity site:irs.gov"), we discover a helpful snippet from an old IRS ruling that has been used as precedent for other rulings, shown here.

The *Friends* does in fact serve *"the general public"* (as opposed to a select class or group), their mission does involve *"a generally recognized public purpose"* (the purpose of the park is defined by

> **Rev. Rul. 67-325, 1967-2 C.B. 113**
>
> * * * Accordingly, since the property and its uses are dedicated to members of the general public of the community and are charitable in that they serve a generally recognized public purpose which tends to lessen the burdens of government, it is concluded that the instant organization is exclusively charitable within the meaning of section 501(c)(3) of the code and is entitled to exemption from Federal income tax under section 501(a) of the Code.

Congress in its enabling legislation), and much of what they do *"tends to lessen the burdens of government."* Searching further, we notice *"Treas Reg"* references in various *Revenue Rulings* and IRS *"EO CPE"* (*Exempt Organization – Continuing Professional Education*) papers, directing EOS's to various Treas Regs.

It turns out these are references to *Section 26* of the *Code of Federal Regulations*, which gives the definition the EOS would probably cite:

> **26 CFR Ch. I (4–1–04 Edition) § 1.501(c)(3)–1**
>
> *(2) Charitable defined.* The term charitable is used in section 501(c)(3) in its generally accepted legal sense and is, therefore, not to be construed as limited by the separate enumeration in section 501(c)(3) of other tax-exempt purposes which may fall within the broad outlines of charity as developed by judicial decisions. Such term includes: Relief of the poor and distressed or of the underprivileged; advancement of religion; advancement of education or science; erection or maintenance of public buildings, monuments, or works; lessening of the burdens of Government; and promotion of social welfare by organizations designed to accomplish any of the above purposes, or (i) to lessen neighborhood tensions; (ii) to eliminate prejudice and discrimination; (iii) to defend human and civil rights secured by law; or (iv) to combat community deterioration and juvenile delinquency. The fact that an organization which is organized and operated for the relief of indigent persons may receive voluntary contributions from the persons intended to be relieved will not necessarily prevent such organization from being exempt as an organization organized and operated exclusively for charitable purposes. The fact that an organization, in carrying out its primary purpose, advocates social or civic changes or presents opinion on controversial issues with the intention of molding public opinion or creating public sentiment to an acceptance of its views does not preclude such organization from qualifying under section 501(c)(3) so long as it is not an action organization of any one of the types described in paragraph (c)(3) of this section.

Thus the *Friends* can easily write about how they qualify under the charitable criterion, expanding on the last part of their mission statement, which says, "*... promote the proper care and maintenance of historic and cultural assets, and serve as volunteers assisting the Sleeping Bear Dunes National Lakeshore in the delivery of rich visitor experiences.*"

What about "educational"? By definition, education involves teaching and learning specific skills. It also involves something less tangible but more profound: the imparting of knowledge, good judgement and wisdom. The fundamental purpose of education is the imparting of culture (all the knowledge and values shared by a society) from one generation to the next. The *Friends* think they serve an educational function, as indicated in the first part of their mission statement says that they help, "*... preserve the history and cultural traditions of Michigan's Manitou Islands. We assist in the collection and preservation of knowledge about the Islands, develop and distribute educational and interpretive materials and programs ...*"

Here's the definition from CFR Sec 26 that the EOS will be looking at:

> **26 CFR Ch. I (4–1–04 Edition) § 1.501(c)(3)–1**
>
> **(3) Educational defined.** – *(i) In general*. The term educational, as used in section 501(c)(3), relates to:
>
> (a) The instruction or training of the individual for the purpose of improving or developing his capabilities; or
>
> (b) The instruction of the public on subjects useful to the individual and beneficial to the community.
>
> An organization may be educational even though it advocates a particular position or viewpoint so long as it presents a sufficiently full and fair exposition of the pertinent facts as to permit an individual or the public to form an independent opinion or conclusion. On the other hand, an organization is not educational if its principal function is the mere presentation of unsupported opinion.
>
> *(ii) Examples of educational organizations.* The following are examples of organizations which, if they otherwise meet the requirements of this section, are educational:
>
> *Example 1.* An organization, such as a primary or secondary school, a college, or a professional or trade school, which has a regularly scheduled curriculum, a regular faculty, and a regularly enrolled body of students in attendance at a place where the educational activities are regularly carried on.
> *Example 2.* An organization whose activities consist of presenting public discussion groups, forums, panels, lectures, or other similar programs. Such programs may be on radio or television.
> *Example 3.* An organization which presents a course of instruction by means of correspondence or through the utilization of television or radio.
> *Example 4.* Museums, zoos, planetariums, symphony orchestras, and other similar organizations.

Although some of the *Friends* activities are educational, they don't exactly match either general definition, and aren't closely described by any of the examples. Moreover, the various revenue rulings published on this subject deal mostly with schools who claim to be nonprofit, narrowly focused publications that claim their main purpose is educating the public, and so on.

It therefore appears that the *Friends'* idea of "educational" isn't the paradigm the IRS has in mind, and to claim exemption on the basis of being an educational organization would make their application somewhat messy. The educational part of their mission could be construed as assisting the government and benefiting the public, so can therefore legitimately be considered a component of charity.

Friends of the Manitous does a lot of things. Not all of these need to, or should be mentioned in the narrative, hence the striking of some items from the full list:

- ~~locates and marks old burial sites on the islands, and helps maintain island cemeteries~~

- publishes an informative free newsletter three times a year

- publishes free visitor guides for the islands

- ~~hosts a reunion/annual meeting in July, with an excursion to the Manitou Islands for members and their guests~~

- plans, organizes and manages maintenance and restoration projects on the islands

- provides grants to the National Lakeshore and other nonprofits for island maintenance and restoration projects

- ~~participates in the Lakeshore's annual "Port Oneida Fair" event~~

- assists with interpretive and security functions at Lakeshore visitor centers, museums and other exhibits

- provides speakers and articles for other organizations' meeting and newsletters, including continuing education seminars at local schools and colleges.

- ~~awards plaques, certificates and scholarships to individuals who have made significant contributions to the purposes for which the Society is organized~~

The bit about the burial sites and cemeteries was scratched because it isn't clear how that benefits the public in any way, or lessens the burdens of the government. As a matter of policy, the National Park Service avoids ownership of old cemeteries if at all possible, unless they have some definite historic significance. The reason is because that puts the government in the position of having to care for what is essentially private property, and graves that are of significance only to the families of those buried there. It seems likely the IRS would take this same position, so mentioning this could raise questions. Moreover, there is a 501(c)(13) category for cemetery associations, which raises the possibility that the EOS might jump to the conclusion that was the proper designation. Since this is not a significant part of what the *Friends* does anyway, it seems prudent to forget about it as far as this application is concerned.

As for the reunion, annual meeting and island excursions – although these things indirectly serve the *Friends'* mission, they are essentially social events, the types of activities that any organization might reasonably be expected to engage in. They would not be significant, so far as tax emption status is concerned, so aren't worth mentioning.

The Port Oneida Fair is an event sponsored by various Lakeshore partners, including the *Friends*, on behalf of the Lakeshore. The main reason partners are involved is that the Lakeshore, as a government entity, is not permitted to solicit grants, and this event is usually funded by grants from the National Council for the Arts and the Michigan Humanities Council. For its part, the *Friends* participates mostly just for the promotional value that results from exposure to the Fair's several thousand visitors, the event not being directly related to our mission. A problem is that exhibitors and demonstrators at the Fair are permitted to sell their wares, and profit personally from doing so. Suggesting that this was a significant *Friends* initiative could raise some rather messy questions about our sponsoring events for personal gain. Although the *Friends* are usually not connected in any way with, or even acquainted with the sellers, the EOS wouldn't know that, and would be obliged to raise questions about the exact nature of the event, who participated, how the transactions were handled, who got what part of the money, and so on. Since this is actually little more than an incidental activity for the *Friends*, it would probably be a mistake to suggest that it was anything more than that by including it in the narrative.

As for "awards, plaques and scholarships," honoring people at annual meetings is, again, nothing special; the kind of thing one could safely assume any organization might do. On the other hand, the appearance of the word "scholarship" will require that you complete *Schedule H*, is guaranteed to ensure against a "merit close," and is likely to result in a letter from the EOS asking for details. In this case, the scholarship was offered as a promotional idea, designed to garner some publicity for the *Friends of the Manitous*, using the familiar essay contest scheme. It was funded mostly by a single board member, using proceeds from the sale of her late father's book about his experiences on South Manitou Island. The money was deposited in the *Friends'* checking account, and the $500 prize was then paid using a *Friends of the Manitous* check. The

---

"Merit Close"

When your application is received at IRS, it'll be routed to a Technical Screener. Technical screeners are highly experienced and technically qualified specialists, who are keenly attuned to areas where the greatest potential for noncompliance exists, but are otherwise capable of efficiently processing the application on its merits. They have the discretion to close determination letter applications on their merit or to limit the amount of review. Applications that cannot be closed are "case graded," and reassigned to an Exempt Organization Specialist capable of dealing with the particular issues involved.

The Technical Screener's first impression and ultimate decision will make the difference between your receiving a letter of recognition in weeks without any further effort, or the process taking months, requiring you to explain items further and justify activities that could be noncompliant. If you're a small, newly organized nonprofit, knowing the ropes and keeping your application simple is likely to please the Screener and you too. Take time to learn how to avoid common mistakes which make it impossible for Screeners to "merit close" new applications.

For more on how the IRS operates internally, you can read the *Internal Revenue Manual* online at www.irs.gov/irm/.

program hasn't been very successful in attracting applicants, or in producing acceptable submissions. The assumption is that the $500 award is not considered significant, compared to the $14,000 to $24,000 cost of a year at regular four-year colleges and universities. In the most recent year, there were no applicants. In view of the complications scholarships bring to exemption considerations and Form 990 reporting, the board would probably be well advised to discontinue this initiative. With these things in mind, it seems prudent to eliminate it from the list of significant *Friends* activities.

Having clarified how to most appropriately present your case – that is; (1) having decided exactly how you qualify for exemption under the Code, and (2) understanding what evidence to cite in support of your claim – it's time to begin drafting the required narrative, answering these questions:

1. When and why your organization was created? Was it a response to some special need, or to capture some special opportunity? Explain.

2. Discuss the things your organization does that qualify it for recognition of exemption under the Code. Tell what, why, when, where and who. Does anyone receive pay in connection with these activities? If so, who? How are their qualifications determined? How is their compensation rate established?

3. Does your organization otherwise have any paid staff. Same questions: If so, who? How are their qualifications determined? How is their compensation rate established?

4. How many people does your organization serve? How many members does it have? Who is permitted to participate? Who is eligible to receive your services, and how is their eligibility determined?

5. How do you do membership recruitment and retention, or otherwise promote your organization?

6. How much money do you raise to support your organization, and how do you come up with it? Do you have dues? Do you sell fundraising items or hold fundraising events. If so, describe how money received is as classified as contributions to your mission or unrelated business income.

7. Itemize approximately how your money is spent on your various mission activities and non-mission functions.

8. Does your organization have own any real or personal property? If so, what, where and what is its approximate value?

Present your case in a reasonably conversational way that will be easy to read, rather than in outline form, tabulated list or legal brief. Proofread, edit and re-write your draft as often as necessary to eliminate redundant content, or anything else that isn't essential to making your points. Refer to attachments rather than describe documents that can be attached.

If your research has turned up government documents such as Revenue Rulings, court decisions, or provisions in the U.S. Code or Code of Federal Regulations that strongly support your case, finish with citations to those references, and attach copies, as appropriate.

The narrative attachment written for the *Friends of the Manitous* example application can be viewed with the completed application on the *SfS* website.

Part V ~ Compensation and Other Financial Arrangements with Your Officers, Directors, Trustees, Employees, and Independent Contractors

Exempt organizations must not, in any way, materially benefit insiders. The purpose of this long series of questions may be intended more as informative, than interrogative. As you read through this series of questions, you can almost hear the IRS saying, "If you're trying to pull a fast one, forget it! If you, or a relative or a friend is going to make any money off your organization, you're going to have to convince us it's perfectly legitimate." The questions reflect the IRS's experience with people who have tried doing just that.

If you are a small nonprofit with no paid staff, as per the example, working through this part of the form is easy. When you check the appropriate box, no explanations will be called for. For the example –

1a: Fill in the blanks, entering *"none"* in the last column for each name. If you have more than five people on your board, enter "please see attachment" on the first line, and attach a list showing all your board members.

1b: Enter *"none"* on the first line in the "Name" column.

1c: Enter *"none"* on the first line in the "Name" column.

2a: *"No"*

2b: *"No"*

2c: *"No"*

3a: In their online article *"Frequently Asked Questions about Form 1023"* the IRS says *"The remainder of Part V asks about various types of relationships between the organization and its governing members. These questions are answered even if no compensation is provided; we are concerned that an organization informs us about the possibility of private benefit to persons who are in a position of control."* Therefore provide the requested attachment whether or not anyone receives compensation of any kind (pay or reimbursed expenses). The example provided on the *SfS* website was written according to the guidelines given in the above referenced FAQ.

3b: *"No"*

4a: *"Yes"*

4b: *"Yes"*

4c: *"Yes"*

4d: *"Yes"*

4e: *"Yes"*

4f: *"Yes"*

4g: Does not apply, since you answered "Yes" to the above six questions.

5a: *"Yes"*

5b & 5c: As you can see by these two items and the note beneath them, if you don't have a conflict of interest policy, you might as well have a board meeting right now and adopt one as a resolution. It's easy; the IRS has already written the resolution for you; as mentioned in the note, you'll find it in Appendix A of the instructions. The attachment used for the example application shows how your board can adopt this boilerplate policy. You'll find it on the *SfS* website, along with a MS-Word version that you're welcome to adapt to your organization.

6a: *"No"*

6b: *"No"*

7a: *"No"*

7b: *"No"*

8a: *"No"*

8b~8f: Does not apply, since you answered "No" to the above six questions.

9a: *"No"*

9b~9f: Does not apply, since you answered "No" to the above six
questions.

Part VI ~ Your Members and Other Individuals and Organizations That Receive Benefits from You

These questions are probably designed to address situations where
nonprofits are organized for the express purpose of providing assistance to
individuals (such as homeless persons or battered spouses) or to other
organizations. However there's nothing here or in the instructions that
limits the scope to that, so until that is clarified by the IRS, interpret these
questions literally (see also *Part VIII, Question 13*). The *Friends*
occasionally provides assistance to the National Lakeshore and to other
nonprofit organizations assisting the National Lakeshore. The answer to
question 1b is therefore "Yes," and that will require an attachment
explaining who is getting the assistance and why (the example attachment
can be viewed with the completed application on the *SfS* website).

1a: *"No"*

1b: *"Yes"*

2: *"No"*

3: *"No"*

Part VII ~ Your History

The reasons for these questions become clear when you review the
attachments you'll have to fill out if you answer "Yes."

Question 1 is partly a matter of simple housekeeping. For example,
it is useful to know if the applicant is replacing an exempt corporation that
is, for all practical purposes, defunct, or has actually been dissolved.
Otherwise, *Schedule G* asks about things that might suggest you're trying
to set up a tax shelter. If you were formerly organized as a business in the
conventional sense and are now reorganizing as a not-for-profit
organization, the IRS will be interested in hearing why, and how that
works. They'll be especially interested in hearing about that if the same
people who were principals in that business are now involved in the
running of your nonprofit. If you answer "Yes" to this question, complete
Schedule G with care, making sure you don't say something that might
suggest a tax strategy.

A "Yes" answer to Question 2 will take you to *Schedule E*, which will establish whether your tax exempt status could apply from the date of your organization's inception or, if not, whether you might alternatively be exempt under Section 501(c)(4) of the code. Otherwise, if granted, it'll apply from the date this application was submitted. The significance of this depends upon your activity up to this point.

Under the Code, an organization that (1) normally has less than $5,000 in gross receipts per year, and (2) which is organized and operated exclusively for tax-exempt purposes, will generally be treated as tax-exempt without any further action (i.e., without having to be officially recognized as such through the Form 1023 process), so if this is your situation, any further consideration is irrelevant. On the other hand, if you were fortunate enough to have received more than $5,000 a year before filing your Form 1023, those receipts will be seen as regular taxable income until the IRS recognizes that you qualify as a tax exempt organization. Technically, you have 15-months after the inception of your organization to apply, in which case your exempt status, if recognized, will apply retroactively to that date. The Code provides for a 12-months grace period, and that is invoked automatically, if needed, hence the "27-months" question. If more than 27-months have gone by between the time your organization was started and the time you filed your Form 1023, then the IRS will want to know if you expect recognition to apply retroactively and, if so, how you justify that. If you can't do that, you might wind up paying corporate income tax on your early receipts, and donors will not be able to treat their donations as deductible charitable contributions. If the amount of money involved is substantial, this can be bad news.

You'll probably answer "No" to both questions. The *Friends* did not replace any existing legal entity, so is not a successor organization. On the other hand, their application is being submitted well beyond the time the organization became a legal entity. So the answers on our example form are:

1:   *"No"*

2:   *"Yes"*

They therefore have to complete *Schedule E;* however since their receipts have never been more than $5,000, they needn't go any further than Question 2a. *Schedule E* provides for certain other scenarios also. Other reasons for filing late could be because your receipts for the past year have passed the $5,000 mark for the first time (Question 2b), you've been covered by a blanket recognition (Questions 3), or predated the Tax Reform Act of 1969 (Question 4).

> ❧ Note: The Tax Reform Act of 1969 introduced the private foundation concept. Before that, organizations that were described in 501(c)(3) were exempt on a *de*

facto basis. The new law, which became effective on October 9, 1969, required organizations formed after that date to submit information sufficient to establish their public charity status. Older organizations who did not submit such information, even those that had old 501(c)3 letters, were presumed to be private foundations. Those that had never filed retained the *de facto* 501(c)3 status.

If none of these apply, Question 5 of Schedule E provides for other possibilities, examples of which are mentioned in the instructions. Otherwise, you must answer "Yes" to Question 6a in order to maintain your eligibility for an advance ruling. You'll provide financial information to support that later. However, if you feel that information will not accurately reflect future sources of support, you may answer "Yes" to Question 6b, then summarize what your expectations for the future are in Question 7.

At this point, if you receive a letter of recognition, it'll begin with the date you mailed your application. Prior to that date you will be considered as having been a taxable entity. If you have a tax liability for the period preceding your application, you might elect to check the box in Question 8 of Schedule E to seek recognition under Section 501(c)4 of the Code for the period between the time your organization was founded and the date of your application.

> ✻ Note: Both charitable and social welfare organizations are exempt from federal income tax. Section 501(c)3 exempts enterprises organized and operated exclusively for charitable purposes, while Section 501(c)4 exempts those operated for the promotion of social welfare. If you feel your application reflects that you were organized and operated primarily to further the common good and general welfare of the community, you may be eligible for tax-exempt status under Section 501(c)4 of the Code as a *social welfare organization*. Donations to 501(c)4's are not deductible as charitable contributions, otherwise this class and the procedure for obtaining recognition, is similar to 501(c)3. 501(c)4 status is ordinarily obtained by filing IRS Form 1024, *Application for Recognition of Exemption Under Section 501(a)*, which is similar to (but not as detailed as) Form 1023. In this case, you would only be required to complete the first page of that form and submit it as an attachment to this application.

Part VIII ~ Your Specific Activities

As in Part VII, the reasons for these questions will also become clear when you review the attachments you'll have to fill out if you answer "Yes."

1:     *"No"* – the restriction is absolute; 501(c)3 organizations may not involve themselves in political campaigns.

2a: Exempt organizations may engage in lobbying activities. However, if that is not specifically a part of your mission, the prudent answer to this question is probably *"No."*

Although lobbying by nonprofits is perfectly legal, certain restrictions apply to 501(c)(3) groups. For example, money received through government grants may not be used to fund lobbying activities. You can choose between two sets of guidelines for measuring lobbying; a measure based on expenditures, and the "substantial" test. Under the expenditure test, lobbying only occurs when there is an expenditure of money. 501(c)3's that choose this alternative can spend up to one-fifth of their budget on efforts to influence legislation, but not more than one-fourth of that can be spent on grassroots or indirect lobbying. To use this test you must file IRS Form 5768 notifying the IRS that this is your choice. Otherwise you'll fall under the "substantial" test, in which lobbying may not constitute a substantial part of your activities. Since the term "substantial part" has never been fully defined, it will be up to the EOS to decide. This situation will usually guarantee against a merit close.

Direct lobbying refers to communications with legislators, either directly by your organization or by encouraging your members to communicate with legislators to influence the outcome of legislation. *Grassroots lobbying* attempts to influence legislation indirectly through appeals to the public by (1) referring to specific legislation, (2) promoting your view in support of opposition to it, and (3) prompting others to take action with respect to that legislation (e.g., "write your congressman").

If these activities are not really part of your mission, leaders in your organization should understand this particular aspect of your exemption status, lest any who might become exuberantly engaged in a certain issue take the organization into territory where it doesn't really wish to go. Discussion of policy matters does not necessarily constitute lobbying. For example, you may provide nonpartisan analyses which need not be neutral or objective, but which present facts fully and fairly, are widely available, and do not include a direct call to action. You can respond to written requests for information or technical assistance from legislators. You can engage in discussions with government officials concerning legislation impacting an organization's existence, powers, duties, tax-exempt status, or right to receive tax-deductible contributions. You are even free to discuss broad policy matters with the general public and government officials, even if legislation is pending. This provides for a wide range of activity, without requiring a "Yes" answer to Question 2a.

Question 3 deals with bingo and other games of chance employed for fundraising purposes.

3a: *"No"*

3b: *"No"*

3c: (blank)

Concentrate on the "do you" part of the question, rather than "will you." If you've tried bingo, raffles, and the like, you've probably already discovered these usually aren't very good fundraisers, and sometimes even prove to be costly. On the other hand, if you're actually making a lot of money on such games, it's quite possible that some of it will be taxable as unrelated business income. This might be a good time to recheck your premises. If you haven't thus far tried games, do not answer "Yes" solely in anticipation of possibly engaging in this sort of activity at some point in the future.

Question 4 provides you with an opportunity to explain exactly how you intend to generate revenue for your organization. Assuming you are applying for recognition as a publicly supported charity, the obvious answer to the first question is –

4a: *"Yes"*

Here again, stick with reality, not dreams. Because you'll need to explain each item checked below this answer, check only items that you actually do, or have developed plans for doing. Anything is possible and you will naturally remain open to all those possibilities. But that is not what the IRS is asking about here. You'll probably check off the "solicitations" (mail, email and personal), and since it's easy to accept donations on your web site, you'll probably check that if you have a web site. Since vehicle donations have recently been identified as a means of abuse, checking that item is likely to raise some eyebrows and might get you a letter asking for more information.

Otherwise check the items that apply and write the required description of the activity as an attachment. Be careful about the words you use. Words like "sell," "distribute," and "publish" suggest the possibility of unrelated business income. When goods or services of any kind are provided in exchange for money, the transaction is, at least in part, a sale, not strictly a donation. Questions also arise regarding the sale of property created by, or services rendered by, others. This will be an issue whenever intellectual property rights are involved with items you are offering for sale, or as a premium to encourage donations, such as books, music CD's or the like, when the copyright holder is someone other than your organization. Remember the part about no benefit inuring to individuals when writing these attachments.

4b: *"No"*

4c: *"No"* – or as appropriate for your organization.

Question 4d may be rather nebulous for organizations that are not strictly local. The *Friends*, for example, solicits contributions from members from all over the United States, such that the definitive listing this question seems to request would obviously be impractical and of little use. The attachment simply so states.

Attachment for Sec VIII, Question 4d

Friends of the Manitous addresses its fundraising appeals to members and other interested parties who reside all across the United States, rather than from persons located within any particular state or government jurisdiction. These activities are conducted solely on behalf of the *Friends of the Manitous*. Except as noted in *Part IV, Question 1b*, proceeds from these fundraising activities are not shared with any other organization, nor does the *Friends* share in proceeds collected by any other organization.

Question 4e is a hot button item, involving "donor advised funds."

Donor-advised funds allow people to give cash, stock, or other assets to special accounts, claim a charitable deduction on their federal income taxes, and then recommend how, when, and to which charities the money in the account should be distributed. This borderline-legal activity has allowed the wealthy to use such funds to pay their children or themselves for their charitable work and expenses, to provide their kids with college scholarships that would be forgiven if they did volunteer work, to use the money to buy tickets (and travel) to charity balls, and to make good on the donor's pledges to other charitable organizations. In 2005 the IRS advised lawmakers that although such funds, which weren't mentioned in the tax code, can have legitimate uses, they have operated largely free of the sorts of regulations that govern private charitable organizations, and many are actually schemes designed to benefit donors rather than to support legitimate charitable purposes. Accordingly, legislation drafted to regulate such funds was signed into law in August of 2006.

4e: *"No"*

If you cannot honestly provide this answer, you probably have financial advisors and they will need to help you with the required explanations and documentation.

In Question 5, the word "affiliated" could be interpreted as meaning "directly connected to" or "answerable to" – a connection to government that goes beyond a cooperative arrangement of some kind, such as a friends organization. If certain government powers have been delegated to your organization, such as certain police powers, you will not qualify for exemption under Section 501(c)3 of the Code.

5:     *"No"*

"Economic development" (Question 6) usually infers some involvement with for-profit business, such as the revitalization of blighted downtown areas, or help for minority-owned businesses. Here again, the potential for abuse is rather obvious, so the IRS would like to know whether or not you are into this sort of activity and, if so, what the extent of your participation is. For most applicants, the appropriate answers are:

6a: *"No"*

6b: (blank)

Another means of abuse is to divert money from your organization to family and friends for services rendered. Question 7 challenges you in this regard. The best approach is not to have dealings with family and other close associates. Of course there might be occasions where such dealings are actually a benefit to the organization, and if that is the case you should be able to explain that the arrangement was fairly offered to all other prospective vendors, and that the work was ultimately granted strictly on that basis.

7a: *"No"*

7b: *"No"*

7c: (blank)

The term "inurement" usually infers the inappropriate payment of money to someone, and that is explicitly prohibited by the Code. Another possibility for abuse of exempt status, which is not expressly mentioned, is *private benefit*. An organization may indeed serve charitable purposes and public interests, yet still not qualify for exempt status if significant benefits accrue to private interests through circumstances that are not strictly incidental to the serving of those charitable purposes and public interests. These situations often arise through partnerships involving for-profit entities. Such schemes frequently involve programs funded by government through tax credits, tax-exempt financing, or grants. Consider the case of charter schools created by a school management company, which then benefits financially by managing all aspects of the schools operations. Nursing homes is another similar example: while a nonprofit nursing home might well serve a charitable purpose and public interest, if it is essentially the contractual captive of a for-profit management organization, the resulting private benefit is probably significant, and not incidental. Government subsidized housing programs offer lucrative opportunities for developers to partner with nonprofits to acquire and rehabilitate blighted real estate at government expense, then operate it profitably while also benefiting as it appreciates in value over the years.

Question 8 asks about arrangements where the possibility of *private benefit* needs to be looked at. Obviously, not all such partnership arrangements lead to a negative determination. However, the EOS will examine your situation very closely, looking for evidence for private benefit that is (1) substantial and (2) not incidental. If you have to answer "Yes" to this question, then the attachment you prepare to "describe the activities of these joint ventures" should be detailed, clearly showing that they are necessary or advantageous to the serving of your charitable purpose or some public interest, and that the for-profit entity will be serving you, rather than you serving it.

8:     *"No"*

Under the Code, child care can be considered educational purposes so long as (1) its purpose is substantially to enable parents to work, to seek employment, or to further their education or training, and (2) the service is equally offered to everyone. The IRS has decided that "substantial," in this case, means 85%. In other words, 85% of the services provided must involve children of working parents. The requirement that the services be available to the general public allows day care providers to be selective about such things as the age of the children and the geographical area they choose to serve, but not about such things as parents' occupations, place of employment, race, economic status, etc.

9a: *"No"*

9b: (blank)

9c: (blank)

9d: (blank)

If you answer "Yes" to Question 9a, you should be able to answer "Yes" to the three follow-up questions. A "No" answer to any of these will require an attachment giving an explanation. Although the requirements seem quite unequivocal, there might be good reasons why you are not able to provide the desired answers at this particular time. As you can see in the instructions, one might be that you are in the process of building your service, and have not as yet achieved the required client base. (Interestingly, the instructions also seemingly attempt to trip you up by inferring that an appropriate answer to Question 9d would be that your are organized to serve the families of a particular employer. That would disqualify you, since your services would not be available to the general public.)

It would be difficult for any nonprofit to answer "No" to Question 10, because almost any organization will create brochures, newsletters, web sites, and other copyrighted matter which could be considered intellectual property. The IRS is specifically interested in knowing about intellectual property that is exploited commercially, not necessarily about material that is made available for free or distributed in support of ordinary fundraising activities.

Commercial activities involve the sale of products or services that have some intrinsic value to the purchaser, as opposed to the intangible value of the good feelings that come from supporting your worthy mission.

For example, a nonprofit association might sponsor the authoring and publication of a series of how-to books, which it sells to the general public and to its own members at a discounted price as a membership recruitment and retention ploy. In such cases, the IRS would want to know all about these projects, and specifically who, if anyone, shares in the proceeds, in order to assure itself that these activities do not violate the rules restricting inurement and private benefit.

If you can, answer "No" to Question 10. You'll probably have to answer "Yes," and attach a brief statement that what is produced is not used for commercial purposes. Include a simple *Intellectual Property Policy*; your EOS might feel you should have one and by anticipating that you might avoid having your application tied up by such a request. An example is provided on the *SfS* website. If indeed you do distribute, or will be selling products or services commercially, your attachment will then have to describe those activities in detail, proving that any sharing of proceeds is strictly on the up and up – preferably incidental and insubstantial.

10:   *"Yes"*

Question 11 addresses non-cash contributions, a significant source of support for many charitable organizations. The tax code provides meaningful and appropriate incentives for giving such items. However, the IRS treats non-cash contributions differently than gifts of cash. Non-cash contributions of $500 or more are reported on the IRS form 8283. In addition, non-cash contributions may require more documentation, especially if the value of all "like" non-cash contributions given in a year to any charitable organizations exceeds $5,000 ($10,000 for gifts of stock). For non-cash contributions at this level, the IRS requires the donors to include qualified, written appraisals with their tax returns.

The concern here is primarily about the use of such contributions as donor advised funds and the valuation of such gifts. These contributions are deductible, in whole or in part, usually according to the fair market value of the property gifted. Although it is the donor's responsibility to substantiate the value, you will be required to sign 8283's to acknowledge their receipt, depending on the type and value of the non-cash contribution. Doing so does not ordinarily signify that you agree with the valuation, nevertheless signing is ill-advised when the value is substantially misstated. Special rules apply to certain types of non-cash donations. Because of previous widespread abuse, the rules applying to donations of vehicles are especially restrictive. If you check "Yes" to this question, you must include an attachment explaining what kinds of property you will accept, under what circumstances, and how you would ordinarily dispose of it. You should also indicate that your organization will have exclusive legal control over contributed assets.

11: *"No"*

Private contributions to domestic organizations with programs in foreign countries are generally deductible. Unless some treaty provides otherwise, contributions to foreign organizations operating identical programs are generally not deductible. Foreign organizations might qualify for exempt status in this country under 501(c)3, with the intention of raising money in this country; however contributions to such organizations for use abroad are not deductible because Section 107(c)2 of the Code requires that such organizations must originate in the United States. Contributions to a domestic organization to support grants made to a foreign organization are deductible only if the domestic organization has control over the use of the money by the foreign organization.

It is generally recognized that donated funds can be appropriately shared with domestic organizations that serve the same, or related charitable interests, and that such funds cannot be diverted to private purposes.

The purposes of Questions 12, 13 and 14 are not clear, although in May of 2003 the IRS published an announcement asking nonprofits to describe their current procedures for making grants and conducting activities outside the United States and to provide suggestions on how existing guidance could be expanded and existing rules improved to provide greater assurance that funds are used appropriately. The Announcement explicitly referred to diversions for terrorist purposes.

Question 13 appears to duplicate what was asked in *Part VI, Question 1b*; however answer the questions on their own merit, rather than referring the examiner back to the previous answer. For this example the appropriate answers are:

12a: *"No"*

13a: *"Yes"*

13c: *"No"*

13f$_i$: *"No"*

13f$_{ii}$: *"Yes"*

14a: *"No"*

A "Yes" answer to any of these questions requires an attachment, providing the required explanatory detail. Answer the questions and make your explanations according to the guidelines discussed in the above two paragraphs. You can review the attachment provided for this example on the *SfS* website.

The IRS has recently become interested in increased scrutiny concerning the compensation paid to officers of tax-exempt organizations. One method of obscuring lucrative arrangements is by having the same people involved in various capacities in two or more organizations. Question 15 probably addresses this interest. *"Close connection"* refers to situations where the same people exercise substantial influence over the organizations; for example, by serving as officers or directors in both organizations simultaneously, sharing facilities or employees, or receiving a substantial part of their funding from the same source.

15: *"No"*

Cooperative Hospital Service Organizations are organized and operated solely to perform, on a centralized basis, certain essential services for one or more nonprofit 501(c)3 hospitals. Examples of such services include data processing, purchasing, warehousing, billing and collection, food, clinical, industrial engineering, laboratory, printing, communications, record center, and personnel selection, testing, training, and education. The patron hospitals may help fund the CHSO, and Section 501(e) of the Code requires that any net earnings of the CHSO be distributed among its patron hospitals. Where CHSO operations involve Medicare or Medicaid clients, these payments can look like illegal kick-backs, so CHSO's are provided with special safe harbor recognition.

16: *"No"*

Section 501(f) of the Code concerns organizations formed and operated to invest funds on behalf of educational institutions, and to pay the resulting income to these institutions. These are called *Cooperative Service Organization Of Operating Educational Organizations.*

17: *"No"*

Charitable Risk Pools came about as a result of the insurance crisis in the late 1980's. When commercial insurers who had over sold and under priced for many years were suddenly faced with a tidal wave of liability claims, liability insurance soon became unaffordable and even unavailable to nonprofits considered high risks. Charitable Risk Pools are set up as nonprofit associations of 501(c)3 organizations which operate as separate tax-exempt entities. They usually offer a variety of programs to manage the insurance needs of their members, provide for legal representation, and provide various risk-reduction resources.

18: *"No"*

School, in the context of Question 19, is used in the conventional sense, referring to an organization offering training or educational services to the public as its primary purpose. This would entail classrooms, teachers, students, and so on, not merely an educational component expressed as part of your organization's mission. If you're still not sure about your answer, have a look at *Schedule B* for a more comprehensive understanding of what this question is all about.

19: *"No"*

Although Question 20 asks about *hospital or medical care*, it refers to hospitals in the conventional sense, or to organizations set up to support a particular hospital and which are closely associated with that hospital. *Schedule C* will provide you with a better feel for what is being asked about here, if there is any question.

20: *"No"*

If your organization provides some sort of housing assistance to people who are disadvantaged in some way, such as by age, infirmity, disability or poverty, the answer to Question 21 might be "Yes." In that case, you'll also have to fill in *Schedule F*, which you might wish to refer to now if there's any doubt about this question. If you're operating a nursing home, convalescent home or similar care facility, you'll probably have to complete both *Schedule C* and *Schedule F*; they are not mutually exclusive.

21: *"No"*

Scholarships have been a notorious method of inappropriately diverting charitable funds to individuals. If this sort of activity is the primary purpose of your organization, the answer to *Question 22* must be "Yes," in which case this will be an area for special attention by your EOS, who will evaluate what you have to say on *Schedule H* very carefully.

Scholarship programs focus on youth and education. Good publicity about these programs can help create awareness of your organization's existence and purposes, and can generate contributions from a diverse audience. Scholarship committees can provide a mechanism for bringing new, and possibly influential, people into your organization. On the other hand, scholarship programs involve a lot of administrative work. Publicizing the program, collecting and reviewing applications, disbursing funds and tracking recipients, are some of the tasks involved.

Since furthering education is a charitable purpose, scholarships are by definition a legitimate charitable activity, so long as they are fairly offered and responsibly administered. Otherwise, there are actually no specific IRS rules regarding scholarship grants to individuals by 501(c)3 organizations, and your plans and procedures for making scholarship grants to individuals do not have to be approved by the IRS in advance. Under current IRS practice, you would also have no tax-reporting requirements in connection with such activities. If your organization is merely thinking about using scholarships for mission or promotional purposes, or if, in any case, this will not constitute a substantial part of your activities, a "No" answer to this question would probably be prudent at this point

22:     *"No"*

> ❧ Note: If and when you decide to go ahead with a scholarship program, you should familiarize yourself with the stringent requirements imposed on private foundations and regulate your activities advisedly in order to ensure that your program will meet muster in the event it is ever scrutinized by the IRS.

Part IX ~ Financial Data

This part of the form has two sections; *Statement(s) of Revenue and Expenses (A)* and a *Balance Sheet (B)*. The first section wonders where you're going to get your money and how you're going to spend it, and the second section wonders about how wealthy you are (your assets and liabilities).

Section A – Revenue and Expenses

The instructions for *Section A* sometimes seem a little more confusing than they actually are –

- If your organization is just starting, you won't have any financial track record, so under *"Current tax year" (a)* enter your best guess for each item, based upon what the situation looks like so far. Then, in the next two columns, *(b)* and *(c)*, enter projections for the next two years.

- If you're finally getting around to submitting your application after having been in existence for at least one full year, what you'll enter under *"Current tax year" (a)* will also be a projection, unless you happen to be filling out this form on the last day of your fiscal year. Enter the actual figures for last year in the next column *(b)*. If you have actual information for the year before that, enter it in the next column *(c)*. If you don't have two years of actual financial data because you haven't been in existence for more than two years, enter a projection for next year in the last column *(d)*, leaving *(c)* blank to signal that the data provided isn't in chronological order.

- If you've been in business for four years or more, simply report your income and expense information for last year (your most recently completed year) under *"Current tax year" (a)*, and the three years before that in the remaining columns *(b)*, *(c)* and *(d)*.

Make sure that these statements jive with what you declared on page one with respect to your fiscal year *(Part I-5)* and when your organization was established *(Part I-11)*. Use simple "cash accounting" (actual money in/money out) unless you have some special reason for using the "accrual" method (credits dues and donations as income when promised or pledged, revenue for products and services sold when billed regardless of when the money is received, and expenses when billings are received regardless of when actually paid).

If you have existing financial statements, you will probably prefer your own format to that used here, and you may in fact submit them as attachments by just marking "see attachments" across the *Part IX* forms. Keep in mind however, that the IRS isn't interested in your bookkeeping capabilities, in minor details, or in how lovely your reports are formatted. In the interest of achieving the quickest possible results, it's good idea to keep things simple and summarize them on the form that the EOS is used to dealing with.

If you have to provide estimates of future income and expenses, they should have some basis other than high hopes or magical thinking. If you have at least one year's experience, that can serve as the basis for projections. Perhaps the years to follow will be about the same. If not, think about why not, and whether what you're projecting seems reasonable given your past history and current resources.

Line 1 – Contributions and Donations: Include regular contributions and donations of money or other things of value on this line. Do not include dues, money earned through the sale of fundraising merchandise or services, or special large gifts or grants. Although the instructions do not call for a breakdown, an attachment indicating the source of these funds might be appropriate, unless they are all from casual contributions received in the normal course.

Attachment for Sec IX, Line 1 – Gifts, Grants and Contributions

Funds Raised at Steering Committee Meetings:
$500 each from three founders
$100 each from 16 "Charter Members"

Funds Raised After Founding
$504 in misc donations from "Regular Members"

Line 2 – Membership Fees: If you assess dues or membership fees, enter the amount collected on this line. The *Friends* has no formal dues structure. Anyone making a donation of any amount becomes a lifetime Member.

Line 3 – Investment Income: Investment income is money earned from financial ventures entered into specifically for that purpose, such as stocks, bonds, mutual funds, and certificates of deposit. Incidental interest earned, such as on a checking account, will be considered insubstantial, and would be listed on line 7 as "other revenue," rather than as proceeds from an investment.

Line 4 – Unrelated Business Income: Unrelated business income is generally taxable. The reason for this is to keep nonprofits from unfairly competing with regular taxable businesses. Unrelated business income involves earnings from trade or business activities that you are involved in on a regular basis, but which are not directly related to your mission. The nature of the activity is the criterion, not what you do with the money earned. There are, however, a variety of exclusions in the Code. Some examples –

1. You decide to sell advertising as a way to finance the cost of the newsletters you regularly mail out. The advertising revenue would be unrelated business income. Aside from the income, promoting Joe's Friendly Tavern, New-2-U Auto Sales and anyone else willing to place an ad, is a regular business activity that is unrelated to your exempt purposes.

2. You come up with the idea of sponsoring a cultural fair as a mission-related educational event. As a fundraiser, you decide to print a colorful advertising-supported souvenir program, which you sell for a dollar. Neither the proceeds from the advertising nor from the sale of the programs is unrelated business income, since this is not an activity that is carried out on a regular basis.

3. You buy an old building you can fix up for use as your headquarters and office. The building has more space than you need, so your plan is to lease the excess space, using the lease proceeds to pay for the building, giving you a free home for your organization. The lease proceeds would not be unrelated business income, because under the Code, rents from real property are ordinarily excluded.

4. Suppose you regularly rent the same excess space in that building as a hall for meetings, banquets, parties, weddings and reunions. Since, rented or not, your hall is available on a regular basis, these fees would constitute unrelated business income. This would be especially true if you also provided any sort of services, such as the use of your equipment, catering, etc.

5. Selling monogrammed merchandise is a great way to raise funds. The proceeds are not unrelated business income for a couple of reasons. First, the monogram promotes your organization, and therefore supports your exempt purposes. Second, if the activity is carried on substantially by volunteers ("substantially" meaning 85% in this case), the Code excludes it as unrelated business income.

As you can see, the call is sometime obvious; sometimes not so clear. Before entering anything on this line, be sure that it is in fact unrelated business income. You can read much more about what is and what is not "UBI" by entering "unrelated business income" in your favorite Internet search engine.

Line 5 – Special Assessments: This line generally refers to public/private partnerships like SID's (special improvement districts), economic development districts, libraries, municipal airports, community centers, and other community initiatives that are managed as nonprofit organizations which are funded in part by special assessments payable (usually) with property taxes. If you weren't sure what this meant, you probably have nothing to report here.

Line 6 – Free Government Services or Facilities: Services and facilities provided by government could include office space for a friends of the park group, meeting space on campus for a college club, a historical society's use of university computer facilities for research and record archiving, and aero club's free use of airport facilities, a marine auxiliary's free use of municipal boat launching and docking facilities, or any number of other things. This line involves facilities and services furnished to you which are not typically made available to the general public. Government more often provides such facilities and services under some sort of reimbursement schedule – often token amounts which are far less than the fair market value. No matter how minimal the reimbursement, those need not be reflected here.

Line 7 – Miscellaneous Income: This is the catch-all line. Whatever income doesn't fit elsewhere goes here. An example is insubstantial earnings from your interest-bearing checking account.

Line 9 – Proceeds from Fundraising: Proceeds from your various fundraising initiatives would go here, as would any earnings derived from facilities or services you provide to others which are consistent with your exempt purposes. As noted in the instructions, although government entities employing nonprofits to do research or special studies in their area of expertise usually refer to the amount paid for the work as a grant, these earnings should be listed here as income. Although the work involved was in line with the organization's exempt purposes, the end product was created for someone else's use, with the nonprofit acting essentially as a hired consultant.

Note that what is expected here is actually a sum, with an itemization of its components provided elsewhere as an attachment.

Line 11 – Proceeds from the Sale of Assets: "Capital assets" refers to things people ordinarily purchase for use over a long period of time; physical things the organization owns, such as business equipment and office furniture, vehicles, land, and buildings.

The gain or loss is computed by simply subtracting the cost or amortized value plus any expense you incurred in completing the sale of the item from the amount you sold it for. However, the IRS wants this broken down into three categories: "Real Estate," "Securities" and "Other." Do that on the form supplied in the instructions, which you must provide as an attachment. Show the sum of these three categories on this line.

Line 12 – Unusual Grants: Remember the one-third support test? An organization will qualify as publicly supported if it normally receives at least one-third of its total support from governmental units, from contributions made directly or indirectly by the general public, or from a combination of these sources. Large gifts or grants can be excluded from the support test if they are indeed abnormal – generally meaning that they were not expected (coming as a special opportunity or windfall), come from an outside source (as opposed to founders and directors) and cannot reasonably be expected to be repeated (at least from that particular source).

Continued reliance on unusual grants to fund an organization's current operating expenses may be evidence that the organization cannot reasonably be expected to attract future support from the general public, in which case the EOS will decide that you are not recognizable as a public charity and will designate you as a private foundation. the IRS understands that founders might well provide such support as seed money at the outset. But if you have anything to show on this line, you should also be careful to offer convincing evidence that you are capable of successfully soliciting support from a variety of smaller donors.

Line 14 – Fundraising Expenses: Fundraising expenses include all the costs involved in soliciting contributions, gifts and grants. Examples of such expenses are:

- publicizing and conducting fundraising campaigns
- soliciting bequests and grants from other organizations or government
- participating in joint fundraising campaigns
- preparing and distributing fundraising materials
- conducting special events that generate contributions

Include expenditures that are directly attributable to revenue above this line; for example, the direct costs of goods or services sold, amounts paid for shipping, packaging materials, and so on. You may also include part of your overhead costs if it can be directly attributed to particular fundraising activities. Although the form doesn't say so, provide an attachment itemizing the components of the sum entered here.

Include only actual expenditures. Do not include "donated costs," such as the value of a volunteer's time or mileage. Although "Total Revenue" (Line 13) and "Total Expenses" (Line 24) do not need to balance, your figures should suggest how excess expenses were financed and how they will be made up in future years, or how excess revenue will be used in future years.

Line 15 – Contributions, Gifts and Grants Paid Out: Nonprofits can legitimately further their mission by providing funds to individuals and other organizations, so long as the money is used for something that serves their exempt purposes. This line refers to money you give to private persons or other organizations as a contribution, gift, or grant, meaning that the ultimate spending prerogatives are essentially theirs. It does not refer to money you spend on mission-related projects or initiatives that you directly manage or control.

It's obvious that this is an area that has great potential for abuse, so if you make such disbursements, the IRS will be very curious about the details. If you enter anything other than zero on this line, you'll need to provide an attachment showing how much was given to whom, and for what purpose.

Money given to government or to other nonprofits is usually easy to justify. Money given to individuals is always suspect, and in such cases you will need to show that the disbursement is entirely in line with your exempt purposes, and that they came by it fairly –

meaning that the opportunity was equally available to others in their particular charitable class. It is usually good practice to disqualify, as a matter of policy, persons closely related to officers and directors from participating in programs that result in such disbursements.

Line 16 — Disbursements To or For the Benefit of Members: If you spend money on anything that benefits your members exclusively, enter the total amount here and provide an attachment explaining who got how much and what for.

What is being asked about on this line are benefits that are available to members only. This is permissible within the definition of certain types of exempt organizations. A labor union, for example, might provide life insurance policies as a member benefit or make disbursements to its members out of a strike fund.

Here again, the word "substantial" comes into play. For example, you might spend money on refreshments for monthly meetings, or even sponsor a banquet as an inducement to members to attend and participate in your annual meeting. There is usually no reason for a public charity to have closed meetings, but even if these are billed as members only events, the amount spent would probably not be considered substantial, and would more correctly be listed as part of your organization's operating expenses. A conventional 501(c)3 public charity would ordinarily have nothing to declare here.

> ❧ Note: This might be a good time to review your promotional literature regarding what you're advertising as member benefits to ensure that you're not advertising perks that would suggest there should be a dollar amount on this line.

Line 17 — Compensation of Officers, Directors and Trustees: Enter a dollar amount consistent with the answers you provided for *Part V*. As noted in the discussion regarding that item, if anyone receives compensation, the IRS will want you to show that the amount paid was legitimately earned.

Line 18 — Other Salaries and Wages: Enter a dollar amount consistent with the answers you provided for *Part V* for persons other than officers, directors and trustees.

Line 19 — Interest Expense: Enter any interest paid on debt directly connected with your mission activities on this line. Interest on borrowed money (notes, bonds, etc.) should be entered here. Interest associated with financed purchases of depreciable equipment, such as vehicles, furniture and fixtures, and the like, can be rolled into the cost of those items and accounted for elsewhere, rather than being treated separately and included on this line.

Mortgage costs should ordinarily be reported as part of your occupancy expense. Insubstantial items, such as credit card finance charges, are probably more sensibly rolled into general and administrative expenses as service charges.

Line 20 – Occupancy: The term "occupancy" refers to physical space your organization occupies, if any. It may be indoors or out, or both. It may be rented, leased, mortgaged or wholly owned. For example, it may be a small rented office space or an eighty-acre farm. In this case, include all costs associated with whatever space you occupy in order to accomplish your exempt purposes. That would be rent, mortgage payments (with interest), bills for utilities, maintenance costs, improvements, and so on. Fees paid for temporary space such as conference rooms, banquet halls and storage sheds do not qualify as occupancy in this sense, and should be expensed elsewhere.

Many nonprofits will have nothing to show on this line, because they have no permanent home or base of operations.

Line 21 – Depreciation and Depletion: *Depreciation* is an accounting strategy, in which the value of an asset decreases over time according to a predefined schedule, with the incremental loss of value being treated as a cost item. Why would you want to bother with this?

Consider the purchase of a $1200 office computer. At the time of the transaction, your net worth, as shown on your balance sheet, does not change since, although your "cash" asset is reduced by $1200, your "office equipment" asset increases by $1200. At this point, you could merely expense the purchase, by adding a $1200 item to the "office expense" line on your statement of revenue and expenses, and many do just that, keeping things simple by not bothering with depreciation schemes. That leaves a $1200 asset in "office equipment" indefinitely, so after a while – after several such transactions over the years – your balance sheet won't mean much since most of your assets will be overvalued. For small-scale organizations, one might pragmatically ask, "Who cares?" since you probably won't have much in terms of assets anyway, and even if you do, they're actually worth no more than someone is willing to pay for them, regardless of their book value.

On the other hand, you might choose to amortize the $1200 cost (1) because you're interested in maintaining a reasonably meaningful balance sheet, and/or (2) because you want to moderate the impact of major expenditures on your expense and revenue statement. The appropriate depreciation schedule for computers is five years, so each year you'll reduce the value of that asset on your balance sheet by $240, and charge $240 worth of depreciation to your statement of revenue and expenses. This is called "straight line depreciation." There are several other methods, all of which seek to more accurately predict the actual market value of the asset at any given time during its useful life. For example, after five years of straight line depreciation, the book value of this computer would be $0, whereas almost any sort of asset has at least some salvage value.

Depletion refers to the consumption of natural resources which are part of an organization's assets. Unless your assets include working oil wells, gold mines, gravel pits or some other irreplaceable natural resource, you'll have nothing to declare by way of depletion expense.

Line 22 – Professional Fees: Here's a slick way to pocket some of your organization's money; pay yourself a fee for your professional services.

Don't even think about it! It's been tried so many times before that this has become an area for special attention by the IRS. What belongs on this line is the total of what you pay accountants, lawyers, consultants, project managers or other outside contractors for services actually rendered and legitimately billed. Even if one of your insiders is fully qualified in one of these professions, hire someone else, or be prepared to explain why an insider is taking this kind of money out of your organization to a suspicious EOS.

Although the instructions don't ask for details, if you have expenses of this kind, provide an attachment indicating who you're paying, for what, how they charge (hourly rate, flat rate, quoted rate, or retainer) and the total amount of their billings for the period.

Line 23 – Other Expenses: Everything else goes in this catch-all category. These might include:

- amounts spent on mission activities, or the direct pursuit of your exempt purposes
- newsletter production and mailing costs (unless the newsletter is actually employed as a fundraising device)
- general administrative (office) expenses
- meeting expenses
- special expenses associated with your annual meeting such as banquet catering and program (entertainment) costs
- training expenses for board members, employees or volunteers

Provide an attachment describing the activity and indicating the amount spent on each item included in the sum entered on this line. Here again, "substantial" is the operative word. Items that are so small that they have no real significance in themselves should be assigned to one of the listed items, else combined into a "miscellaneous small expenditures" item.

Section B – Balance Sheet

The balance sheet is much easier to complete, since it involves only your current situation. If you were organized more than a year ago, use the figures pertaining to your situation at the end of your most recently completed fiscal year. Otherwise show what your expectations are for the end of the current fiscal year based upon the information you have available at this point.

Line B – Year End: This must the end of your fiscal year, as previously stated in Part I, Item 5. Enter the year-ending date, not just the year – either last year's or this year's.

Line 1 – Cash: – all the money you can readily get your hands on, including petty cash (money in your cigar box), checking accounts and passbook savings accounts.

Line 2 – Accounts Receivable: Receivables are money legally owed to you for goods or services you provided. Grants successfully applied for but as yet unpaid would also be included here. Pledges, which are merely statements of intent to donate that are not legally binding, would not be included, nor would unpaid dues, since the payment of dues ordinarily constitutes the discretionary renewal of membership. Payments due on loans or other notes will be included on Line 4.

Line 3 – Inventories: As used here, "inventories" refers to stocks of marketable material that you are keeping on hand. This could include office supplies, promotional items such as brochures, and fundraising items such as monogrammed coffee cups, tee shirts, and caps. Enter the total value of these items based upon their original cost, rather than what you think they might be worth.

Line 4 – Bonds and Notes Receivable: This can be another hot button item, since interest-free or casual loans to insiders is a frequent abuse of nonprofit funds. On the other hand, if you have a significant amount of reserve capital, lending it can yield higher returns with less risk than investments.

　　※ Note: Lending the organization's money to its officers, directors or insiders is usually considered improper. Officials approving such deals can be considered personally liable for repayment of the debt.

Notes and bonds are similar debt instruments. Notes are formal contracts written by lenders, while bonds are basically certificates of debt, or IOU's, provided by borrowers. Both indicate the amount of the loan and stipulate the date when the loan will be repaid, the interest rate and how the interest will be paid (i.e., over a specified time period, or with the principle when the bond matures). Notes usually set up a schedule of payments, which include both principle and interest. Bonds are usually redeemed at a specified future payment date, unless they are "callable," meaning that the borrower has the option of paying them off before that date, paying only the interest earned up to that point.

Although any income resulting from securities loan agreements is exempt from tax as unrelated business income, such lending can be construed as unrelated business activity if not properly handled, with any related earning becoming taxable UBI.

> ❧ Note: The rules are simple, however. If interested, refer to IRS Publication 598, *Tax on Unrelated Business Income of Exempt Organizations.*

If you have anything to declare on this line, provide an attachment giving the details for each item; to whom the money was loaned, for what purpose, at what rate, when and how it is to be repaid.

Line 5 – Corporate Stocks: If your organization has investments, enter the total current value here (fair market value) and provide and attachment naming each corporation and the exchange where the stock is traded, indicating the number of shares you hold and their value. For stock held in close corporations, name the corporation, summarize its capitalization, and indicate the number and value of shares you hold.

Line 6 – Loans Receivable: This line addresses loans made to individuals, as opposed to business, nonprofit or institutional borrowers. These usually take the form of simple loan agreements, land contracts or mortgages. Enter the total current value of such loans here (principle and interest), and provide the usual attachment naming the borrower, the amount and purpose of the loan, the interest rate and repayment terms.

Line 7 – Other Investments: The current total value of government bonds, developed real estate, land and other items *held as investments* and not covered elsewhere goes here. Attach a summary describing each item and listing its current book value.

Line 8 – Depreciable and Depletable Assets: This is somewhat of a misnomer, since what it refers to is assets you use to accomplish your mission (or your exempt purposes), rather than assets held as investments, and this can include real estate (buildings), which would not ordinarily be considered "depreciable." Furthermore, "depreciable" and "depletable" are used here as merely descriptive terms. Included here are items accountants might customarily commit to a depreciation or depletion schedule. Whether or not you've chosen to do that, enter the total value of such equipment, and provide the usual attachment; a summary describing each item and listing its current book value.

Line 9 – Land: If you hold title to land as part of your organization's exempt purposes (e.g., land conservancies, etc.), enter the total book value here. Use an attachment to provide details; a description of the holdings and the value of each.

Line 10 – Other Assets: The total value of other assets *not held as investments* should be indicated on this line. This can include intangible assets such as rights to intellectual property, prepaid insurance, and so on.

Line 12 – Accounts Payable: Enter the sum of all amounts owed by your organization. This includes, but is not necessarily limited to:

- bills for goods and services
- salaries
- payroll
- interest payments
- unpaid taxes

Although the instructions don't require any detail, if the amount on this line is substantial, an itemization provided as an attachment might help expedite your application if your EOS wonders about this amount.

Line 13 – Contributions, Gifts and Grants Payable: If you are obligated to make any of these kinds of voluntary disbursements, or have any balances due on such commitments, enter the total amount here. An attachment is advised.

> ❧ Reminder: Disbursements of this kind should clearly comply with your exempt purposes.

Line 14 – Mortgages and Notes Payable: This is the flip side of Lines 4 and 6, you being the payer instead of the payee. "Notes" are loan contracts, the loan applying to the purchase of vehicles or equipment, or money borrowed for some other purpose. Notes can be *secured* or *unsecured*, meaning guaranteed by some sort of collateral or not. Mortgages are similar, except usually applying to real property – land and buildings – which also serve as collateral for the loan. The purpose of these contracts is to formalize the lender/borrower agreement, indicating the amount of money loaned, the interest rate, repayment terms and default consequences.

If you are the named debtor on any such contracts, indicate the total principal amount currently remaining on this line. Attach an itemized list of any such debts, giving the details of each obligation:

- purpose of the obligation
- name of the lender
- original amount of the contract
- original date and length of contract
- interest rate
- repayment terms

Line 15 – Other Liabilities: Enter the total of any obligations not included on Lines 12, 13 and 14. These might include balances due on other kinds contracts such as insurance programs and leases, unpaid fines and legal judgments, and so on. An explanatory attachment is required, explaining each component of the sum entered on this line.

Line 17 – Total Fund Balances or Net Assets: A nonprofit's assets often wind up being distributed among separate funds which have certain restrictions on their use. For example, you might elect to set aside a minimum amount of cash as a reserve fund to ensure that operating money will be available even in the leanest of times. Or perhaps someone makes a very generous donation and mentions that they would like to see the money used for some particular purpose, so you set aside that money as a donor advised fund informally designated for that purpose. When an organization uses *fund accounting*, separate balance sheets (assets, liabilities, fund balance) are formally maintained for each fund.

Although most nonprofits wind up with what they consider to be special funds, few volunteer treasurers in small organizations will have ever heard of fund accounting. If they use the term *fund balances* at all, it usually means "net assets," the difference between total assets and total liabilities, being preferred over "net worth," since that term doesn't seem as appropriate for nonprofits as it might for businesses or individuals. A simple note is often then included on the balance sheet showing how the assets are distributed among an "unrestricted fund" and other named funds.

If you use fund accounting, enter the total fund balances. Otherwise subtract Line 16 from Line 11 and enter the value of your net assets on this line:

Line 17 (Net Assets) = Line 11 – Line 16

Line 19 – Substantial Changes in Assets or Liabilities: The question asks whether there have been any *substantial* changes in the financials *since the period reported above*. If your information is current, the answer to this question will probably be *"No."* If you have reason to answer *"Yes,"* include an attachment explaining the situation.

❧ Note: Attachments where required or advisable for these financial statements, as they appear on the example form, are included on the *SfS* website.

Part X ~ Public Charity Status

As mentioned in the *"Private Foundation or Public Charity?"* discussion earlier in this section, the IRS will designate your organization as a private foundation unless you specifically claim and can provide convincing evidence that you are a public charity. This section of the application provides an opportunity for you to help your EOS make the proper determination.

As mentioned before, public charities must meet the test of having broad public support. However, certain other situations automatically qualify an organization as a public charity:

- churches
- government units
- hospitals
- safety test labs
- schools
- nonprofit subsidiaries of other public charities

Question 1 asks directly whether you are a private foundation. Assuming that you wish to qualify for recognition of exemption as a public charity –

1a: *"No"*

If you answer "Yes" to 1a, then –

1b.   (checked)

– and provide the attachment as directed. If you are applying as a private foundation, your Articles of Incorporation must include specific restrictions on the corporation and assertions about how its money will be distributed. the IRS provides these boiler-plate provisions for you on page 27 of their *Publication 557 (March 2005)*. If you have not already done so, amend your corporate charter by adding an article called "Provisions Required by IRS for Private Foundations" (or whatever you wish to title it) and insert the IRS paragraphs verbatim. Then cite that article in a brief attachment. As explained in the instructions, forty-nine of the fifty states provide these assurances as a matter of state law. However there are often certain conditions and exceptions. If you choose to rely on state law instead of writing these provisions into your articles of incorporation, refer to the appendix provided in the instructions to ensure that your assertion will be acceptable.

Question 2: If you checked "Yes" to Question 1, indicate whether or not you are a "Private operating foundations" at Question 2. Private foundations that actively conduct their own charitable, educational, or other exempt programs and activities are called "operating foundations." Museums, zoos, research facilities and libraries are often organized as operating foundations. Private foundations otherwise usually provide grants to other organizations or to individuals for charitable or other exempt purposes, and are called "non-operating foundations." The income distribution rules for operating foundations are somewhat more liberal, and donations to these organizations are more highly deductible.

Question 3: If you checked "Yes" to Question 2, Question 3 provides an opportunity for you to submit financial reports that will readily demonstrate that you are indeed functioning as an operating foundation. If you have such financials, check "Yes" and attach them to your application.

Question 4: If you have been so recently organized that such financial reports are not yet available, Question 4 offers you an opportunity to attach statements from your accountant certifying that future reports will indeed show that your are an operating foundation. Lacking that, you may attach a document of your own indicating why you feel your organization can be described as an operating foundation rather than a regular private foundation.

Question 5: If you answered "No" to Question 1, you must now indicate how you think you qualify as a public charity. Section 509 of the U.S. Code was drafted by Congress in the 1960's to more precisely define the term "private foundation." It also defines "public charity" by describing these as organizations that are not private foundations for various reasons. Section 170 of the code deals with the nature and deductibility of charitable contributions and gifts.

Read the choices carefully and check the appropriate box. Most applicants will check box *h*. The main difference between *g* and *h* is that organizations described as 509(a)(1) / 170(b)(1)(A)(vi) may receive a substantial amount of their support from a governmental unit or the general public, while 509(a)(2)'s are organizations that can meet the one-third public support test (previously described).

Question 6: If you identified yourself as anything other than a *g*, *h*, or *i* type organization, you'll automatically qualify for a *definitive ruling* as a public charity. Otherwise the question of your status, public charity or private foundation, hinges on your being able to demonstrate that your public support is substantial, preferably meeting the one-third support test. The difference is that public charities are exempt from certain taxes imposed on private foundations. The 501(c)(3) designation is not the issue.

Part a: You might not be able to provide convincing evidence at this time because your organization is too new to have accumulated such history, or because you have not kept accounting records adequate to the task. In this case, the information you have provided should be sufficient to allow the IRS to conclude that your organization *is likely to* be publicly supported, and you should check this box. Under an advance ruling you'll be treated as a public charity for up to five years, during which you will be expected to accumulate convincing evidence supporting that designation. If you do, you will then receive a definitive ruling. If not, you'll be designated a private foundation and may be liable for taxes during the advance ruling period.

> ❧ Note: If you will have soon completed at least eight months of your tax year and, on the basis of that, can satisfy the public support requirement, you might elect to delay your application until you can apply for a definitive ruling.

Since the advance ruling assessment period can be extended up to 100-1/2 months, but the statute of limitations in the revenue code is three years, if you request an advance ruling you will also be asked to voluntarily wave the statute of limitations.

If you feel that the information you've provided clearly demonstrates that you are indeed publicly supported to the extent required by the category you checked, do not request an advance ruling.

Part b: If you feel that the information you've provided clearly demonstrates that you are indeed publicly supported to the extent required by the category you indicated in Question 5, check this box, then answer questions (i) and/or (ii), depending upon which option you checked in Question 5.

> ❧ Note: The term *"disqualified person"* generally refers to insiders:
> - a substantial contributor
> - a foundation manager
> - a person owning more than 20% of an organization that is a substantial contributor
> - family members of someone described as a "disqualified person"
> - another organization in which such persons hold more than a 35% interest
> - another organization which is effectively controlled by the person or persons in control of the foundation in question
> - a government official

Obviously, the purpose of these questions is to evaluate the nature of your financial support. You can show that you are publicly supported either by meeting the one-third support test, or if that is not possible, the facts and circumstances test. The facts and circumstances test accommodates the reality that new organizations are often funded by seed money provided by founders and special enthusiasts, by applying certain minimum conditions and a variety of subjective considerations to determine whether or not the applicant is likely to be publicly supported. These are discussed in detail in the *"Qualifying as Publicly Supported"* section of IRS Publication 557, *"Tax Exempt Status for Your Organization"* which is available online at the "Forms and Publications" line on the IRS web site.

Question 7: "Unusual grants" are gifts, donations or bequests which might be large enough to adversely affect your classification as a public charity, which were not anticipated and come from "disinterested persons" (the opposite of a "disqualified person"). If the financial information you provided in Section IX includes any receipts of this nature, you have the opportunity to explain that here.

7:     *"No"*

Part XI ~ User Fee Information

Your check or money order in the amount of either $300 or $750 must be submitted with your completed application form. The fee depends only upon your actual or expected *annual gross receipts*, over the four-year period you reported or projected in Section IX. Divide the sum you entered at Section IX-A, Line 10e by 4 to calculate your average gross receipts. If the number is less than $10,000 your application fee is $300. Otherwise remit $750. Your check or money order should be made payable to the *"United States Treasury."*

Submitting Your Form 1023

Congratulations! Sign and date your form any you will have completed the hard part. Go to the last two pages of the form and work through the check list to make sure your application is presented to the IRS just exactly as they like to have it.

Some items on the check list are somewhat less than intuitive.

- The purpose of the third check box is to remind you that everything you include with your application should be identified by your FEIN number.

- "An exact copy of your complete articles of organization" (sixth check box) means a "conformed copy" of your "creating document," which is the copy your state sent back to you as proof that your form had been properly filed, and indicating the official date of filing. Compare the citations you provided in *Part III, Lines 1 and 2* to the copy of the state form you're including with your application to make sure you have this right.

- Who signs? This doesn't make a lot of difference. It's an good idea to review your assembled package with the board, and then have it signed off by your executive officer. Why? Complications can arise, and in that event it will be emotionally easier on everyone if finger-pointing can be avoided by virtue of the fact that you did your best as a team. Otherwise any duly elected officer or director may sign.

- You'll probably be tempted to present your application in a nifty binder of some sort; but don't do it. Assemble the papers as directed, and then put them in a regular 9" x 12" envelope to keep them in order during mailing.

- There is no real need for special handling of your application. Because of the weight of the documents USPS *Priority Mail* service makes sense, and the post office will provide you with a nice rugged official-looking outer envelope for free. If you use the online *"Click-n-Ship"* to print the label, you'll also get free delivery confirmation. The IRS will not bother to advise you that your application has been received, but you may call the IRS Customer Service for Applications (1-877-829-5500) whenever you wish to inquire about its status.

Your Letter of Recognition

More than half the applications received are merit closed. If you're lucky, yours will be one of them and you'll receive a letter of recognition sometime within the next 60-days. Otherwise, you'll receive a letter from your EOS asking for clarifications or more information, and allowing you 21-days to respond. How long the process will take in that case depends upon how promptly and successfully you respond. By all means respond within the 21-day limit, else your application will be round-filed and your have to start all over again.

Remain confident; almost 80% of applications are eventually approved. The other 20% are cases that wind up being classified as 501(c)-

somethingelse's, or are abandoned by the applicant. Less than 1% receive denials.

You'll probably receive an advance ruling, via a copy of IRS Form Letter 1045. If you're among the few who successfully apply for a definitive ruling, it'll be Form Letter 947. Letters of recognition are surprisingly bare-bones, as you can see by the examples provided on the *SfS* website. But these are important and valuable documents. Scan your letter, and then put the original in your safe deposit box with your other important papers.

Advance Ruling Follow-ups

New organizations claiming to be public charities ordinarily receive advance rulings, because they simply have not been around long enough to accumulate the donor history required to demonstrate that they are publicly supported. As mentioned above, the IRS will begin with a presumption that your organization is a private foundation. It then falls to you to make your case that you are a public charity, not a private foundation.

The practical definitions of "private foundation" and "public charity" are given above. The IRS, however, relies on Section 509(a)(1) and Section 170(b)(1)(a), or Section 509(a)(2) of the Code. This is mentioned here because the advance ruling follow-up form, IRS Form 8734, *Support Schedule for Advance Ruling Period*, addresses these sections when asking you to evaluate your public support experience. Confusingly, the IRS defines what a public charity is by saying what a private foundation is not and, of course, that definition is verbose and convoluted with referrals to subparagraphs and other sections of the Code. No explanation is provided regarding the differences between Section 509(a)(1) / 170(b)(1)(a) organizations and 509(a)(2) organizations.

These organizations both qualify as public charities, except that 509(a)(2)'s are organizations that ordinarily receive some form of compensation for the services they perform. These are therefore sometimes called "service provider" charities. Examples might include symphony orchestras, amateur theater companies, children's camps, drug rehabilitation centers, hospice organizations, and others whose primary mission is to provide a service for which a fee is ordinarily charged. Most small nonprofits, therefore, qualify under Section 509(a)(1) and Section 170(b)(1)(a), rather than under Section 509(a)(2).

Form 8734 seeks to verify your status by evaluating your experience during your five-year advance ruling period. Ideally you'll be able to show that you meet the one-third test on Line 12. If not, but your public support amounted to more than 10%, you can still claim recognition under the facts and circumstances test by making your case in a written statement and attaching that to the form.

When applying for an advance ruling, you should familiarize yourself with the follow-up process and set up an appropriate record-keeping system; one that will capture all the data needed to successfully complete the process five years later.

Adverse Determinations

If the IRS decides to deny the exemption, the organization is notified before the determination is finalized. The organization may generally supplement its application with additional information to try to correct the problem. If the IRS does issue a final adverse determination, then the organization may appeal the decision to the IRS Appeals Office or, if appropriate, IRS Headquarters. Once the organization has exhausted its administrative appeals, it may, subject to numerous requirements, file an appeal in the federal courts.

Application for Sales Tax Exemptions

*Unless you're in Arkansas or Hawaii, you can
preserve donated resources with a sales tax exemption.*

All but five of the fifty states currently have some sort of sales tax. Most provide certain exemptions for nonprofits. Purchases are usually nontaxable, and sales (e.g., of fundraising merchandise) are often not taxed until gross sales exceed a certain limit.

Most states still issue exemption certificates, or "sales tax licenses." The application process usually involves filling out the state's unique form and sending it in with a copy of your conformed articled of incorporation and your IRS letter of exemption attached. You will then be registered as tax-exempt and given a "sales tax number," which is often the same as your EIN. To make tax-exempt purchases, you will usually have to provide the seller with another form for their files, which identifies you as a *bona fide* tax-exempt buyer.

A few states, Michigan being one of them, no longer issue exemption certificates, relying on articles of incorporation and IRS letters of exemption as evidence enough of tax exempt status. Tax exempt purchases are made by providing an exemption declaration form with these two documents attached for the sellers' files.

To find out about your state's law, search the Internet –

texas "sales tax exemption" nonprofit	Search

This book is written with small NPOs in mind, so it's not likely you'll be spending big bucks. Sales taxes average around five or six percent, so if you spend $5,000 a year, that amounts to only $250 to $300. Nevertheless, paying sales tax when you don't have to means that some of the money donors gave you won't be used for the good purposes they had in mind when they gave it. A little extra time taken to take advantage of sales tax exemptions will fulfill your duty of due diligence, and your frugality will demonstrate to contributors that you are a good steward of donated funds.

3

Meetings

Planning prevents meetings from turning into gab fests.

— ❧ —

3
Meetings

The Secretary's Role(s)

So many hats – and only one head!

Nonprofits are managed by consensus. Consensus is most easily accomplished by getting together to express feelings and ideas and share relevant information. The get-togethers are called "meetings."

Incorporated membership organizations have two kinds of regularly-scheduled meetings; periodic board meetings and an annual meeting. These meetings will be prescribed in the bylaws. Your bylaws probably specify that an annual meeting of the general membership be held at the same time and place every year, and that the board of directors must meet at least quarterly. Provisions for special meetings of the membership will also be included.

The responsibilities for meetings usually fall to the secretary. These usually include:

- complying with the requirements in the bylaws
- arranging for meeting space
- assembling and disseminating agendas
- issuing the formal call
- providing for amenities
- serving as parliamentarian during the meeting
- recording and publishing the minutes

Complying With the Bylaws

Who is responsible for seeing to it that obligatory meetings happen?

For small NPO's, the President is usually also the corporation's chief executive officer, so compliance with governance mandates is their responsibility. The reality is, however, that presidents are often the chief public relations officer, chief fundraising officer, board team captain and chief schmoozer. Being able to get individuals to pull together as a crew all rowing the same boat is a huge benefit to any organization. Networking with other organizations and interested third parties is also essential for any successful nonprofit. Unfortunately, the same personality organization that makes a president a great leader and a great networker is not likely to engender a concern for minor details.

Worse yet are presidents who do not fit the above description, who are impatient and say things like, *"A camel is a horse that was designed by a committee!"* and see no reason to waste time talking about things they already have their minds made up about – independent go-getters who feel they already know what to do, and do it. But the very worst are the neurotic turf protectors who are intentionally secretive, guarding their inside information like a junkyard dog, or the control freaks who think they're the only ones who know how to get things done and done right.

Under the best of circumstances, the secretary usually becomes the closest member of the board to the president – often actually the president's adjutant. Under the worst, the secretary might be forced to serve as the board's go-between or watchdog, either working around a problem president, or keeping them honest. Whatever the case, it'll probably fall to you to *ensure* that the rules about meetings are complied with.

Not to worry! There's an easy way to keep the monkey off your back.

Before any and every meeting is adjourned, bring up a motion to set the time and place for the next scheduled meeting. Be definite, naming a date, time and place in your motion; *"I move that we next meet on Saturday, March 17, 2007 at two o'clock in the afternoon at Midwestern Community College in Kalamazoo, Michigan."* Motions have to be properly disposed of, so the matter of your next meeting cannot simply be ignored. To make sure that in the heat of a successful meeting you won't forget this detail, include notice of your motion in the agenda you prepare for each meeting. If there is a move to table or postpone consideration of your motion, you will have ample opportunity to remind everyone that the meeting in question is required under the bylaws.

— ❧ —

Arranging for a Meeting Place

Small nonprofits rarely have facilities of their own, so this assumes you don't either. That's not a problem, since facilities abound. Many of these are available to you at reduced rates, or with no charge at all.

If you have a large group and the plan includes a catered banquet, potluck or serious *hors d'oeuvres*, you'll probably need a room with kitchen facilities. The choices are:

- township halls
- churches
- museums

Township halls usually have a published rate schedule, since they're ordinarily available for private use (family reunions and wedding receptions) as well as public functions. As a nonprofit, you fit somewhere in between. If the schedule doesn't list a nonprofit rate, ask for that special consideration. Mainline churches always have banquet facilities and are usually, as a matter of outreach policy, readily willing to make their rooms available without charge to nonprofits. Museums usually have auditoriums or classroom facilities for meetings and seminars, often with adjacent food service facilities. Contacts are the township clerk, the church secretary or business manager, or the museum's business office. Naturally, in exchange for any special consideration, you'll agree to leave the facility as you found it, or better, ready for the next event.

For small meetings, such as board or committee meetings, the possibilities are:

- a private home
- churches
- museums
- county or township offices
- community colleges
- community centers
- another nonprofit's offices
- service clubs

A private home does not necessarily have to be the residence of one of the meeting's participants. People who do not feel interested in, or up to the task of, serving on the board or a committee are often readily willing to contribute in other ways, such as hosting meetings in their homes. As an additional attraction, these are often showplace homes – comfortable places in wonderfully scenic or interesting locations.

Churches of any size will have facilities for small meetings. Again, most mainline churches are eager to accommodate exempt organizations as part of their outreach or local mission, so there is ordinarily no charge for the use of their room.

Museums, county or township offices, community colleges, and community centers also always have rooms suitable for small meetings. These publicly supported entities, as a matter of fairness and political correctness, usually have to charge a fee for the use of their facilities, often called a "cleaning fee." The fee is usually very affordable, but that shouldn't discourage you from asking for special consideration based upon your also being a publicly supported organization as opposed to a private group. The payment of a cleaning fee does not mean you should feel comfortable leaving a lot of work for the janitor.

Other nonprofits and service clubs include organizations like the Chamber of Commerce, Jaycees, AA/Alanon, the Elks, Eagles, Moose, VFW and American Legion. These groups typically have idle facilities which they're willing to share simply for that reason. Because they are nonprofits, they're often willing to make space available to other nonprofits without charge. As a good steward of donated funds, there is no reason you should feel shy about asking for that consideration provided your use of the room won't add anything to the organization's overhead. That means you do all the setup and, without fail, the tear-down and cleanup.

Most of these organizations are not in the hall rental business, so may not spend a lot of their time as hospitality managers. Halls are often controlled by volunteer buildings and grounds committees, which are usually more concerned with maintenance issues rather than event hosting. When you make arrangements for the use of someone else's facilities, if they have no formal agreement of their own, write a letter on your letterhead immediately confirming your reservation, noting the day, date and time and anything else you verbally agreed to (or took exception to). If a fee is involved, include a check for the whole amount with their reservation form, user agreement, or your letter. If you rely on a verbal reservation with a pay later agreement, on the day of your meeting you might find that those in charge of the building have had no notice of your coming or, worse yet, the facilities have been made available to someone else.

— ❧ —

Notice of Meetings – Issuing Calls

The *call* of a meeting is a written notice of the time and place, which is distributed to all members of the board, committee, or organization, a reasonable time in advance. Meeting calls have a special significance under parliamentary rules. The purpose of the rules is to *ensure* that everyone's rights are protected, with all having ample opportunity to adjust their personal schedule and prepare for the meeting.

The rules about previous notice require that notice of meetings be provided in a timely manner, and it's your duty to see to it that these rules are complied with. The meeting can otherwise be declared illegal and any business conducted or decisions made during the meeting can be vacated. Therefore you'll want to make this an area for special attention.

Requirements for previous notice of meetings are probably defined in your bylaws; otherwise your parliamentary authority rules. The requirements vary, depending upon the situation; for example, whether the meeting is a regularly scheduled event, whether matters will be taken up that require a majority vote, and so on. In the latter case, the call must also include notice of the motion(s) that will be put before the group at the meeting. Review the notice requirements in your bylaws, and the rules for previous notice in your parliamentary authority.

In most cases, the requirement will be between ten and thirty-days. In some cases the period of advance notice might be limited, as in statements like "ten-days and not more than thirty-days." To simplify the job, you can decide to go with thirty-days as a matter of habit, and include an agenda for the meeting with the call. Whatever the time requirement, the clock ordinarily begins ticking the day your notices are mailed, and stops the day before the meeting. Weekends and holidays are counted. For example, notices for a meeting on July 31 should be mailed on July 1 to provide exactly thirty days prior notice.

Whether required or not, calls should be provided for all meetings as a courtesy to those involved. For the time being, at least, relying on electronic forms of communication as a means of giving prior notice is not considered acceptable. Regular mail is legally considered to be reliable. Notices should be printed and mailed using regular first class service. Notice of annual meetings of the general membership can usually be provided in the issue of a newsletter that precedes the meeting, thereby avoiding special mailing expense.

Examples of calls are provided on the *SfS* website.

Preparing Agendas

Every meeting should have a printed agenda, which should be included in the call.

The agenda gives everyone a snapshot of what will transpire at the meeting, and a sense of its purpose and importance. For large meetings, such as annual meetings, it serves as a program which enables people unfamiliar with the process to easily follow along and understand what's going on. For smaller meetings, such as board and committee meetings, it can help motivate participation by showing that the business at hand justifies the contribution of one's personal time and expense, and that the value of the contribution is recognized by the care being taken to manage the meeting effectively.

In all cases, the agenda serves as a tool for keeping business meetings focused, preventing them from degenerating into social events or undisciplined gab fests which drag on interminably with only some members participating. When that is permitted to happen, meetings are usually unproductive and the most dedicated participants often become frustrated to the point of excusing themselves from future meetings or even leaving the organization entirely.

What goes into the agenda largely depends upon the purpose(s) of the meeting. Some items might be carry-overs from the previous meeting. Other items will be matters that have arisen since the previous meeting. Begin keeping a simple grocery list of what will be dealt with at the next meeting before the present meeting is adjourned. Add to it as things come up between then and the next meeting. Finish your list by polling key members and board members for items they think should be included on the agenda for the next meeting. Then compile a draft of the agenda for the next meeting, and submit it to whoever will preside, ordinarily the president, for their final input and approval.

Regardless of the size or nature of the meeting, the written agenda should consistently follow the *order of business* outlined in the bylaws or whatever parliamentary authority you rely on. This usually takes the following form:

- determination that a quorum is present
- call to order
- opening ceremonies and welcoming comments

    1. roll call (board and committee meetings only)
    2. adoption of the agenda
    3. reading and approval of the minutes
    4. reports of officers and committees

5. special orders
6. unfinished business and general orders
7. new business
8. adjournment

- open discussion
- announcement
- program or social hour

All meetings have three components, the call to order, the formal business session, and optional closing activities. The numbered items in the above list represent the business session, preceded and followed by the informal functions.

In small meetings, the agenda need not necessarily have the significance attributed to it under parliamentary rules written with respect to larger assemblies or more formal meetings. The reason you should include its adoption however, is to provide an easy way to keep your meeting focused. When adopted in this matter, the agenda becomes the orders of the day. If the meeting begins to digress unproductively, it's an easy matter for the presiding officer to politely cite that, and suggest that the meeting return to the agenda or, lacking that, for any member to call for the orders of the day. Adopting the agenda might seem like an unnecessary formality for a small, informal meeting, but the simple act will raise everyone's awareness that the meeting will be carefully managed.

It is customary for the Secretary to stand and read the minutes of the last meeting, after which anyone may move their approval. For your small meetings prepare copies of the minutes for as many as will be attending so that the presiding officer can simply refer to that draft and suggest a motion to approve the minutes as written, or even say something like, "If there is no objection, the chair will declare the minutes approved by consensus as written."

With the exception of the treasurer's report, other officers and committee chairs may have nothing to report. Find out who actually will have something to report. In the interest of courtesy and efficiency, include only those who do on the agenda. After the captioned reports have been presented, it will be sufficient for the presiding officer to ask, "Does any other officer or committee have anything to report?" Reports should also be written up with copies made available for each person at the meeting so that they can be accepted as written, rather than the officer or committee chair having to speak for any purpose other than to answer questions or clarify complex or subtle aspects of their report. Reading reports to the meeting after having provided printed copies is usually unnecessary and inappropriate.

In the context of small meetings, "special orders" are usually limited to items mandated by the bylaws, such as the nomination or election of officers or the appointment of board or committee members. However, this could also be a particular item of business that has, for some reason, been assigned for consideration at this particular time. For example, if something requires input from an outside authority who does not wish to sit out the entire meeting, that item could be assigned for consideration at this time, and thereby becomes a special order.

Unfinished business and general orders are often called "old business." This refers to matters that were not resolved in, and have been carried forward from, the previous meeting, as reflected in the minutes for that meeting. If there are no such matters, do not include this item on the agenda, and it will be understood that there is no old business. (The presiding officer should not ask, "Is there any old business?" since the reading of the minutes from the previous meeting has already answered that question.)

The agenda should list all known items of legitimate business that members wish to introduce by motion or otherwise. The presiding officer can then call upon these individuals in order to present their motion, proposal, or information, and have the matter discussed, debated, voted or otherwise appropriately disposed of. Following that, the presiding officer must ask if there is any other new business, and recognize members as they are able to obtain the floor when no question is pending. Anyone with standing (able to vote) cannot be prevented from making appropriate motions or introducing legitimate business at this point, regardless of possible fatigue and time pressures.

It isn't really necessary to show "adjournment" on the agenda. Because of the above rule, it isn't possible to set a precise time for adjournment, even though many "how to manage a meeting" articles suggest doing so. However, indicating where the official meeting is expected to end serves to establish an expectation that will help prevent the meeting from speciously continuing on beyond that point.

Examples of agendas for an annual meeting of the general membership and for board meetings are included on the *SfS* website. These can be used as templates.

Amenities Make a Difference

Most people aren't big on meetings, and justifiably so. Almost everyone has experience that suggests that meetings are typically an unproductive waste of time. A little attention to creature comforts and human nature can help your meetings be perceived as comfortable, maybe even enjoyable, and productive.

Small Meetings

Choose a location for your meeting that is suitable for meetings, one that is free from outside noise and disruptions. Pay attention to seating, making sure there are seats for everyone, all of the same quality and comfort. If note-taking is required, everyone should have a surface to write on. No one should sit behind or to the side of your speakers, or off to the side of other attendees. A round-table format is ideal for small meetings, since it literally keeps everyone *in the loop.*

If seating has to be arranged auditorium-style, people will typically tend to choose a seat behind those already seated. Before beginning, ask everyone to move up to the front seats, vacating the space towards the back of the room. This will help make sure visuals are visible, and that everyone can hear. It will also facilitate the non-disruptive passing of handouts, props or samples around the room. Invite speakers to come forward to say what they have to say, else at least stand at their seat.

Food and drink often relaxes the atmosphere, helps make people feel comfortable, helps sustain positive energy levels and promotes social interaction. Consider the possibility of differing tastes among your group:

- offer assorted fresh veggies and fruit (assorted grapes and berries) in addition to small Danishes and donuts (cookies, cakes, breads, cheeses and crackers are not recommended as refreshments)

- light candies are also appropriate, such as butter mints and candy-coated almonds
- drinks should include water (plain and flavored), coffee (freshly brewed regular and decaf) and tea (assorted packets of regular and herbal or, in season, a choice of regular and raspberry iced teas); alcoholic and carbonated drinks are not recommended
- provide appropriate glasses and cups, also small paper plates, napkins and disposable tableware; many find it distasteful to drink from bottles and eat with fingers in indoors settings

The refreshment table should be located in the end of the room opposite the speakers or head table. Set the table nicely, using a paper table cloth and matching paper and plastic ware. All these things can be purchased very inexpensively at specialty stores such as *Party Express* and *Let's Throw a Party!*

Indicate the location of convenient and private toilet facilities before calling the meeting to order, so that everyone knows where to go without having to ask, preferably by exiting the room at the end opposite the speaker or head table.

Large Meetings – Banquets

For small nonprofits, "large meetings" usually means the annual meeting. Annual meetings are usually mandatory compliance affairs. That fact isn't lost on the general membership, most of whom probably care a lot about what your organization does, but don't give two hoots about its administration and governance. In good times (i.e., when things are going well and there is no contention in the ranks), attendance at your annual meeting will vary directly with how much party and showmanship you provide. If you want a good turn-out, you'll have to give people good reason to come.

If you have problems with the idea of spending money to boost attendance at your annual meeting, recheck your premises and find another argument for doing that. Think about it as —

- a membership recruitment and retention event
- a fundraising event
- – or both

Regardless of whether your meeting has serious business to deal with or is only *pro forma*, plan on providing food and entertainment. Your affair will probably be held on a Saturday because that's when most people will be free to attend. A luncheon works best if prospective attendees —

- have to travel any significant distance to make your meeting
- have children they can, or must, bring along
- are active people who are likely to have Saturday nights booked

If you have a choice, set the room up with round tables. If only long sixes or eights are available, arrange them separately, rather than in long rows, to promote social interaction and facilitate movement around the room. A diagonal arrangement of rectangular tables will eliminate the need for some of the people to turn all the way around to see speakers and presentations. A head table is not recommended. Better to have your officers and board members mingle, rather than set them apart from the others.

Schedule your business meeting before lunch. Do not try to coerce participation in your meeting by holding your luncheon guests hostage. Open the room an hour before the meeting. Refreshments need not be provided at this time. Those who wish to participate in the meeting will arrive during this hour, and may want a few moments to collect and review whatever handouts you have provided, and to discuss issues and concerns with others. Those who show up too late for the meeting (but just in time for lunch) might someday prove just as helpful to your organization in other ways. The important thing is that they come.

Make Your Meeting a Show

Think of your meeting as part of the show, rather than as a dreaded, but necessary evil. No matter how small or informal *you think* your organization is, manage your meeting so that it comes off as an interesting and worthwhile experience for everyone in room. This does not mean turning the meeting into a roast or joke fest. It means planning and conducting your meeting with a level of propriety appropriate to the doing of your corporation's business, yet casual enough to make everyone comfortable. A casual atmosphere arises when those participating are familiar enough with their role to be comfortable in it and able to play their part smoothly and confidently, rather than embarrassedly stumbling through it. Participants, especially the presiding officer, should perceive their role as part of a performance. Rehearsals, at least a quick run-though of the agenda, are essential.

Staging is also important. Set up two tables, one either side of a lectern (if available) at the front of the room as a panel. When the meeting begins, the panel members will then take their seats at the front of the room, the presiding officer to the left of the lectern (from the audience point of view) and the Secretary on the right, with others seated as they wish on either side. If there is no lectern, seat the presiding officer at the middle of the table. All speakers use the lectern, because that focuses attention on them and what they have to say. If there is no lectern, speakers should stand and try to speak with a clear, strong voice. A sloppy, casual decorum on the panel does not project an image of a board that has a lot on the ball and takes its responsibilities seriously.

Speakers from the audience, when recognized by the presiding officer, should be invited to stand when taking the floor, and come forward to speak if what they have to say is lengthier than a few sentences. If the room and the gathering are large enough, use the room's public address system if there is one, otherwise borrow or rent a portable PA system. If much audience participation is expected, a portable microphone will also be helpful. If there will be award presentations, hand-shaking or any other sort of activity that is likely to involve picture-taking, provide enough space in front of the panel for those functions. Casually shaking hands or passing awards from behind the panel or lectern inappropriately diminishes whatever honor and recognition you are trying to convey.

When the meeting is adjourned, the panel is vacated, with the panel members returning once again to the gathering.

Lunch; Simplicity, But With Chic

Have it catered. Potlucks don't work very well anymore, since busy families don't have time to manage a home restaurant and aren't into food preparation. If people feel they have to bring something, that'll be a disincentive for many. Besides that, potluck tables are nowadays more likely to feature buckets of KFC chicken, boxes of Little Cesar's pizza and bland potato salad, coleslaw and pistachio jello salad from the supermarket deli, rather than good old fashioned home cooking. Same old stuff – not much to come for.

As an alternative to professional catering, if your meeting place has kitchen facilities (church facilities, township halls and so on often do), and you can recruit a kitchen committee, it can be fun to cater the event yourself. Meal planning is easy; just enter "catering lunch menus" on your favorite Internet search engine.

As they say in the restaurant business, "Presentation is everything!" Creating a favorable impression for your members and guests as they first enter the room will get things started off on the right foot. Set your room up nicely with paper table cloths, matching paper and plastic dinnerware and napkins. Provide ice water with clear plastic glasses at each table. Candy dishes with mixed nuts and butter mints are always a nice touch. These items do much to dress up an otherwise bland room, while also covering the blemishes on well-used tables. As suggested above, they can be purchased quite inexpensively at party specialty stores. Simple centerpieces such as small arrangements of silk flowers or some other appropriate item (for example, model boats if your organization has a nautical connection or Christmas decorations at that time of year) will complete the table decorations. Such items are very inexpensively available at *Hobby Lobby* and other stores selling imported merchandise. As an added bit of fun, the table decorations can be given away after lunch as prizes using a simple drawing, or some other little game.

You can recoup a substantial part of the cost of this affair by collecting donations. As noted in the fundraising section of this book, you should always provide an opportunity for people to make contributions, regardless of the size or nature of the activity. In this case, provide small wicker baskets containing contribution envelopes on every table. Announcements or signs explaining the purpose of these baskets are not required or appropriate. Before the end of lunch is a good time for each officer, board member or other "plant" to quietly, but visibly, fill out one of the envelopes and enclose a contribution. Everyone will get the idea, and with a little luck a bandwagon effect will cause them to follow suit. Selling meal tickets is not a good idea, because it serves as a disincentive. That might also put you in the position of receiving unrelated business income, whereas you are otherwise simply providing a free meal and receiving free-will contributions.

What About the Kids?

Activities for children, both during the meeting and during the program following lunch, will also help promote attendance. If you plan something that will attract the interest of the children, they'll often drag their parents along. These need not necessarily be highly planned activities. A nearby park, playground or beach might easily take care of this need. Special drinks and snacks for the kids will not be needed if there are grocery stores, ice cream shops and the like in the area. Kids have more fun shopping for their own treats than having to settle for the healthy treats adults are likely to provide for them.

Parents of younger children will need to know that capable care is being provided. This is a great opportunity for older teenagers to participate, by planning and supervising these activities and events. Publicity about your annual meeting should include notice that child care and events for children will be provided.

Programs and Entertainment

A special presentation is another ideal way to promote attendance at your annual meeting. Coming up with a good program, however, is often not an easy task.

For example, spending contributed money on something that is pure entertainment is sure to raise some eyebrows. There are exceptions, of course. For example, if prospective adult participation includes lots of families with children, you can probably justify spending a reasonable amount on an entertaining program for children that runs parallel to a more mature presentation for adults. Otherwise this reality makes it difficult to provide a program that is purely entertaining. Amateur entertainment isn't likely to be a big draw, and professionals are usually not able to work for nothing.

Towards coming up with a low cost or no cost program that your meeting will find enjoyable and worthwhile, think about your particular group's interests. Why do they participate in your organization, and why are they at the meeting? Having figured that out, is there someone who could share their knowledge or skill as a speaker? Perhaps there's a highly relevant documentary film; you can find documentary films at online rental services at reasonable prices. Speakers are not usually as easy to afford, but don't discount local talent. Is there someone in, or associated with, your group who can speak with authority? How about someone from another nonprofit; one with a similar or related mission? Perhaps you can create a documentary presentation of your own covering all the great fun and accomplishments during the past year. With today's technology, a creative high school student can put together a surprisingly polished and professional-looking presentation on DVD, with little cost beyond that of the media.

If you have some money in the budget, arts and humanities touring programs are often a great source of programs suitable for adults and for children. Most areas have some sort of arts and humanities council or alliance, connected with the National Endowment for the Arts (NEA) and National Endowment for the Humanities (NEH). These programs are often edutainment, rather than purely entertaining or purely educational. They are usually not free. Even if presenters are willing to perform for free, they still ordinarily need to have their expenses reimbursed. However, the fact that this kind of entertainment is more culture-based might make any related expense more palatable to the watchdogs in your group.

* * *

Annual Reports

Annual reports aren't mandatory, but they are a nice touch as a handout for your annual meeting. Some of the information you'd include in an annual report, such as financial reports, would be handout material anyway. Beyond that, a nicely bound annual report –

- will impart an image of competence and professionalism
- provides a useful way for attendees to fill dull moments
- serves as a conversation piece during socializing periods
- will likely be a valued take-home piece or souvenir
- can be an interesting coffee table item
- is useful during the year as a handout to new members
- is a great tool when soliciting the support of large individual and corporate contributors

Your annual report might include –

- Executive's summary of the year
- Events and Accomplishments
- Challenges
- Membership – Honor Roll of Contributors
- Volunteer Recognition
- Comparative Financial reports (this year vs. last year)
- Statistics (membership, attendance, literature distributed, etc.)
- Officers, Board Members, Committee Chairs
- Contact Info

Annual reports are usually 8-1/2" x 11", and that size is also recommended as a practical matter. The annual report is a one-time publication that you'll usually be putting together on short notice, and a standard letter size document is easier to set up and easier to produce than odd sizes. A little creativity is in order here. Do what you can to make your document attractive, as well as informative. Print the covers on 67 lb. cover stock, print the pages double-sided on 24 lb paper, and staple the report on the left edge to create a booklet. An example is available on the *SfS* website which you might choose to use as a template. Or you might discover a standard or third-party Microsoft Word report template that you like.

Parliamentarianism

Strict adherence to parliamentary rules and procedure isn't usually necessary, or even desirable, in meetings of small organizations or committees. For example, people are likely to offer motions to do something, even when such actions do not require a motion. Others may second motions that do not require seconding, or second a motion by saying "Support!" (which is not the same thing as seconding the motion – one can only support a motion when it's time to vote). The presiding officer might not adhere strictly to the agenda, or there might not even be a prepared agenda. These sorts of things can be overlooked.

However, to the extent that the rules apply to fairness and protecting the rights of minorities, they must be carefully adhered to. This is a practical matter, not just a concern for ethics. If you don't comply with the rules and someone feels their rights have been infringed upon, the offending meeting or procedure can be declared an illegal, which will usually result in the action in question being automatically rescinded.

Someone at your meeting should be at least familiar enough with Robert's Rules, or whatever parliamentary authority you are using, to be able to find the relevant information in the manual if and when questions arise. Being able to field such questions or situations knowledgably and comfortably gives an appearance of competence. Fumbling through the rule book for several minutes without being able to find the answer has just the opposite result.

The "someone" will probably be you. If that is the case, consider participating in a seminar or workshop on parliamentary procedure. These are frequently offered by organizations supporting nonprofits or nonprofit associations. As a minimum, read through Robert's Rules, or whatever manual you are using, and familiarize yourself with its index system.

Minutes or Minutia?

As the Secretary, it's your job to record and publish the minutes of each meeting. The minutes are a record of what was done, not what was said. The minutes of a meeting should not be a transcript of what went on in the meeting. The minutes of meetings include only facts; no anecdotes, opinions or other superfluous commentary.

After minutes are formally approved and signed, these documents have standing as a legal record of the meeting having occurred, and of actions taken, or not, at the meeting. In the event of a legal action, these documents can be subpoenaed as evidence, and will usually enjoy an assumption of credibility. This is mainly why it is unwise to include anything other than the minimum of essentials.

Be aware that any notes taken by the Secretary (or some other board member) for the purpose of ultimately writing up the minutes of a meeting can also be subpoenaed, and can also rise to the stature of having legal standing in a court of law. This happens under the theory that a board member has certain fiduciary responsibilities, including one of honesty. Thus, notes taken by such a person will ordinarily be considered reliable. Whatever notes you take in order to ultimately prepare a formal write-up of the minutes of a meeting should be destroyed after the formal document has been accepted and signed off. Minutes are ordinarily kept in a special binder as a historical record. Do not file your notes with the formal document.

The minimum contents of the minutes should be as follows. The header should contain the following information:

- The type of meeting (regular, special, etc.).
- The name of the organization (or committee, etc.).
- The date, time and location of the meeting.
- The name of the presiding officer and secretary (with an explanation if someone is substituting for the regular chairperson or secretary).
- Action taken with respect to the minutes of the previous meeting (approved as read, or as corrected) giving the date of that meeting.

The body of the document should then have:

- A paragraph for each motion brought before the meeting, giving:
    - The name of the person(s) bringing the motion (do not record the names of those who second motions).

- The exact wording of the motion at the time it was adopted or otherwise disposed of.
- Mentioning whether the motion was debated or amended prior to its being disposed of.
- Giving the disposition of the motion (passed, defeated, tabled, etc. When there is a formal count, enter the numbers, counting anything other than a "Yes" or "No" vote as an abstention, or "Not Voting".).

- Notice of motions, if any (re: giving previous notice).
- Points of order and appeals, if any, indicating whether sustained or lost, and how ruled by the chair.

The final item in the minutes is the time of adjournment.

After the minutes of a meeting have been reviewed and approved (ordinarily at the next meeting), they must be signed by the Secretary and properly filed. Optionally, the presiding officer may also sign.

The minutes may be written in either outline form (see the example on the *SfS* website) or narrative form (an example of which may be found in Robert's Rules), but recalling that the collection of these documents comprise a formal, legal record of your proceedings, consistency is highly recommended. If no standard has been adopted, following the form of previous secretaries is good practice.

Note that the format of the minutes closely follows that of the formal agenda. Hence the value of preparing a formal agenda. With that in hand, recording and preparing the minutes can be as simple as making appropriate notes on your copy of the agenda during the meeting then, in essence, rewriting the agenda in the form of minutes.

— ❧ —

4

Office Routine

Tables and Queries and Forms ...
Oh, My!

—⚜—

4
Office Routine

The Membership Database

Let's turn people into numbers!

How will you, or do you, keep track of the names, addresses, donation history and other details for members and others connected with your organization? How do you maintain a mailing list? How can you print up a batch of mailing labels on short notice? Can you produce a list of people who contributed to your organization during the past year? What's the average of last year's contributions, and is there a seasonal distribution?

What is a "RDBMS"?

A database is simply an organized body of related information. A collection of 3x5 recipe cards is a database, maybe arranged alphabetically and functionally, by breakfast, lunch, dinner and dessert recipes.

A "flat file" database is an organized list, such as your personal check register. A flat file database could also work just fine for your membership list, as long as the questions you were asking about each member had only one answer; for example, the date they joined, their street address or their cell phone number. However flat file databases become rather messy when you wish to keep records of meeting attendance, contributions, volunteer participation, and other items where there may be several items to record under a single name. For example, every time a certain member made another contribution, you'd have to add a new record, but that record would necessarily include all the other fields – name, address, city, state, phone, cell, etc., etc. – along with the fields containing information about the donation – date, check number, amount, and purpose or occasion.

A "relational database" is a system that can help you store, manage and retrieve related information in a more efficient manner. This system essentially consists of a set of related flat-file databases, which are called "tables." For example, one table might contain members' names and addresses, and another table could hold information about contributions. The two tables each have a numeric "key" field which links all the records that belong to a certain member. The key can be any number, but could be, for example, a "member number."

☙ Example: "John Doe" is uniquely identified as "0001" in the member information table, which contains John's name, address and other personal information. Each time John makes a contribution, the date, check number, amount and purpose is added to the contributions table, along with the key "0001." Although there is nothing in the contributions table that directly identifies the donor, we can look up "0001" to see who it was. On the other hand, if John would like to see his contribution history, we can simply go to the contributions table and find all the entries with the key "0001", and by combining the information on both tables, we could print a nicely formatted report. Notice that the contributions table contains only four fields besides the key field. None of John's personal information needs to be repeated every time he provides another contribution.

A record system of this kind is called a *Relational DataBase Management System* or *"RDBMS,"* and these are naturally computer-based systems. In fact, this has become one of the most important computer applications in the business world, and database design and programming is one of the most highly-paid careers in the field of information technology. Microsoft Access is one of the leading RDBMS software systems. Access is a desktop application, and therefore lacks much of the power and capability of larger networked systems. However, its integration with other Microsoft Office applications provides a level of familiarity and intuitiveness that makes it ideal for small projects that must be maintained by regular office workers, rather than database programmers.

The *SfS* Database

Access databases are composed of *objects, tables, queries, forms, reports* and *macros,* all of which are stored in a single computer file. Users who are quite familiar with the program often work with these components directly. But Access also has features that permit programmers to set up *applications.* These allow people totally unskilled in RDBMS technology to successfully maintain and use the database. Users work with simple control panels and forms, with the underlying complexity remaining completely transparent.

SfS DataBase
Record Keeping Functions and Reports

- Information about people
  - members
  - prospective new members
  - interested third parties
  - vendors

- information about receipts
  - membership fees
  - contributions
  - memorial gifts
  - grants
  - bequests

- information about disbursements
  - accounts payable
  - donations and grants
  - scholarships

- reports
  - mailing list
    - mailing labels
    - individual mailing list record
    - mailing list
      - alphabetical
      - by Mailing List ID
      - grouped by Address List ID
  - receipts
    - by individual Address List ID, sorted by date
    - by date range, sorted by receipt type and activity
  - disbursements

The *SfS* Database is such an application. It is free for you to use if you wish, and does not need to be licensed, because it is not a stand-alone application; you must have MS-Access 2002 installed on your computer in order to run it. The *SfS* DataBase provides for the record-keeping and reporting functions shown in the sidebar. Anyone skilled in the use of Access can extend these capabilities, and one doesn't need to become a database programmer in order to develop such skills in the use of Access.

❧ Note: The *SfS* Database application is free; you can redistribute and/or modify it under the terms of the GNU General Public License as published by the Free Software Foundation version 2, or any later version. Microsoft Access® 2002, which is required to run this application, is not free, but is usually available at a discount to nonprofits under Microsoft's donation program at www.techsoup.org/stock/.

The diagram below illustrates how the database is organized. As shown, there are four tables, named –

- MailingList
- Disbursements
- AddressList
- Receipts

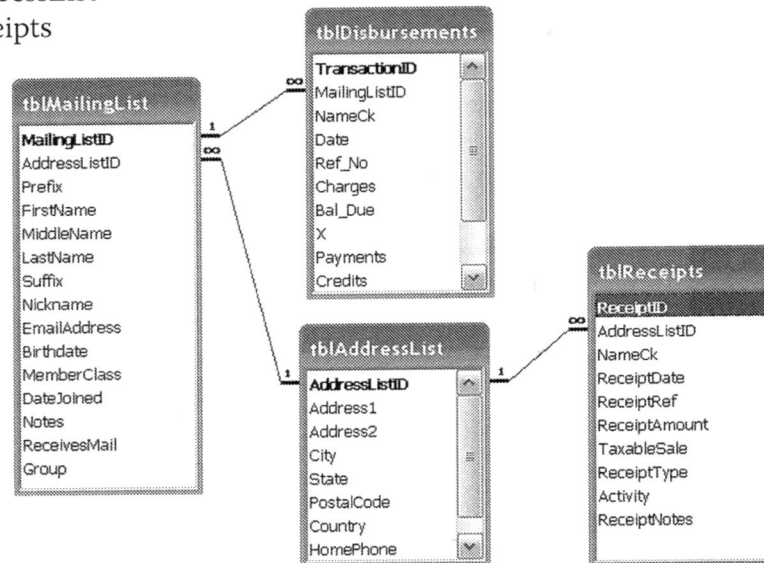

You can see what sort of information each table contains in its several *fields*. You can also see how the tables are related to each other. The fields whose name ends in "ID" are keys, and you can see that the tables are linked by these fields in "one-to-many" relationships (signified by "1" to "∞"). For example, one *record* in the AddressList table might be linked to several records in the MailingList table, to accommodate family memberships, where two or more members reside at the same address. Receipts are linked to addresses, instead of individuals, as a rather arbitrary solution to the problem of properly crediting contributions to households, rather than individual family members who might have happened to sign the check.

You work with the database by entering the information in the fields using a form. You'll never see these underlying tables. The primary keys, shown in boldface type, are assigned automatically by Access each time you create a new record. Keys shown in regular type are called foreign keys because they belong to some other table. These may also be entered automatically if the database is able. In other cases you will enter the foreign key value, but you won't ordinarily perceive it as a key, but rather as a member number, or some other logical identification number. The point is, you should be able to easily learn how to use the *SfS* database application without having to learn much about MS-Access or the database's underlying structure.

Getting Started

When you open the database by clicking on the desktop icon, you will be presented with a simple *control panel* form. The buttons on the "Main Switchboard" provide you with four choices:

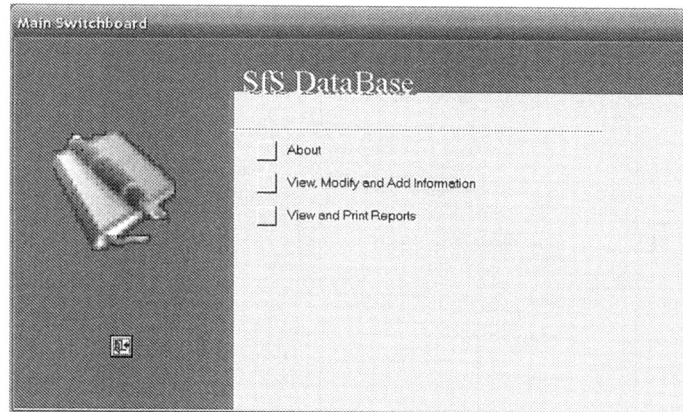

- About: View information about the application, licensing and contact information.

- View, Modify and Add Information: This button brings up the main member information page, which is the main work area for the database. You can add new records, update existing records or simply view information by clicking on this button.

- View and Print Reports: View or print selected information, such as membership lists and mailing labels.

- Quit: Close the database (small icon in lower left corner).

The Main Member Information Form

This is a very busy place. Let's begin by seeing what all these fields and buttons are for.

The two uppermost ID fields show the keys associated with this record. You cannot change these values. When you create a new record, they will be assigned automatically when the new record is saved.

> ✺ Note: The application takes care of saving automatically. When you close the database, everything will be saved just as you left it. If the database isn't sure whether or not a partial new record or some change you've made to an existing record should be saved, it'll ask.

The next six fields provide spaces for the individual's complete name. A complete name might be:

Mr John C McCann Jr ("Jack")

The *ReceivesMail* field can be checked for individuals who should be included on the regular mailing list. A typical use for this field involves situations where there are two or more members in the same household, and it doesn't make sense to send individual copies of the newsletter and other mailings to each one.

The *Status* field provides an important way to group records according to the individual's relationship to your organization. Typical entries are "Member," "Prospect," "ITP" (Interested Third Party), "Deceased," "Supplier," etc. You can enter anything you want in this field, but do it advisedly. Think about how you might, at some point, wish to sort people into various groups according to their status or relationship to your organization, and create your own list of standard entries for this field.

Use the "... *Notes*" boxes to enter any kind of information you wish; ordinarily memoranda. For example, if a person is an accomplished keyboard player, you might wish to make a note of that on their record so you could possibly tap into that talent someday when you need some music for a special occasion. The two boxes are associated with two different tables. Notes entered in the *Mailing List Notes* box will appear whenever you access that particular individual's record. Notes entered in the *Address List Notes* box will appear whenever you access the personal record of anyone living at that address. Therefore information entered in the lower box will ordinarily be something relative to everyone at the associated address — possibly information applicable to a whole family, such as the name of an important ancestor, or other members they are related to.

The familiar array of navigation buttons at the very bottom, left-hand corner of the form permit you to toggle back and forth through the records one at a time, to jump to the first record or the last, or to bring up

a new blank form [►*] when you wish to create an all new record.

Just above this array is a special box labeled "*Who's at Address No. ...*". This *subform* is equipped with its own array of navigation buttons, and will permit you to see the names of everyone sharing this address. When you wish to add someone to this address, click the *Add New Resident* button [►*] at the right end of the subform to bring up a blank *Add New Resident at This Address* form.

> ❧ Note: If you add a new individual any other way, the address you enter will be considered unique, and will be given a new primary key. The database does not worry about duplicate addresses. The new record will therefore not be related to any others that share that same address. When adding an individual who shares an address with someone already in the database, be sure to use the *Add New Resident* button within the "*Who's at Address No. ...*" subform.

The functions of the buttons in the array of seven controls at the right-hand side of the *Personal/Company Information* form are as follows:

🔍	Search this Field
📝	Edit this Record
➕	View and Add Receipts
▶*	Create New Record
🗑	Undo All Changes
🖨	Print This Record
🚪	Exit This Form

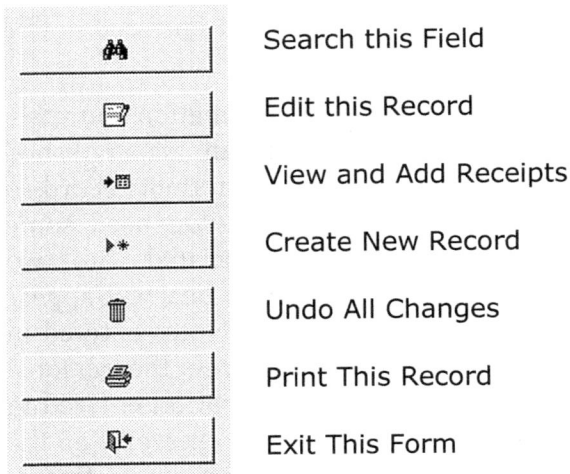

You can use Search this Field to find records by clicking on the field you wish to search on, then clicking this button to bring up a familiar Windows "Find and Replace" dialog box. (The "Replace" tab will be available only while the record is editable.)

Records are automatically locked when saved, to prevent accidental changes. While the form is locked, you will not be able to add or change information in any field. If you wish to change something in the record you are viewing, click the Edit this Record button. When you try to move to another record or exit the form, a dialog box will appear asking whether or not you wish to save the changes you made. Click "Yes," "No" or "Cancel," as appropriate. When you use this button, only the record you are viewing becomes editable. All others remain locked, so you will need to click this button for each record you wish to edit.

To record contributions, donations, gifts and grants, click the View and Add Receipts button. This will bring up the *Receipts* form, which is described below.

To enter a whole new record, click the Create New Record button to provide a new, blank form. Enter as much of the information as you have available, then exit that record by using the back or next navigation buttons, searching for a different record or exiting the form. The dialog box will appear asking if you want to save the newly created record; click "Yes," "No" or "Cancel."

What happens if you are editing a record when the phone rings, the cat walks across the keyboard, or before you save your changes you realize you have been editing the wrong record? You can click the Undo All Changes button to return the form to its original state.

Click Print This Record to provide a scratchpad notation of this individual's contact information. A print preview sheet will appear. Use the small toolbar at the top of the window to do whatever you want with this page. The choices are:

- Close
- Print
- Print Setup

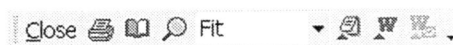

Close 🖨 📖 🔍 Fit ▾ 🔲 ﷼ 📊 ▾

- Magnify
- Zoom
- Send to Notepad (or NoteTab)
- Send to MS-Word

Exit This Form dismisses the *Personal/Company Information* form, returning you to the *Main Switchboard*.

The Receipts Form

Clicking the *View and Add Receipts* button on the *Personal/Company Information* form will bring up the *Receipts* form. This form permits you to view contributions previously received from individuals at this address, and to record contributions newly received.

To review all the receips on record, use the forward and back navigation buttons at the bottom of the form. Note that the number of existing records for this address is indicated ("2" in the above example).

To create a new record, click the *Add New Contribution Record* button [▶*].

Enter the *AddressListID* as it is shown at the top of the form, unless you wish to associate the receipt with some other known address.

The *NameCk* field is a provision for capturing entry errors, permitting the manual cross-checking of this field against the *AddressListID* field should there ever appear to be any possibility that contributions were credited to the wrong individuals. You can make up anything you feel would be distinctive for this field, but generally use a LASTNAMEFIRSTNAME format. The field will accommodate only the first eight characters you type and, if necessary, will convert them to upper case.

The *Taxable* field is a provision for sales tax. If you are selling fundraising items to which sales tax applies, enter "Yes" in this field to indicate that the value in *Amount* includes sales tax.

What you enter in the *ReceiptType*, *Activity* and *Notes* fields is up to you, and how your organization might wish to use the information this form captures. Whatever you decide, be consistent. For example, you might someday wish to compare the financial results of various kinds of activities, or of selected activities. Suppose newsletters are one of your major fundraising initiatives, and you publish them quarterly. Contributions received in response to newsletters might be coded "NL2005Q1", "NL2006Q2", and so on. If you wondered about the results of the summer 2006 issue, you would be able to select data where [Activity="NL2006Q2"]. On the other hand, suppose you were asked how much money the newsletters have brought in altogether? The answer could be had by selecting data where [Activity includes "NL200"].

> ❧ Note: This would involve building a simple query, which requires some knowledge of MS-Access running in full mode.

The four buttons at the right-hand side of the form are similar in function to those on the *PersonalCompany Information* form:

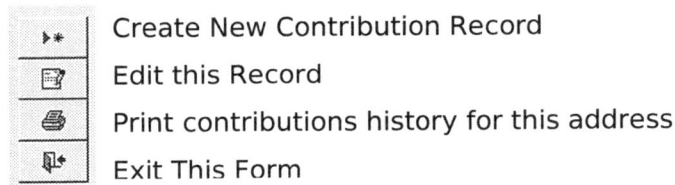

▶✳	Create New Contribution Record
▤	Edit this Record
☷	Print contributions history for this address
▯✦	Exit This Form

Viewing and Printing Reports

Clicking the *View and Add Reports* on the *Main Switchboard* to bring up the *Reports Switchboard*. This panel provides you with five ways to view and print the records in your database.

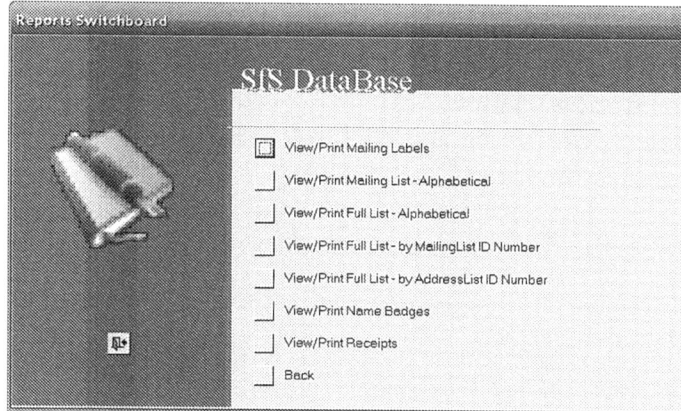

For mailings, *View/Print Mailing Labels* will provide a print preview showing all the records marked *Receives Mail* formatted for printing on standard Avery 5162 (Laser) or 8162 (Ink Jet) 1-1/3" x 4" 14-per sheet labels. You can browse through the pages to check for errors, duplicates, and problems using the back and forward navigation buttons at the bottom of the print preview pages. To immediately print all the labels, simply click the printer icon on the small toolbar at the top of the page. To bring up the printer dialog box, use "Print ..." on the "File" menu or touch Ctrl+P instead. This will allow you to print a test page or selected pages, or to adjust printing options.

The next four choices provide:

- View/Print Mailing List – Alphabetical: A list of records marked "Receives Mail" in alphabetical order.

- View/Print Full List – Alphabetical: A print-out of the entire set of records in alphabetical order.

- View/Print Full List – by MailingList ID Number: A print-out of the entire set of records ordered according to MailingList ID numbers – useful for maintenance (auditing and editing) purposes.

- View/Print Full List – by AddressList ID Number: A print-out of the entire set of records ordered according to AddressList ID numbers – also useful for maintenance purposes.

For meetings and special events, *View/Print Name Badges* can be used to print personalized name tags to Avery 5163 (Laser) or 8163 (Ink Jet) self-adhesive 2" x 4" 10-per sheet labels. The label will show first and last names, and where the individual is from (city and state).

> ❧ Note: With a little knowledge of MS-Access, the name badge template can also easily be customized with your organization's logo and the name of the event. The underlying query selects only those records where the "Status" field contains either "Member" or "ITP." With a little knowledge of MS-Access, other selections are easily achieved.

View/Print Receipts will provide a list of all receipts, organized by source (donor) during whatever calendar period you specify in the pop-up dialog box that appears when you click this button. Enter the date range of interest, then click the "OK" button to provide a print preview of the report. Use the small toolbar at the top of the page or use "Print ..." on the "File" menu to further format and print your report.

To exit the *Reports Switchboard* and return to the *Main Switchboard*, click the *Back* button.

Use the small *Quit* icon in lower right corner of the *Reports Switchboard* to close the database directly without returning to the *Main Switchboard*.

frmPrintReceipts : Form 7/2/2007 · 15:38:41 · W.
Select Report Criteria
Enter Start Date: 01/01/1997
Enter End Date: 12/31/1997
[OK]   CANCEL

DataBase Installation & Maintenance

The *SfS* DataBase downloads as a single compressed file. Save the download at a location of your choice, then right-click the file and choose "Extract Here" on the pop-up menu. See the Readme file to provide a desktop shortcut. Microsoft Access 2002*, ordinarily provided with Microsoft Office Professional*, is required to run the application.

Maintain the database by periodically compacting it and saving a backup. See the Readme file to learn how.

❧

Handling Contributions

Deposit the money and acknowledge the gift immediately!

Donations and gifts will be received at meetings, by mail, and possibly online. Donors sometimes simply casually hand checks and cash to other board members.

Record Where the Money Came From

It is important that donors be identified:

- So that contributions can be properly acknowledged.
- To capture the names of prospects for future solicitations.
- For IRS reporting purposes.

It is not unusual for board members or others to bring in a handful of cash, without being able to recall who it came from. This usually happens at special gatherings and events. Everyone in a position to receive such money should understand that its source must be recorded. In a pinch, this can be as simple as writing the name of the giver and the amount given on the currency itself.

When money is received, *immediately* record the date, donor's name, check number, amount and the nature or purpose of the donation or payment. This information should go into your membership database. If not using a database, this information can be recorded in an Excel spreadsheet.

Deposit the Money Immediately

Deposit all receipts immediately. Even if you do not reside in the same place where your organization's bank is physically located, most major banks have branches or affiliates throughout the country, and you may make deposits at any branch.

Acknowledge the Gift Immediately

An immediate acknowledgement is a good way to let donors know that their giving is important and that their contribution is appreciated. These acknowledgements must be treated as an integral part of your fundraising strategy, not as a simple courtesy or afterthought. The receipt of contributions is part of your fundraising strategy, not the end of it. People who give once are likely to give again, unless discouraged by a callous reception of their generosity, or board bumbling that results in contributions not being properly documented and appropriately acknowledged.

This applies to all contributions. Small donations must be accepted just as graciously as large gifts. It's often much easier for a wealthy patron to hand you a check for $1,000 than for an aged shut-in to put two one-dollar bills in an envelope and send it by mail.

The section on *Graphic Arts Ideas* (Section 6) includes an idea for a simple, but classy and effective, contribution acknowledgement card that you can easily personalize and print as needed.

Contributions will most often be received by the Secretary, assuming the Secretary receives the mail. Regardless of how they are received, contributions should be routed through the Secretary in order to ensure that they are properly recorded and acknowledged. Establishing a routine or a system will enable you to handle contributions effectively without much effort:

1. Record the details of the contribution, by name, date, check number, amount, and purpose or occasion of the contribution. These entries can be made in the membership database introduced above, otherwise create a simple flat-file database using a spreadsheet to record this information. There is an example of a form designed for this purpose on the *SfS* website.

2. Print the acknowledgement card and envelope.

   ❧ Note: To ensure that mistakes are avoided, consider doing these two steps independently for each deposit. When things get confused and the donor is credited with the wrong amount, or the card for one donor is mistakenly put in the addressed envelope of another donor, such mistakes can be very embarrassing. With a little organization, you can easily make the database entry, then print a corresponding acknowledgement card and envelope before going on to the next item.

3. Endorse the checks and prepare a deposit slip, with a duplicate.

4. Bring the money to the bank, having the teller stamp the duplicate deposit slip as a receipt (whether or not they print any other sort of receipt).

5. Advise the President and Treasurer of the deposit by email. (Save a template in your email client's "draft" folder that you can quickly and easily make use of to report deposits.)

6. Mail the deposit receipts to the Treasurer with your regular month-ending report.

> ✤ Hint: With a little ingenuity, you can create Excel forms to endorse your checks and print your deposit slips. Examples are provided on the *SfS* website. Why pay for a custom endorsement stamp, or computer form deposit slips? Get your bank's logo from their web site, and pick up a stack of blank deposit slips at the bank, then create an Excel form to suit. Using your form will help avoid errors by assuring legibility and math accuracy.

> ✤ Note: You must use the bank's blank deposit slips. You cannot design and print your own because the OCR data that appears at the bottom of the slip is printed with magnetic machine-readable ink.

— ✤ —

Record Keeping

Keeping track of cash receipts and disbursements;
avoiding overdraft fees, over-limit fees and late fees.

Rudimentary Accounting

The board of directors is responsible for the quality of financial reporting, and is duty-bound to ensure that accounting and financial reporting adheres to legal and ethical standards. Donors and creditors often rely on audited financial statements and Form 990's submitted to the IRS, so their accuracy and quality is an important part of meeting the organization's obligations of accountability and transparency to the public.

Nonprofits are required by generally accepted accounting principles, as well as by the IRS, to divide their total expenditures into three categories:

- program costs
- general and administrative expense
- fundraising costs

Program spending ratios (program spending divided by total expenses) and fundraising efficiency ratios (total fundraising costs divided by total contributions) are important measures of a nonprofit's effectiveness, and are therefore of interest to prospective donors and grant committees. However, the generosity even of small casual givers will be tempered by their opinion of how much good their money is actually doing. Whether they think in these financial terms or not, everyone will be looking for a high program spending ratio and a low fundraising efficiency ratio. The averages (see www.charitynavigator.org) appear to be approximately:

- Program Spending Ratio: 71%
- Fundraising Efficiency Ratio: 9%

In order for anyone to know what's going on in your organization, someone has to keep track of the money and provide coherent periodic reports about how much is being received and what you're doing with it. This doesn't mean you need to be a CPA or skilled at double-entry bookkeeping. For small organizations, all you really need is

- good templates for financial statements
- a system for collecting and organizing the data for the reports

Cash or Accrual Basis?

There are two ways to think about your financial activities as far as these reports are concerned.

The easiest is called the *cash method of accounting*. This is simply money in – money out. In other words, revenue is recorded when you actually receive money, and expense happens when you actually pay money out. As you can easily imagine, if your Statement of Activity, is based strictly upon this method, it may not provide a truly accurate picture of your financial situation if someone owes you money, or you have unpaid bills or other debt.

Accountants therefore prefer the *accrual method of accounting*, which records revenue when it is earned, and expense when incurred, whether or not you actually receive or pay out any money. If you ever become large enough that your financial statements need to be professionally audited, they will have to be based on the accrual method. At that point, in the interest of simplicity, many choose to ordinarily maintain their accounts according to the cash method, and then convert their data to the accrual basis for their year-ending reports.

Small nonprofits do not ordinarily have significant accounts receivable and accounts payable or hold depreciable assets of significant value. Because of this, reports prepared on a cash basis or an accrual basis would come out just about the same, so for these simple situations, the cash basis is perfectly acceptable.

Templates for Financial Statements

Treasurers change from time to time. It is helpful if financial report formats remain consistent in spite of that reality. That can happen if you develop reporting formats that are easy to use and which are easily understood. Keep the reports simple, and avoid using financial and accounting terms that are unfamiliar to the average person.

The following templates are provided as a guide to what is necessary and appropriate for a small nonprofit. They are based upon recommendations provided in a study of nonprofit financial reporting (http://ksghome.harvard.edu/~ekeatin/finassess.pdf) by Keating and Frumkin of the Kellogg Graduate School of Management at Northwestern University of Illinois, and the Kennedy School of Government at Harvard University. Feel free to modify these to more appropriately suit your situation. Copies are available on the *SfS* website.

Statement of Financial Condition

The Statement of Financial Condition, which business' often call a *Balance Sheet*, provides a snapshot of your financial situation at one point in time, usually the end of your fiscal year. In a personal or for-profit setting, the difference between assets and liabilities would be called "net worth," "owner's equity," or the like. Since nonprofits have no owners or stockholders, the term "net assets" is used instead.

Assets always balance Liabilities and Net Assets since assets must be funded either by resources provided by others (liabilities) or resources of your own (net assets). By convention, assets are usually listed by order of liquidity, meaning how easily they can be converted to cash. You may choose to list zero items if you feel it is meaningful to indicate that there are no such assets or liabilities. Footnotes are often helpful as a way to explain the scope of various items without making the report messy with detail.

Net Assets sometimes involves funds, and until about ten years ago were usually called "Fund Balances." Funds necessarily arise when money is set aside for a particular purpose. For example, a donor might provide a gift on the condition that the money be used for a particular pet project of their own but, of course, one that falls within your exempt purposes. Another donor might provide a sum of money as an endowment of sorts, stipulating that it be invested for the purpose of creating continuing revenue for your organization. These would be shown as restricted funds under Net Assets.

You might also hold money in other funds because the donors, upon giving you're the money, expressed a hope or intention that it would be used for a particular purpose, if possible, or in a particular way, but without creating any sort of contract requiring you to comply with their wishes. These are actually donor advised funds, but since that terminology has taken on connotations that raise IRS eyebrows, such funds are now often referred to as "temporarily restricted," meaning that until they decide otherwise, the board chooses to voluntarily honor the donors' wishes.

In fund accounting, any value left over is simply called "Unrestricted." In the example below, Net Assets might be shown as follows:

Total Liabilities 654

Net Assets
     Unrestricted 879
     Temporarily Restricted[1] 1,000
     Permanently Restricted[2] 2,500
        Total Net Assets 4,379
Total Liabilities and Net Assets .... $ 5,033

[1] Willard K Jones memorial, informally designated for lighthouse restoration
[2] Mary Watson Keller memorial endowment

If you have any funds, list them this way. Consider adding footnotes to explain what they are.

STATEMENT OF FINANCIAL CONDITION

Friends of the Manitous, Inc.
Year ended June 30, 2007

ASSETS

Cash[1]	....	$ 3,526
Inventory		
Promotional items[2]	....	325
Materials and supplies for projects[3]	....	1,126
Office supplies	....	56
Investments	....	0
Property and equipment		
Land, buildings and improvements	....	0
Equipment	....	0
Total Assets	....	$ 5,033

LIABILITIES

Liabilities		
Accounts payable	....	$ 654
Contributions, gifts and grants payable	....	0
Payroll[4]	....	0
Commissions and fees payable	....	0
Other liabilities	....	0
Total Liabilities	....	654

NET ASSETS

Net Assets	....	4,379
Total Liabilities and net assets	....	$ 5,033

[1] checking accounts and certificates of deposit
[2] brochures, visitor guides, tee shirts, etc.
[3] lumber, drywall, paint, fuel, etc. for island projects
[4] salaries, wages, withholdings, employment taxes and agency fees

Statement of Activities

The Statement of Activities provides a picture of actual operations for the period covered by the report. The statement measures activities according to resources received and spent. More simply put, this statement shows how much money was received and who from, and how much was spent and what for. In business, this is variously called a "statement of revenue and expenses," "income statement," or "profit and loss statement," and the final figure would be called "net earnings" or something like that.

For nonprofit purposes, the bottom line is more appropriately called "Change in Net Assets."

Organizations that doing fund accounting might provide this report in four columns to show how these activities are distributed among the three fund accounts shown above (unrestricted, temporarily restricted, and permanently restricted) and the general account. The simple example provided below shows only a total amount for each item. Even if you have funds, you might elect to keep things this simple.

Expenses are distributed into three categories:

- Program Expenses – costs directly attributable to projects and activities you do in fulfillment of your exempt purposes or your mission.

- Fundraising Expenses – include the cost of publicizing and carrying out fundraising campaigns and events, maintaining donor mailing lists, distributing fundraising literature, and any other activity specifically involved in soliciting contributions or memberships.

- Administrative Expenses – general expenses and managerial costs such as office expense, office supplies, record-keeping expense, meeting expenses, bank or credit card fees, and anything else that might ordinarily be considered overhead – items not directly related to program or fundraising activities.

Again, you might wish to show revenue and expense items with zero balances, if you think it would be helpful for some to see that there was no activity of that kind during this period, or even if there never is any such activity.

STATEMENT OF ACTIVITIES
Friends of the Manitous, Inc.
Year ended June 30, 2007

REVENUES

Grants, gifts and contributions received	$	7,350
Membership dues		0
Income from investments		0
Miscellaneous income		0
Total Revenue	$	7,350

EXPENSES

Program Expense

Building stabilization project on South Manitou $	1,150
Fence repair project at North Manitou cemetery	300
Volunteer interpreter on South Manitou	8,500
Visitor Guides for North and South Manitou	540

Fundraising Expense

Manitou Island Excursion	120
Port Oneida Fair	190

Administrative Expense

Professional fees	0
Personnel[1]	0

Office Expense

General office supplies	97
Occupancy, utilities and equipment	0
Telecommunications[2]	0
Printing and postage	0
Miscellaneous administrative expense	47

Meetings

Quarterly board meetings	422
Annual meeting	470

Total Expenses	$	11,836
Change in Net Assets	$	-4,486

[1] Includes salaries, wages, withholdings, employment taxes and agency fee
[2] Includes land line, long distance, toll free service and DSL Internet service

Other Kinds of Reports

Nonprofits also sometimes publish two other reports. If you apply for a major grant, you might be asked about such reports.

The *Statement of Functional Expenses* provides expanded detail with a more careful distribution of costs in the three functional expense categories, program, fundraising and administrative. For example, in the above statement you can probably see that some of the items listed under "Administrative Expense" should probably be distributed over all three categories. In other words, was the telephone ever used in connection with program and fundraising? The obvious answer would be "Yes." At your level would it make sense for you to account for your expenses with this much detail?

The *Statement of Cash Flows* presents a more detailed picture of how money moved through your organization during the period, separating activities into three categories; operating activities, investing activities and financing activities. Small nonprofits do not often become involved in investment and financing activities, so this statement is seldom relevant in that setting.

Experienced granters will understand that for most small nonprofits, these two statements are optional, since the information they provide can be gleaned from the statements of financial condition and activities.

Performance Ratios

Performance ratios are sometimes interesting, if not necessarily informative or authoritative. These are mentioned here only so that you will be familiar with the terminology. People who are considering giving you money should be interested in knowing something about how efficiently and effectively you use your funds, and performance ratios can be a way of quickly providing simple answers to such questions.

Performance ratios can also be used as a way to compare your performance to other nonprofits. You should understand, however, that such comparisons are only valid when comparing apples to apples. Nonprofits differ in terms of what is normal or average for organizations of their type. For this reason, rating organizations analysts more often refer to *peer benchmarks*, comparing organizations of similar size and purpose when talking about performance ratios.

Some popular benchmarks are:

- Program Spending Ratio (total program expense divided by total expenses (higher is better)

- Fundraising Efficiency Ratio (grants, gifts and contributions received divided by total fundraising expense (lower is better)

The figures on the next page show the typical ranges of these ratios for various kinds of nonprofits.

Average Program Expenditures of Nonprofits by Subsector

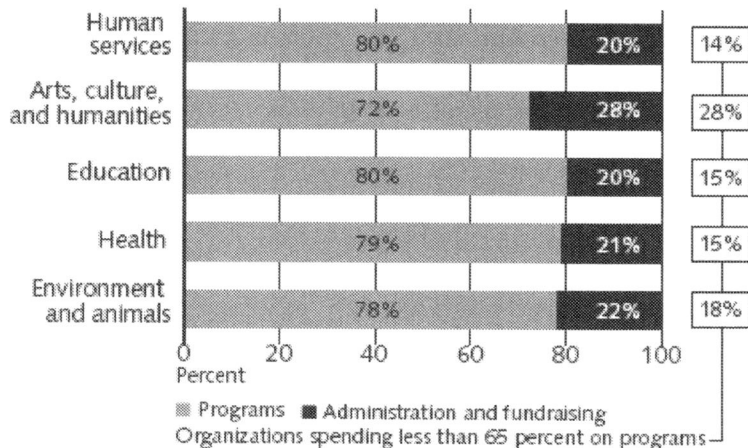

Subsector	Programs	Administration and fundraising	Organizations spending less than 65 percent on programs
Human services	80%	20%	14%
Arts, culture, and humanities	72%	28%	28%
Education	80%	20%	15%
Health	79%	21%	15%
Environment and animals	78%	22%	18%

Average Amount Spent to Raise $1 in Contributions by Subsector

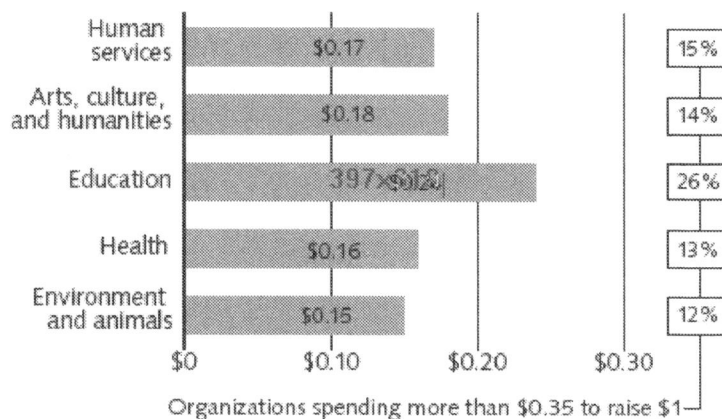

Subsector	Amount	Organizations spending more than $0.35 to raise $1
Human services	$0.17	15%
Arts, culture, and humanities	$0.18	14%
Education	397×$0.24	26%
Health	$0.16	13%
Environment and animals	$0.15	12%

(From   http://nccsdataweb.urban.org/kbfiles/521/brief%205.pdf   - "*The Pros And Cons Of Financial Efficiency Standards*"; Center On Nonprofits And Philanthropy, Urban Institute and Center On Philanthropy, Indiana University)

You can find a variety of interesting statistical information at (http://nccsdataweb.urban.org/FAQ/index.php?category=31) The National Center for Charitable Statistics, the national repository of data on the nonprofit sector in the United States. Its mission is to develop and disseminate high quality data on nonprofit organizations and their activities.

Chart of Accounts

Information for your financial reports can be easily captured and organized using a *Chart of Accounts*. This is merely a list of the items that make up your reports, with each item on the list having a unique account number. When posting receipts and disbursements, you mark each one with the appropriate account number. When subsequently collecting data to compile your reports, you sort all the items by their account numbers to ensure that everything falls into the correct categories.

In an attempt to help nonprofits improve their financial reporting practices, in terms of both uniformity and accuracy, a standardized chart of accounts is in development. The *Unified Chart of Accounts (UCOA)*, currently a joint project of The California Association of Nonprofits, and the National Center for Charitable Statistics, is cross-referenced to IRS Forms 990 and 990EZ, and to other frequently used reporting standards. Its aim is to help ensure that line items on financial statements have the same meaning for everyone; in other words, that everyone calls apples "apples," and oranges "oranges."

The UCOA is intended to be broadly applicable to nonprofits that are big enough financially to require the filing of 990 returns. It might therefore seem detailed and

Simplified Chart of Accounts
Adapted from Unified Chart of Accounts (UCOA) v3.0
(www.solutionsforsecretaries.com)

UCOA Acct No		990 EZ Line No
Statement of Financial Position		
	Assets	
1000	Cash	22
1400	Inventories:	
1410--	Promotional items	24
1420a	Materials and supplies for projects	24
1420b	Office Supplies	24
1500	Investments	22
1600	Fixed operating assets:	
1610	Land, buildings and improvements	23
1640	Equipment	24
	Total assets	25
	Liabilities	
2000	Payables:	
2010	Accounts payable	26
2020	Contributions and gifts payable	26
2100	Accrued liabilities:	
2110	Payroll	26
2150	Commissions and fees payable	26
2500	Other Liailities	26
	Total liabilities	26
	Net Assets	
	Total net assets	21 & 27
	Total liabilities & net assets	n/a
Statement of Financial Activities		
	Revenues	
4000	Grants, gifts and contributions received	1
5200	Membership Dues	3
5300	Income from investments	4
5400	Miscellaneous income	5a
	Total revenue	9
	Expenses	
7000	Program expenses	
7010--	Program-related projects	10
7020--	Grants to other organizations	10
7500	Fundraising expenses	13
8100	Administrative expenses	16
7540	Professional fees	13
7550	Personnel	13
8110	General office supplies	16
8120	Occupancy, utilities and equipment	14
8130	Telecommunications	16
8170	Printing and postage	15
8590	Other administrative expense	16
8670--	Meetings	
8670a	Quarterly Board Meetings	16
8670b	Annual Meeting	16
	Total expenses	17
	Net Change in Assets	n/a

comprehensive beyond the needs of your small NPO. However, you may still adopt this standard for your organization; just use what applies and ignore what doesn't. Where the chart captures detail you don't need, simply combine the sub-categories into the main category.

Citing that your chart of accounts is based upon the UCOA will lend increased respect for your credentials and credibility to your financial reports. For this reason, adapt the UCOA to your situation. A simplified chart of accounts based upon the UCOA is available on the *SfS* website, illustrating how that can easily be done.

Financial Statements Spreadsheet

Also provided on the *SfS* website is an MS-Excel spreadsheet template based upon the simplified chart of accounts, showing the Statement of Financial Condition and Statement of Activities monthly, with the total for your fiscal year. The items are arranged by account numbers, with fiscal year totals indexed to Form 990EZ line numbers.

You can use this spreadsheet without much knowledge of Excel. Just fill in the numbers. Calculated and non-entry fields are protected, so you can't make a mistake by entering amounts in the wrong fields. The calculations are done automatically for you as you enter your information. If you maintain this record on a monthly basis, there will be no need to panic as the end of your fiscal year or the date of your annual meeting approaches.

Modify the spreadsheet as desired by inserting whatever additional rows you want. In order to do so, you will need to momentarily unprotect the sheet (click *Tools|Protection|Unprotect Sheet* ...). When you insert rows, be sure to check the formula bar *(fx)* to ensure that Excel understood your action.

SfS DataBase Financial Capabilities

The *SfS* Database has simple provisions for financial record-keeping. You simply post receipts and disbursements as they occur. Then you can print a report which summarizes and totals all the transactions for each UCOA account number for a period you specify, usually a calendar month. That data can then be manually entered on your financial statements spreadsheet.

Distributing Joint Costs

As suggested above, many expenses are jointly applicable to two or more activities. How you decide to distribute such costs is strictly up to you. Your decision should be based upon what seems reasonable and prudent, remembering that your reports are being prepared to help others understand what's going on in your organization, not just as an exercise or filler for the annual report.

Using the above example, it will probably be sufficient for observers to understand that your organization is run out of a small office ordinarily manned by a volunteer who wears many hats. When the phone rings that person will often have to change hats, depending upon who's on the other end of the line. Keeping close track of telephone usage would be a waste of that volunteer's time, and any attempt to estimate an appropriate distribution would be nothing more than a guessing game. Therefore the best you can do is dump telephone expense into G&A, and apply the expense equally to all your activities as overhead.

An exception to this might arise in connection with major grants that create restricted funds – money provided for a particular activity. A more careful allocation of costs might be desired, lest general revenues wind up funding costs that should be supported by the grant.

Audits

Corporate financial statements are customarily audited by a professional and independent certified public accountant (CPA). Auditors examine financial statements, accounting practices and procedures, management practices and financial controls, to form an opinion on the accuracy and validity of the financial statements, which they then publish. Financial statements provided without an auditor's report must be taken on faith, but could be pure fiction.

Depending on your size and funding sources, you might be required to have an annual financial audit. In most cases this will not be necessary, so people will have to rely solely on your honesty and integrity if they want to believe your numbers. Should it become necessary, in connection with a grant application, for example, your situation will probably be simple enough that you can appropriately invite a local independent auditor to help you out on a *pro bono* basis.

— ❧ —

Budget Discipline and Decorum

Most of us don't bother with budgets in our personal life. Budgeting isn't fun. It seems miserly, confining and even demeaning, as in having to openly admit we're not rich enough to throw our money around with blithe indifference. We prefer to remain "financially flexible," dreaming that someday our ship will come in. While we're waiting, we waste a significant amount of money through impulse spending and foolish deals.

It's quite possible you won't bring this attitude to your nonprofit board, because the subject of doing a budget might never come up anyway if you all think alike. Does it need to be said? That's not good stewardship of your donors' generosity! You realize that, of course. What you probably don't realize is that financial flexibility will eventually result in misunderstandings and contention among board members, hard feelings, and resignations.

In order to avoid all that misery, you need to sit down as a full board and write a budget. During the process you'll each find out where everyone else is coming from — what's big on their agenda; their hopes and dreams; what they think of yours. In the end, the process might well pay bigger dividends in communications than in financial control. This is a really good opportunity to justify a weekend retreat.

If your organization is brand new, an attempt to budget might very well seem like a waste of time. If you have little more to go on than vague notions about financial support and possible programs and activities, you'll feel like the budget is nothing more than a wish list. However, if you're going to apply for recognition of exemption, you'll have to have something to put into the form by way of financial projections. You'll all just have to roll up your sleeves and do your best.

After you've been around for a few years, the process becomes much easier. Simply make of list of the things you always do — board meetings, the annual meeting, regular events — and things you'd like to do; new ideas or opportunities. Then, using previous revenue and expense data and your chart of accounts as your guide, estimate the revenue and expense impact of each item and total out the whole program (a good spreadsheet application).

Ideally, projected revenues, possibly including carried over surplus from previous years, will exceed projected expenses. (As a rule of thumb, most nonprofits plan for lean years by keeping enough cash in the bank to pay for two-years of general and administrative expense.) If not, you have some tweaking to do. Maybe you'll decide to defer some activities to next year, or maybe you'll decide you can make up the difference with a more aggressive approach to fundraising this year. Maybe you have the opposite problem – more revenue than your projected expenses can accommodate, meaning that you'll be able to do even more this year, or think about carrying over a handsome surplus to help finance a really big initiative next fiscal year!

Once you have a budget that seems more or less acceptable to everyone, it's time for the board to formally vote its approval. It's a formality, of course, but one that's important for political reasons. The debate preceding the vote gives everyone a fair opportunity to voice their opinions, pro or con, about anything and everything in the budget. Then any board member who doesn't like it can go on record as having voted "No!" That probably won't happen, leaving everyone officially recognized as having voted "Yes." During the program year there is certain to be talk about how inappropriately the board allocated resources, especially when pet projects seem to have been slighted. It's therefore important to have the entire board onboard, rather than have one or two board members ally themselves with the nay-sayers. (Sad, but true; all this applies regardless of the small size of your organization. It's just human nature.)

The budget is, of course, also a management tool. Unforeseen circumstances arise, and assumptions prove wrong. That's simply part of the process. Whenever the board meets, the agenda should include a review of the budget to determine how closely the actuals are tracking the projections. It isn't likely that the match will be exact, so making mid-course corrections, either by juggling the budget or adjusting specific programs and activities, will be an important part of the board's business meeting.

Once again, the *whole board* needs to be involved in the budget process. As the Secretary, you'll wind up having to document the details. With the help of the Treasurer, you'll also provide a lot of input information for the whole board's consideration. Take care not to make budget decisions by default while engaged in these supporting activities. The board should recognize that these are merely necessary supporting clerical functions; that the actual writing and adoption of the budget is the board's joint responsibility.

Simple Cash Journal ("Check Register")

Check Register is a somewhat dated term in this new era of debit cards and online banking. Today's checking accounts are more accurately viewed as deposit accounts where withdrawals can be affected by paper checks, electronic charges against the account using a debit card or by electronic fund transfers (which include online payment and automatic bill-pay transactions). While money has traditionally been deposited in checking accounts as cash or checks received from third parties, money may now come into these accounts through automatic deposit arrangements and online payment systems.

Keeping track of all these transactions using a traditional paper check register is entirely okay, but is inconvenient and error prone. It is inconvenient because it isn't easy to correct errors and doesn't provide a very portable record. Doing the necessary arithmetic manually is a process that is hampered by illegible entries, misread figures, mistakes in manual arithmetic or errors in keying in figures when using a calculator. The spreadsheet helps eliminate these problems.

All banks now offer customers online access to their accounts. These systems are usually timely, user-friendly and intuitive, so you might be tempted to live with that, and not bother keeping up a journal of your own. If you have a lot of extra money in your account and don't have to worry about overdrafts and the high penalty charges that accrue from them that might be okay. But the bank never knows about outstanding items, so their balance at any given moment might not reflect how much cash you actually have available. Since checks you write might lay around for a while before finally being deposited, and debit card transactions do not always come through the system instantly, you'll probably need to keep your own up-to-date record.

While there are many check register programs for computers, a regular spreadsheet, such as Microsoft Excel, is ideally suited to this task. Although Excel's capabilities are much broader than those employed here, this simple application has virtually no learning curve. You'll be able to use Excel quite successfully without having to learn much about it. A template worksheet is provided on the *SfS* website. Just follow the instructions given below.

> ❧ Note: These instructions seem rather lengthy and involved. That's only because it's often more difficult to describe a simple process than it is to actually do it. Once you get used to using the cash journal, you'll see that the process is easy and readily understandable. It's mostly just a matter of entering your transactions by filling in the blanks.

Looking Over the Example

1. Open the example file *cashjournal_monthyear.xls*.

2. The first cell (A1) contains the filename of this record, which also serves as a caption for the sheet.

3. Row 3 contains the titles for each column. Columns B through E are for disbursements; columns G through I are for receipts.

4. The red corner in cell A3 signifies that there is a comment attached to that cell. Hold the cursor over the cell to see what it says. This is a handy place to keep your account information for easy future reference. Right-click the cell and choose "Edit Comment," then enter your information.

5. Row 4 contains carry-forwards from the previous month's record, including the total of unreturned items and the actual balance in the account when the previous record was closed out at the end of that month.

6. Column J calculates a running total of receipts and disbursements, showing how much cash is actually available in the account.

7. Column F is for unreturned items, meaning items that have not yet been posted on the bank's record. Whenever you post a disbursement or a deposit, you also enter an offsetting amount in this column. When you justify your record against the bank's record, you'll delete these entries and paint the corresponding disbursement or deposit blue to show that these items have been reconciled.

8. At the bottom of the record are three special fields which show the sum of the unreturned items, the balance from the bank's record, and an imbalance flag. When you reconcile your record with the bank's record by entering a new value in the "Bank's Online Balance" cell and deleting items in the "Unreturned" column that have cleared the bank, the "Imbalance at last entry" cell will ultimately return to "0.00". Otherwise it shows the amount by which the bank's record disagrees with yours, which will help you find out why the two do not agree.

Getting Started

9. Open the example file *cashjournal_monthyear.xls*.

10. Save the example as *cashjournal_october2006.xls*, or whatever month you wish to begin with.

11. Delete all the data in cells A5 ~ I42 of the newly saved file.

12. Update the date in cell A4, and then enter the previous month-ending "Unreturned" and "Balance" carry-forward amounts on Row 4.

13. Save the file.

Posting Transactions

1. Post expenditures (checks, debit card transactions, etc.) and receipts (deposits) as they occur. Develop the habit of doing this promptly; for example, immediately upon returning from shopping trips. Otherwise, it'll soon become evident how easy it is to forget.

   ❧ Suggestion: to help make this convenient, create a shortcut to the current file on your desktop. You'll need to update the shortcut's properties every month to reflect the new filename. To make a shortcut now, do this:

   - if you have other applications open, minimize those windows
   - double-click the Excel title bar or click its "Restore Down" button
   - click on *File* | *Save As* …
   - the "Save As" dialog box pops up; right-click the filename
   - in the context menu that pops up, click "Create Shortcut"
   - click on the shortcut, then drag it out of the window onto the desktop, then close the box

2. Post these amounts as shown with double entries, each item in the Amount columns having an offsetting amount in the "Unreturned" column.

3. As you work with this file, watch the Imbalance at Last Entry value. It should always be "0.00". If not, find out why and correct the error immediately.

   ❧ Note: Excel isn't very good at updating the running balance formulas in Column J as you add or delete rows. Therefore, occasionally copy cell J5 to the clipboard, then paste it over all the other cells in Column J, up to the cell immediately preceding the "Unreturned Items" row.

Periodic Maintenance

Assuming that you have access to your bank account through online banking, log in periodically and justify your journal with the bank's record. How frequently you need to do this depends upon your activity. If you do several transactions every day, you will probably find it easiest to take a few moments to justify your record every two or three days.

1. After logging on to your online banking account, delete all the items in the "Unreturned" column which have appeared on the bank's record since the last time you checked it.

2. If you forgot to post something, notice an electronic payment or direct deposit, you'll probably need to add an item to match the bank's record. Highlight the row number where you wish to insert the item, right-click and select "Insert." The new row will be inserted at that point, with everything else shifted down one row.

   ❧ Note: Excel will not update the running balance formula in Column J when you insert rows in this manner. Therefore, copy cell J5 to the clipboard, then paste it over all the other cells in Column J, up to the cell immediately preceding the "Returned Items" row.

3. Update the amount in the "Bank's Online Balance" cell with the amount currently shown on the bank's record.

4. The "Imbalance at Last Entry" value should return to "0.00". If not, find out why and correct the error immediately.

5. For items returned from previous months, see below.

6. Change the text color of all the returned items to blue, indicating that these items have been successfully reconciled.

7. Save and close the file.

Handling Last Month's Unreturned Items

If any unreturned items were carried forward, the bank's record will ultimately show these items as having finally cleared. To handle this situation and keep your record in balance, do this:

1. Open the previous month's record, and delete all the items in the "Unreturned" column which have finally appeared on the bank's record.

2. Reduce the amount shown in "Bank's Online Balance" by the sum of the items deleted above.

✤ Suggestion: Change the value in that cell to a formula showing the original amount, minus the returned items. This can be helpful if you need to backtrack later. For example, change the original value "1256" to "=1256-(9.52+54.26+134.15+12.96)," rather than just entering the new value "1046.11".

3. The "Imbalance at Last Entry" value in this file should then return to "0.00". If not, find out why and correct the error immediately.

4. Change the text color of all the returned items to red, indicating that these items have finally been successfully reconciled.

5. Enter the new month-ending "Unreturned" carry-forward amount on Row 4 of the current month's record.

6. Save and close the previous month's record.

Month-Ending Maintenance

1. Close this journal out at the end of the month, adding the bank's service charge, if there is one, then save the file.

2. Save a second copy of the file, named for the next month (e.g., *cashjournal_november2006.xls*)

3. Enter the previous month-ending "Unreturned" and "Balance" carry-forward amounts on Row 4.

4. Delete all the data in cells A5 ~ Ixx of this file.

5. Save this newly created file.

6. Update the properties of your desktop icon with the filename of this newly created file (right-click the desktop icon and choose "Properties").

— ✤ —

Simple Credit Card Record

Oops! You forgot to send in your credit card payment until the day before it was due? That'll cost you $29, but don't feel bad; they love people like you! Over limit by a couple of bucks? Not to worry; that's only another $35 fee tacked onto your next statement, and your APR just went from the 6.27% which enticed you to sign up for the card to 27.5% (read the fine print in your credit card agreement).

All credit cards provide access to your account and accept payment online. If you organization uses credit cards, register for online access and set up your account so you can pay your card by electronic transfer from your bank account. If you pay by sending paper checks through the mail, pay statements as soon as you receive them. However, if for any reason the payment is not received, credit cards won't provide the courtesy of a reminder; they'll just charge a late fee to your account and will probably also increase your APR to the maximum rate.

You can use an Excel spreadsheet similar to the cash journal discussed above to manage your credit cards. The Excel credit card record is actually even more simple and easy to use than the cash journal. Unlike the cash journal, which you keep on a monthly basis and close out at the end of each month, it usually makes sense to use a continuous record for credit cards. A template is provided on the *SfS* website. Here's how it works.

The First Month

1. Open the example file *creditcard-nnnn-1a.xls*. This is an example showing the first month's activity with a new card.

2. Cell A1 contains the record's filename and also serves as a caption for the sheet.

3. Row 3 contains the captions for each column. The purpose of most columns is obvious, with the possible exception of "E" – the "Memo" column.

4. The "Date" cell also contains a comment box where you can record account information for this card.

5. Column E shows charges occurring between the time the credit card rendered your last monthly statement and the date you decide to make a payment, duplicating the dollar amounts shown in Column D.

6. Columns G and H show the actual balance, according to your record, and the credit card's statement balance, which should be equal to your actual balance, minus the amounts left in Column E.

7. In this example, you made various charges during the month of October, but the credit card usually issues your statement around the 8th of each month, so some of your charges do not appear on the first statement. The statement you received in the mail shows that your payment due date is November 1st, so you decide to pay this card before the end of October.

8. Enter the payment information on Row 9. Since these charges are less than thirty days old, there is no finance charge on this statement, so enter "0.00" in the "Amount" column.

9. Delete the items in the "Memo" column of your record which appear on the statement, and paint the corresponding values in the "Amount" column blue to show that they have been reconciled. The balance in your "Statement" column should then agree with the balance shown on the statement you received.

10. Although the minimum payment is just $15.00, you decide to pay the statement balance instead. You open your cash journal and record the $155.60 payment in that account. Then enter that same amount in the "Payments" column on your credit card record for October 27.

11. Log on at your card's web site and complete the online payment process. When your payment is accepted, the online payment processing system will generate a screen indicating that the transaction was successful, and providing a confirmation number. Copy that number to a comment in the corresponding cell in Column C, as shown in this example.

Month One Alternative

12. When you log on and view your record at your card's web site, you would see that the current balance is different than your paper statement, because the $46 charge to seanic.net has been posted. The balance shown online is therefore $201.60 instead of the $155.60 amount shown on the statement.

13. At this point you could decide to pay the $201.60 balance. Update your record by deleting the "$46" item in the "Memo" column of your record and changing its corresponding value in

the "Amount" column to blue, then update your cash journal, replacing "155.60" with "201.60".

14. Complete the payment process online, and enter the payment confirmation number on your record as shown in the example *creditcard-nnnn-1b.xls*.

As you can see, with online access to your credit card account there's actually no need for paper statements, and cards typically offer you the option of stopping them. Most then provide an email notification when your online statement becomes available each month. The choice is up to you, but since there's usually no real advantage in going paperless you might opt to leave well enough alone. You'll probably get into the habit of managing your card using its online record. At that point the paper statement will serve only as a reminder, and something to file.

Month Two

1. Open the example file *creditcard-nnnn-2a.xls*.

2. There were three more charges since your last payment. Two of these preceded this month's closing date, so they appear on your paper statement. The third charge occurred after the statement was rendered, so your online balance will probably not agree with the statement. None of these charges have carried over from one statement to the next, so again there is no finance charge.

3. When you log on at your card's web site, you find the online record does not match either the statement or your record. What's the problem? Are there other charges which you forgot to post, automatic debits for electronic payments, or fees of some kind (such as annual fees, late payment fees, or over limit fees)? Looking at your card's recent activity screen, you see the "Deerings Market" item, as expected. There's also an automatic charge on 11/3 for $34.24; your office telephone bill; you remember authorizing AT&T to charge your new card every month, rather than send you paper bills.

4. To insert this item in your record, highlight Roe 12, right-click and select "Insert" from the pop-up menu. Enter the information about the phone bill in Columns A through E.

5. Notice that Excel didn't update Cells G12 and H12, which are now blank, and the running totals are incorrect beginning at that point. To fix this, highlight the two cells immediately above those two blank cells (i.e., G11 and H11), right-click and select

"Copy." Then highlight the two blank cells and all the cells in those two columns below that point that contain the formulas (Cells G12 through H43); right-click and select "Paste." Your worksheet will now look like *creditcard-nnnn-2b.xls.*

6. This time your payment due date is November 30th, so you're getting in just under the wire. Had you assumed it wouldn't come up until after the first of next month and procrastinated until the 30th, the card might have still accepted your payment, but would probably have charged you an express payment fee, usually around $15).

7. Your new balance is $335.52, and the minimum payment is $15. Since your cash situation looks a little tight right now, you decide to pay $35.52, leaving a balance of $300 even.

8. Open your cash journal and record the $35.52 payment in that account, make the appropriate housekeeping entries on your credit card record for November 28, then go ahead and complete the online payment process.

9. Again, when your payment is accepted, the online payment processing system will generate a screen indicating that the transaction was successful, and providing a confirmation number. Copy that number to a comment in the corresponding cell in Column C, as shown in *creditcard-nnnn-2c.xls.*

... And So On

There'll be a finance charge on your next statement, since you're carrying over $240.12 worth of unpaid charges *(see creditcard-nnnn-2d.xls).* Otherwise the monthly procedure will be the same as described above, month after month.

— ❧ —

Government Reporting Requirements

Tax exempt does not mean tax free!

State Information Updates

Having successfully filed your articles, you must keep your information up to date by filing some sort of information update form, usually each year. Your state will probably send this form to your registered agent when needed. Failure to file can put your corporation at risk of automatic dissolution. Since these forms are easy to fill out (see the example on the *SfS* website), and the associated fee, if any, is usually low ($20 in Michigan), there's little reason to procrastinate. Several states, including Michigan, now make it possible for you to do such filings online, and prefer that you do so (see www6.dleg.state.mi.us/corpsfilings/).

Exempt Organization Return (IRS Form 990)

Almost every tax-exempt organization must file an annual information return. The most widely used returns are IRS Form 990, *Return of Organization Exempt from Income Tax*, and Form 990EZ. Form 990EZ is a shortened version of Form 990 designed for use by small organizations. Form 990EZ is available if your annual gross receipts are less than $100,000 and its total assets at year end are less than $250,000.

Unless specifically excluded (religious organizations, etc.), every type of tax exempt organization which has annual gross receipts of more than $25,000 is required to file Form 990 or Form 990EZ.

Form 990 is an information return or reporting form, not a tax return. The organizations that file these forms do not pay federal tax on income related to their exempt purposes and programs. Nonprofits with unrelated business income report that on Form 990-T, which is a tax return. 990's become public information, and are available upon request from IRS, and often online at www.guidestar.org.

The filing deadline for Form 990 is the 15th day of the 5th month after your organization's accounting period ends. For example, if your fiscal year ends on June 30, your 990 will be due the following November 15. You can get an automatic three-month extension by submitting Form 8868 to the IRS, and another three-month extension is usually permitted if you submit a second Form 8868. Thus, you can therefore legitimately file Form 990 eleven months after your fiscal year ends.

If your gross receipts are less than $25,000 you may feel relieved that you are not required to file this return. Consider voluntarily filing anyway, for these reasons:

- Although at first glance the form may look intimidating, it is lengthy, but otherwise not complicated. If you were able to file your Form 1023, you'll certainly be able to handle the 990, especially if you can use the 990EZ. Download the online fillable PDF version, and the instructions in PDF, and you should easily be able to complete your return in an evening.

- Filling out the form each year is a good way to create records for your internal use that can be helpful to newly elected or appointed officers and board members, and anyone else with a serious interest in your organization.

- Submitting the return on a regular basis will ensure that you meet the requirement of keeping the IRS advised of changes in your organization's address, activities or structure, and will also ensure that you are not removed from their list of qualified charities (IRS Publication 78).

- Assuming you received an advance ruling in response to your Form 1023 *Application for Recognition of Exemption*, filling out the 990 each year will provide you with all the information you will eventually need to complete the *Advance Ruling Follow-Up* when your advance ruling period ends.

- Filing the return establishes a start date for the IRS's three year statute of limitations with respect to potential audits. There is otherwise no limit.

- Submitting 990's is simply good business practice. The availability of a 990 on your organization, even when not required, creates a positive image of a well-managed organization with a professional board.

For the organization example used as a basis for this book, no return would actually be required. However, as an exercise and illustration, the 990EZ was completed, and is available on the *SfS* website for your inspection and use as a guide.

Federal and State Employment Taxes

It's nice to be able to provide employment opportunities, and rewarding to watch the looks on those faces when you say, "You're hired!" However, to be an employer is also to be a tax collector.

When you hire help for the first time, you'll likely be tempted to find some way around having to collect state and federal withholding, FUTA, SUTA and FICA and having to file all those quarterly and annual returns. Maybe you can call them "independent contractors" rather than employees, or just pay them cash under the table. Beware! They have a special place set aside in IRS Hell (Leavenworth, Kansas) for employers who fall short of the glory of the Code. By misclassification of employees, outright cheating or intentional neglect, you set yourself up for a fate worse than death. The reason is simple; unscrupulous employers cheat their fellow citizens out of much-needed tax revenue, and their employees out of future retirement benefits.

If, when you filled out Form SS-4, you made the mistake of indicating that you have, or expect to have, any significant employment activity, you'll probably eventually find a letter from the IRS in your mailbox with a Form 941, *Employer's Quarterly Federal Tax Return,*. If you had no payroll for the quarter, or have no employees, you aren't obligated to file. However *complete the return and send it in anyway*. If you don't, you will surely be hearing from the IRS, who will have decided that you are delinquent. File the form as a final return, indicating on Line 16 that you have stopped paying wages (no more relevant choice is provided on the form), and attach an explanation of your situation.

There are situations when people you hire really are independent contractors. In that case you are obligated to report awards, fees or similar forms of compensation amounting to $600 or more using IRS Form 1099-MISC, *Miscellaneous Income*. Send the individual their copy no later than January 31st. Also send a copy to the IRS, along with a Form 1096, *Annual Summary and Transmittal of U.S. Information Returns* no later than February 28.

For more information on employers' obligations and guidance on classifying workers, see IRS Publication 539, *Employment Taxes.*

An easy and legitimate way to avoid becoming an employment tax collector is to use temps. Temporary-help agencies find individuals looking for work and place them in jobs at client organizations. Hiring agreements can be for a prescribed term, or open-ended. Most agencies pay the wages, employment taxes, and workers' compensation for the people they place. Clients pay the agency a flat hourly rate, which covers these costs, plus an administrative fee for the agency.

State employment taxes are usually combined with sales tax returns.

State Sales, Use and Withholding Taxes

Most states have sales and use taxes, with businesses reporting and paying quarterly, then submitting a final annual return. Employment taxes — state withholding and state unemployment tax — are usually integrated with these returns. If you will be responsible for withholding or obligated to pay any of these taxes, you must register with your state's treasury or revenue department, which will then provide you with the proper instructions and forms.

The Internal Revenue Service, in cooperation with various state partners, has established a new electronic filing and payment program for employment taxes called FSET (Fed/State Employment Taxes). This program enables the filing of both federal and state employment tax returns using online forms that have been developed for this purpose. Initial state partners included California, Connecticut, Iowa, Illinois, Massachusetts, Maryland, Minnesota, Montana, New Jersey, New York, Pennsylvania and South Carolina. The program is now open to all states. Information on FSET and how it works is contained in the *Fed/State Employment Taxes (FSET) User Guide* and other publications available from the IRS.

— ❧ —

5 Desktop Publishing

"If you are free to start your desktop publishing system from scratch, both hardware and software--start with a Macintosh. There are many things that IBM computers do well, but when compared with the Macintosh, desktop publishing is not one of them."

J. Scot Finnie
The Magazine for Magazine Management
December 1988

— ❧ —

5

Desktop Publishing

Desktop Publishing in Perspective

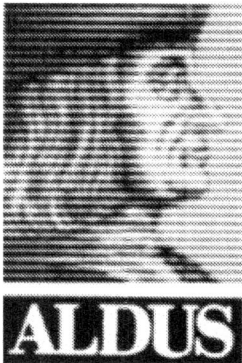

Paul Brainerd, founder of Aldus Corporation, is credited with coining the term "desktop publishing" in mid-1985 to promote the company's new flagship product.

The personal computer had advanced beyond the original DOS-ANSI-dot matrix paradigms. Graphical interfaces and displays were suddenly enabling PC users to create "WYSIWYG" document layouts on screen, then immediately print them on high resolution laser printers. Apple was leading the way, with increasingly capable computers, displays, printers and software tools which were revolutionizing the typesetting and printing businesses. Aldus' new product, called "PageMaker," would raise the bar and become an industry standard. As these new hardware and software tools became increasingly compact and affordable, ordinary PC users found themselves able to provide for many of their own needs. Today, only twenty years since the term was coined, desktop publishing has all but eliminated small time mom and pop print shops.

For our purposes, we use the term in its original context, referring to desktop publishing as projects involving the creation and production of printed pages. Examples are form letters, reports, booklets and even books. Over the years however, the term has been popularly broadened, or perhaps corrupted, to include all kinds of graphical and printing applications, even web pages. Let us choose to refer to these other sorts of applications by what they are. In the next section, you'll encounter several other valuable uses of the same tools you use for desktop publishing, but we'll refer to these activities as "graphics arts."

This section is about publishing in the conventional sense; preparing and issuing printed material created for the purpose of communicating information to readers. The scope is limited to requirement that any small nonprofit is likely to encounter in the normal course. These are:

- brochures
- small booklets (programs, annual reports)
- fliers (special events, news briefs)
- newsletters

You'll find examples of these items on the *SfS* website, and in the following pages:

- a discussion about how they were authored and designed
- step-by-step instructions for producing each item

Mission Statement, Logos & Tag Lines

You'll want to use various versions of your logo in most of these projects. Some also provide opportunities to use your mission statement or tag lines. If these are available in advance, you'll be able to easily walk right through the needed customizations. If these items are not yet available, you might wish to revisit Section 2 before going further into this Section.

— ❧ —

Brochures

Brochures are good marketing tools. As a hand-out when making cold calls or greeting visitors to your exhibit, they're great ice-breakers and conversation starters. They come in very handy as an insert when responding to inquiries about your organization. In a brochure rack or as a small stack left on the counter at the library, or other appropriate offices or business places, your brochure will work to promote your organization and further your mission full-time, and at no cost!

How to Write Fetching Copy

Deciding on content is easy. If you were to try selling someone on your organization face-to-face, what would you tell them? You'd tell them precisely what they want to know:

1. *WWWWWH? (Who, what, why, where, when and how?)*

2. *What's in it for me, right now? (What can I do; where would I fit in?)*

3. *Sounds great, but how much is this going to cost me in terms of both time and money?*

First, the facts: who you are, what you do, why you do it, where, when and how. That's easy within the context of a conversation. Because you have limited space in your brochure, this will require some very creative writing. For now, just write it up as you would say it conversationally. Think about these questions:

- *Who – Would I be comfortable with these sorts of people? Do I already know anyone who's involved?*

- *What – Do I know anything about this? Is this the sort of thing I'm interested in, or could become interested in?*

- *Why – Is what they're up to really important or worthwhile? Do I really care?*

- *Where and When – Would participation be convenient for me? Do I have time for this?*

- *How – Do I have personal skills or assets that could be of value to this group? Or does it just sound like fun?*

Did you notice these are all about *I* and *me*? Don't bother blowing your own horn. Talking about how great you are, all the wonderful things you've already done and all the good times you've already had is likely to leave your prospects feeling that they'll be late-comers, on the outside of an established hierarchy looking in. Your brochure is primarily a membership recruitment tool, not a public relations blurb. This is the *X-Generation*. "GenXers" have plenty of opportunities, and are not especially altruistic. You're not doing them a big favor by offering them something to do, and they probably won't buy into the notion that sacrificing for a worthy cause is always a good thing.

So next, cut to the chase; what's in it for them? Perhaps by becoming involved with your organization they'll –

- broaden their interests,
- learn new skills,
- acquire experience,
- meet new like-minded or socially compatible friends,
- make valuable business or professional contacts,
- have more fun, or
- enhance their resume by showing they're good citizens, who are active in public service activities and support volunteerism.

Here's another writing challenge; you can't say some of these things explicitly. They need to be written between the lines. People reading your brochure should realize that participation will be personally rewarding in these ways, although nothing in what you've written actually addresses opportunities for social or vocational advancement, or personal fulfillment.

Finally, what's the cost in terms of time and money? Say it plainly. When prospects receive proposals that avoid this subject, they're bound to suspect there's a reason why, and are likely to anticipate a hard sell later on. Rather than expose themselves to that possible annoyance and embarrassment, they're apt to simply toss the brochure in the trash and forget about it. Don't try to explain, excuse or justify these requirements. They are what they are. If your prospects don't feel they have the price of participation now, that's not likely to change no matter how much arm-twisting you try on them later. If your prospects make a rational value judgment and typically but incorrectly conclude that what they're likely to get out of it won't justify what they're asked to put into it, that's your fault; your brochure isn't working.

The Mechanical Layout

Tri-fold templates usually provide a brochure that measures about 3-5/8" x 8-1/2"; in other words, an 8-1/2" x 11" sheet printed in landscape with three equal columns. Professionally printed brochures are often designed as self-mailing pieces, approximately the same size as a regular No.10 business envelope. Smaller brochures based on the simple tri-fold template make for odd-size mailing pieces, and when placed in brochure racks alongside professionally printed brochures, they look cheap and puny.

These disadvantages are easily avoided by designing your brochure with a smaller third panel, which will be folded into the brochure. Arrange the inside side like this:

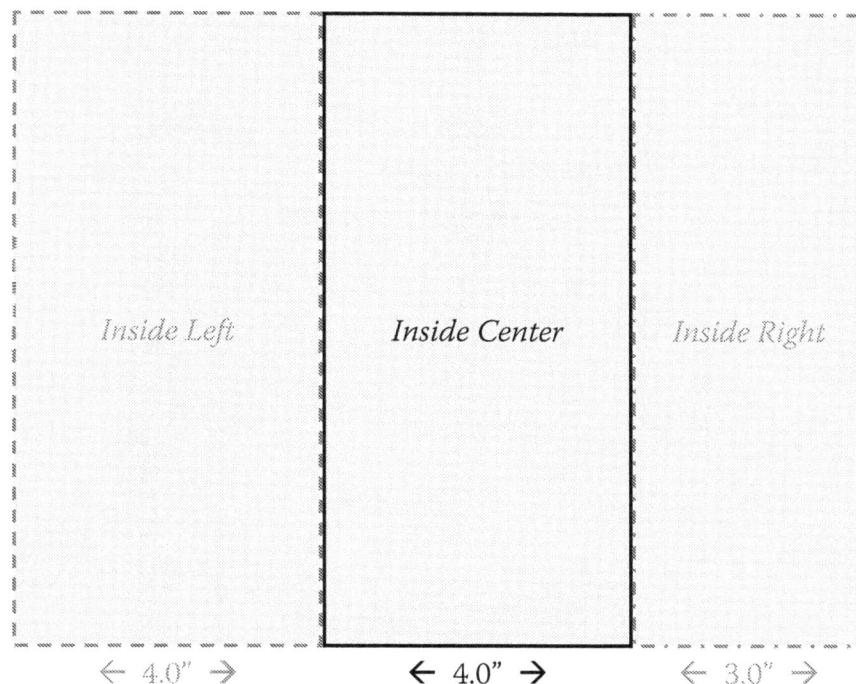

Inside Left   Inside Center   *Inside Right*

← 4.0" →   ← 4.0" →   ← 3.0" →

It is possible to set this up using Word's column formatting; however because the amount of copy is small, and the paragraphs short, it's easier to simply use text boxes. Provide plenty of white space by making the text boxes 2.5" wide in the left two panels, and 1.87" wide in the right panel. When the text boxes are centered in their respective panels, the left and right margins are 1/2". Leave about 1.5" of white space at the tops of the panels, and about 1" at their bottoms.

Set the internal text box margins to 0" all around (*Format Text Box, Text Box* tab), then type your copy into these boxes and position them as appropriate in their respective panels. The boxes themselves vanish when you format them choosing *No Line* and *No Fill* under the *Colors and Lines* tab. Arrange whatever pictures and graphic you wish to use as appropriate.

For printing purposes, before inserting graphics in your document, they should be saved at 300 dpi (*dots per inch* or *pixels per inch*). The uncompressed TIFF image format is preferred, but if another format is used, JPG for example, be sure to set the compression to zero before saving the image.

Word doesn't like to place other objects within text boxes. If you need to insert an image inside a text box, the work-around is to insert it outside the text box, and then position it as desired on top of the text box. Before doing this, you might have to set text wrapping to *None* (Word97) or *Other* (later versions). If necessary, right-click this second object and choose *Order* to place it above or below whatever else is in the text box. Control wrapping by manually arranging the text using spaces and line breaks.

Save the above as *"brochure-inside.doc"*, then choose *Save As...*, and save it again as *"brochure-outside.doc"*.

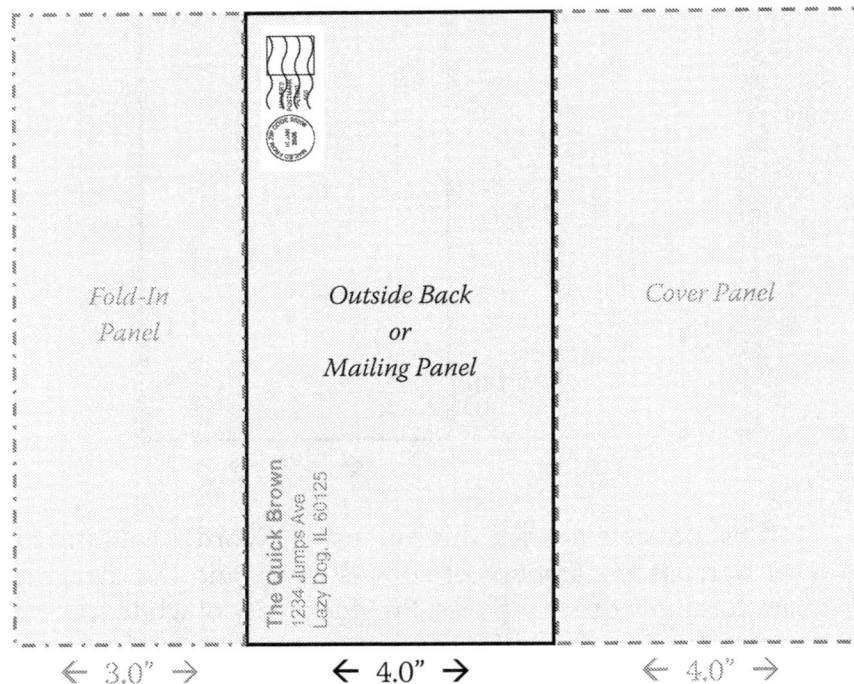

Fold-In Panel   *Outside Back or Mailing Panel*   *Cover Panel*

The Quick Brown
1234 Jumps Ave
Lazy Dog, IL 60125

← 3.0" →   ← 4.0" →   ← 4.0" →

Now rearrange the outside of the brochure as shown above, replacing the content with the text and images that go on this side.

If you intend to use the brochure as a mailer, use the back panel as the mailing panel, and set it up as shown here. This places the fold at the bottom of the piece as it passes through the automatic sorting machines, with the loose ends at the top, and will help prevent mechanical damage to the piece as it passes through the system.

If your brochure will more often be distributed in brochure racks, mailed with other literature and used as a hand-out, setting it up as a self-mailer will probably waste a lot of real estate that could better be devoted to additional information. Unless you have a definite reason for doing that, it is not recommended.

Assuming that your brochure is a membership and fundraising tool, you'll need to include a convenient way for people to sign up and send you money. That usually implies a form for applicants or donors to fill out, which will take up even more of the brochure's limited space. A better approach is to let the brochure be a brochure, and insert a separate reply/remittance envelope inside. Your brochure will fit neatly into a standard No.10 business envelope, which can easily be addressed using your printer, and which will guarantee that it'll reach the addressee in pristine condition.

Printing and Finishing

Unless you have a particular reason to choose something else, consider printing your brochure on 67 lb. white cover stock (such as Hammermill No. 18624-0). If you happen to have a color laser printer, consider using 32 lb coated paper (glossy or slick paper, such as Hammermill 16311-0), which produces a more professional-looking result. Coated paper is not recommended for use with inkjet printers, because the ink does not soak into the paper; the drying time is very long, and the ink is prone to smearing even after having dried for several days.

To fold your printed brochures, tape a straight-edge exactly 4" from the edge of your paper cutter (Ingento #1142, or equal). Use that as a guide to accurately make the cover panel/back panel fold, then the back panel/fold-in panel, and then tuck the fold-in panel inside. Making the first fold just slightly less (e.g., 1/32") than 4" will improve the mechanical appearance of your piece and make it easier to open up.

Because desktop printing is slow and expensive, it's likely that you'll eventually need to have your brochure printed in quantity. Most printers prefer to receive files in Adobe PDF format, rather than Microsoft Word format. Although there are many ways to convert Word documents to PDF, the method recommended when you need to provide such files for a commercial printer is to save the word files as print files, then use Adobe's *Acrobat Distiller* (comes with the Adobe Acrobat program) to convert them to PDF. This ensures that mechanical aspects will be maintained and all fonts will be faithfully reproduced:

1. Select *File|Print (or Ctrl+P)*
2. Select *Printer-Name: Acrobat Distiller*
3. Check *Print to File*
4. Click *OK*
5. The *Print to file* dialog box appears.
6. Navigate to *C:\Program Files\Adobe\ Acrobat\Distillr\In.* (If the *Distillr* folder doesn't contain an *In* folder and an *Out* folder, create these two folders.)
7. Provide a name for your print file in the *In* folder.
8. Click *OK*
9. Select *Start|Programs|Acrobat Distiller*
10. When Distiller starts, it will search the *In* folder for *.prn* files, convert whatever it finds to PDF format and save them in the *Out* folder.
11. Open the files found in C:\Program Files\Adobe\Acrobat\ Distillr\Out using Acrobat or the Adobe Reader, and inspect them carefully to ensure that your documents have been faithfully converted.
12. These two files can be transmitted to the printer electronically or on disk.

A printable example of a color brochure is provided on the *SfS* website. Download the example, open it in Word and print it to get a better feel for setting up and printing a similar presentation piece of your own design.

— 🙢 —

How to Make Booklets

Making 4" x 7" or 5-1/2" x 8-1/2" Booklets is Easy!

Regular old 8-1/2" x 11" reports are fine for many applications, but you can easily turn these common-looking documents into something special, just by changing their layout and size. Booklets are also often a good way to do simple handbooks and instruction manuals, since their small size suggests simplicity. Use this idea to make programs for special events, giving your guests the impression that you cared enough to make the extra effort, getting things off to a good start, with the notion that the entire program is likely to be equally well done. As a very practical solution, if you're preparing a document that included several bound pages, there is no cheaper way to bind them than saddle stitching, which means stapling on the fold.

Although the instructions that follow seem to suggest this is a complicated and time-consuming task, making booklets really isn't difficult, once you get the hang of it, and the results are always rewarding enough to justify the effort. You'll find examples of these two formats on the *SfS* website. 5-1/2" x 8-1/2" booklets are the easiest to do. These are simply regular letter-size sheets folded in half. The pocket size 4" x 7" booklet is not quite as simple, but has the additional advantage of fitting in a regular No.10 business size envelope for mailing.

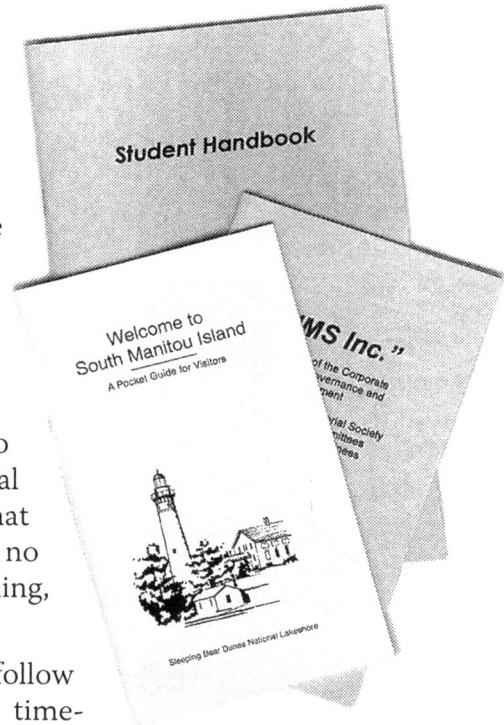

Getting Started – Making a Mockup

Booklets have to be carefully paginated. The pages in the printing layout do not follow each other in sequence. For example, the first side of the first sheet will have the front and back covers printed on one side, and the inside front and back covers printed on its other side. So the same piece of paper will serve as the beginning and end of the booklet. Likewise, the next sheet will have the first page and the last page on one side, and the second page and next-to-last page on the other. Doesn't sound simple? It is, but it's easy to become confused, so you therefore need a system to make sure everything comes out right.

1. The first step is to prepare your project as a regular letter size MS-Word document, printed in book format (printed on both sides of the page, sometime called duplex printing). This can be printed in draft mode, since you'll only be using it as a mechanical model, or mockup.

Here are some hints that will help your booklet look professionally done. You should number your pages, using Word's footer capability, and provide a Table of Contents. The first few pages of your booklet, which are usually referred to as "front matter," should be numbered with lower case roman numerals; "i," "ii," "iii," "iv," etc. The pages containing the main content should be numbered in the usual way; "1," "2," "3," "4," etc. The covers and any extra blank pages at the end should not have page numbers. By convention, with a book or magazine lying open in front of you, the even-numbered pages are always on the left, the odd-numbered pages on the right. New headings should never begin on even-numbered pages, while odd-numbered pages should ordinarily never be left blank. From time to time, you might need to add blank pages to your document to comply with these conventions.

> ❧ Hint: When using Word's footer capability, keep in mind that you must use the *section break* to isolate sections of the document which are to have different footers or no footer at all, and make sure the *Same as previous section* box is not selected.

To make things come out right in your booklet, the font size used here should be larger than you would ordinarily choose. For example, to create a 5-1/2" x 8-1/2" booklet, you'll simply copy 'n paste content from these pages to the new, smaller pages, reducing it as necessary to fit. 14pt Times New Roman on the mockup reduced to 11pt will work quite well. There is no formula, however, since the final look of your booklet is a matter of personal preferences, and the mechanics vary considerably, depending upon what fonts you choose. So you'll need to determine what font sizes to use for text and headers by experiment. As a starting point, you might choose these:

For	Font	Mockup	Booklet
Headers	Arial Bold Upper Case	18pt	14pt
Subheaders	Arial Bold Title Case	14pt	11pt
Text	Times New Roman	14pt	11pt
Footnotes	Times new Roman	9pt	8pt

Before you begin to convert the mockup to booklet form, your project should be complete so far as content is concerned. Minor revisions are possible once the content is rearranged, but changes that cannot be accommodated without forcing content to spill over to the next page might be difficult to incorporate.

2. When working with lengthy documents, Word ordinarily handles page breaks automatically, according to certain rules of its own and preferences you can set. When you make changes in your document, Word updates its layout automatically. When converting the contents of the mockup to booklet form, this will be a nuisance. Therefore, go through the document now, replacing each automatic page break with a hard page break (menu: *Insert|Break...|Page break|OK*).

> ✻ Hint: Customize the standard toolbar by adding a Page break and a Column break icon. These will prove very handy. Get creative; edit the column break button image so that it looks like the page break button, rotated 90-degrees, as shown below.

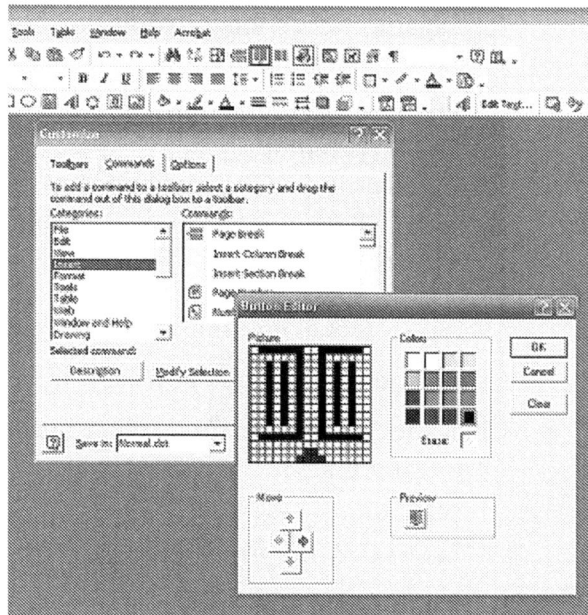

3. Next, count the pages in your printed document. If necessary, add a blank sheet at the end to provide an even number of sheets. If you have included the covers, this extra sheet should be inserted just before the back cover.

4. Lay out pairs of these pages as they will relate to each other in the booklet, and tape them together in the middle. For example, rather than just stapling the collated document as you ordinarily would, take it apart, laying the first page face-down on the left, then the last page face-up on the right, then using two or three small pieces of tape to hook them together in the middle, forming a single tabloid size (11" x 17") page. Mark the bottom side of this page "1A" and to top side "1B".

5. Do this same thing with the next top and next bottom page, until all the tabloid-size mockup pages have been assembled. Mark these pages "2A" and "2B," "3A" and "3B," etc.

6. Having stacked these in 1-2-3 order, if you pick up the stack and fold it on the middle seam, you'll have an 8-1/2" x 11" mockup of the booklet you're about to create. However, leave these pages unbound so you can work with them separately.

5-1/2" x 8-1/2" Booklets

This is the easier of the two formats, since it is simply made by laying out regular letter-size pages in landscape mode with a two-column format. However, before you begin, make sure your page layout is set correctly. Here again, there's lots of room for creativity, but here is a basic setup you can use as a starting point:

- paper size: standard letter size (8-1/2" x 11")
  - orientation: landscape
- margins: 0.5" all around (top, bottom, left and right)
  - header and footer: 0.0" (none)
- columns: 2
  - space between columns: 1"
  - equal column width: checked

7. Open a new document, and set it up as specified above.

8. Click the *Show/Hide* ¶ toolbar button so you can see the page formatting marks.

   a. Place the cursor in the left column of the page and click the *Insert Column Break* button.

   b. Then place the cursor anywhere in the right column and click the *Page Break* button.

   c. Word opens another new page. Repeat these two steps to provide as many columns as there are pages in your mockup document.

   d. Save this as "booklet.doc", or whatever you wish to name it.

You can't do page numbers in columns using headers or footers, but you can duplicate what you have on your mockup using text boxes. There is, of course, an easy way to do this, and it is very helpful to have the page numbers in place before you begin transferring content.

9. Place the cursor in the left column, and create a small text box.

a. Click the *Textbox* button on the drawing toolbar (menu: *Insert|Textbox*)

b. Double-click on the text box's frame, to format it:

    i. Fill: "No Fill"
    ii. Line: "No Line"
    iii. Height: 0.45"
    iv. Width: 1.5"
    v. Wrap: "None" (or Layout: "Other")
    vi. Text Box: Internal Margins: "0"

c. Click within the text box, then enter whatever content you wish to include, and the number "0". Format the content as you wish (8pt and 10pt Times New Roman is shown here).

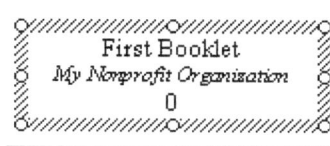

> First Booklet
> *My Nonprofit Organization*
> 0

d. Double-click the text box's frame again, and set it's absolute position with respect to the page:

    i. Horizontal: 2.0"
    ii. Vertical: 7.5"

10. To make a copy of the text box for the right column, hold down the Ctrl key, then click and drag a copy of the text box over to the right column. Position this one to:

a. Horizontal: 7.55"
b. Vertical: 7.5"

> ⚜ Hint: The anchor ⚓ for these text boxes should be in the same column they are in. When copying things by clicking and dragging, the anchor usually doesn't move. So click the new text box, and if the anchor isn't in the same column, click on it and drag it to one of the paragraph marks in that column.

11. To provide an identical text box at the bottom of each column, select the first one, in the left column of the first page, then press *Ctrl+C* to copy it to the clipboard. Click anywhere in the left column of the next page, and press *Ctrl+V* to paste a copy in that column.

a. Move down to the left column of the next page and press *Ctrl+V* again. Repeat this process for every page.

b. To place identical boxes in the right columns, do the same. Copy the text box in the right column of the first page, and then paste copies in the right column of each succeeding page.

c. The pasted text boxes will probably be somewhere close to the correct position at the bottom of each column, but you will need to double-click each one, and set its horizontal and vertical position to exactly the values given above; 2" x 7.5", and 7.55" x 7.5".

d. Now edit these boxes so that they contain the correct page numbers, using the mockup as the reference. The first page of the booklet corresponds to the mockup page marked "1A," the second page to "1B," the third to "2A," and so on. For pages that shouldn't have a page number (such as the covers), simply delete the text box.

Having prepared the basic booklet template, it's time to cut and paste the content, from the mockup document to the booklet document.

12. Load the mockup document, then save this copy as "mockup-work.doc" (or something similar), in order to preserve the original.

13. Go through the mockup document one page at a time, reducing the headers and text to the booklet size you've decided on (under Step 1, above). Images and text boxes can also be proportionately reduced so they will look right on the smaller pages. Again; no formula for this. Just use your judgment, working with these objects until you're satisfied that they look right.

> ✷ Hint: Images can easily be resized in Word, but the embedded file remains unchanged. This allows you to click the *Reset Picture* button whenever you wish to return the image to its original state. Consider doing this: after adjusting image sizes, use the *Format Picture* button to see the new width and height, use an image editor to change the image to that size, and then replace the larger embedded image with the reduced version. Word will then be able to handle your file more efficiently and the resulting file size will be considerably smaller.

14. Now transfer the pages from the mockup to the booklet. To do this, select all the headers and text on a mockup page, press *Ctrl+X* (cut). then place the cursor on the corresponding booklet page and press *Ctrl+V* (paste).

> ✷ Hint: When this is done, any objects associated with the page (images and text boxes) will ordinarily accompany the highlighted text, because its anchor is associated with it. If that doesn't happen, return to the mockup page and press *Crtl+V* (undo), then find the anchor and drag it back onto that page.

15. Save the booklet file frequently during this process, and after the task has been completed. The "mockup-work.doc" file can then be deleted.

Printing and Binding the Booklet

Print the booklet file in the duplex mode (double-sided), like any other print job. Textured cover stock makes an attractive cover.

> ❧ Hint: Wausau Paper No. 27427, with its natural-color Antique Parchment Finish, is often a good choice. It's available from most office supply stores.

16. Fold the printed pages in half, to 5-1/2" x 8-1/2".

> ❧ Hint: Rather than trying to fold the whole booklet at once, fold just three or four pages at a time. Otherwise the middle pages sometime develop unwanted wrinkles and creases.

17. With the booklet properly folded and assembled, bind it by stapling its seam. Two staples are usually sufficient.

> ❧ Hint: A long-reach stapler will be needed. An inexpensive choice is the Stanley-Bostitch Model B440LR – about $22.00 from online sellers.

18. The top and bottom edges of the booklet will be trim and even. The long edge, however, may need trimming in order to give the booklet a professionally produced appearance.

    a. Do not try using a paper cutter.

    b. Hold a straight-edge firmly against the long edge of the booklet, 1/16" back from the edge of the covers, and then use a common 6" plastic box cutter to neatly cut off the uneven edges. Use several light passes, rather than trying to trim all the pages off at once.

4" x 7" Booklets

This is made by laying out regular letter-size pages in portrait mode with a two-column format. Smaller font sizes are usually appropriate for these booklets. As a starting point, you might consider these:

For	Font	Mockup	Booklet
Headers	Arial Bold Upper Case	14pt	11pt
Subheaders	Arial Bold Title Case	11pt	9pt
Text	Times New Roman	11pt	9pt
Footnotes	Times new Roman	8pt	7pt

19. Create a mockup document as outlined above (Steps 1 thru 6).

20. Next, create the template document for the booklet (Steps 7 and 8).

a. Set up the booklet page layout as desired, else as a starting point use these parameters:

- paper size: standard letter size (8-1/2" x 11")
  - orientation: portrait
- margin – top: 0.5"
  - left and right: 0.57"
  - bottom: 4.0"
  - header and footer: 0.0" (none)
- columns: 2
  - space between columns: 0.64"
  - equal column width: checked

21. Refer to Steps 9 thru 11 to see how to apply text boxes with page numbers. Because of the smaller format, these parameters are suggested:

   a. Height: 0.15"
   b. Width: 0.3"
   c. Left Column Position: 2.0" x 6.75" (H x V)
   d. Right Column Position: 6.2" x 6.75" (H x V)

22. Cut and paste the content from the mockup document to the booklet document as explained in Steps 12 thru 15.

Printing and Binding the Booklet

Print the booklet file in the duplex mode (double-sided), like any other print job.

23. These printed pages must be accurately trimmed to 8-1/2" x 7". Use a paper cutter to cut 4" off their bottom edge. To ensure accuracy and uniformity, tape a ruler atop the paper cutter as a guide, so that all pages will be trimmed to exactly the same length.

24. Fold the printed pages in half, to 5-1/2" x 7".

   ❧ Hint: Rather than trying to fold the whole booklet at once, fold just three or four pages at a time. Otherwise the middle pages sometimes develop unwanted wrinkles and creases.

25. With the booklet properly folded and assembled, bind it by stapling its seam. Two staples are usually sufficient.

26. The top and bottom edges of the booklet should be trim and even. Trim the long edge to the desired size, giving the booklet a professionally produced appearance:

   a. Do not try using a paper cutter.

b. Hold a straight-edge firmly against the long edge of the booklet, 4" to 4-1/16" from the stapled edge, then use a common 6" plastic box cutter to neatly cut off the excess width. Use several light passes, rather than trying to trim all the pages off at once.

News Briefs

The 5-1/2" x 8-1/2" format is also useful for mini-newsletters. Two sheets of paper provide an eight-page piece. Stapling isn't necessary. A six-page piece can be produced by printing two copies of pages 3 and 4 on a single piece of paper, then cutting it in half and inserting it within the folded page.

Publishing Easy, But Effective, Newsletters

Make 4, 6 or 8-page newsletters that look professionally done.

Newsletters are important for several reasons. First, they are powerful membership recruitment and retention tools. Second, they are a very effective fundraising idea. Finally, they are a thoughtful and unobtrusive way to touch base, and keep in touch with interested third parties (such as vendors, newspaper editors and politicians) and the general public (through distribution at libraries, museums, or other venues likely to be visited by people with an interest in what the organization does).

When visiting the offices of a company or organization, if the premises are cluttered and messy, it suggests that the operations are probably much less efficient and effective than they could be; that this organization might not be the best place to invest one's money or time. The same holds true for the paperwork an organization publishes and distributes. In the case of newsletters, many readers will never have an opportunity to visit the organization or become personally acquainted with its officers and members, so the newsletter is the first and last chance to create and maintain a favorable impression. Newsletters that are crudely typed and mimeographed, or badly photocopied, are not very effective, and might even be a detriment since they do not represent the organization at its best.

Good news! There's no economic reason to settle for that anymore. What you can achieve on your desktop is limited only by your creativity, imagination and energy. This applies whether you are distributing tens, hundreds or thousands of copies.

You'll find the MS-Word layout for the newsletter pictured here in the "examples" section of the *SfS* website. The following pages will teach you how to produce a piece of this quality for your organization.

Coming Up with Content

But first things first! What goes into the newsletter, and where do you get it?

Wouldn't it be nice to have a newsletter committee? Or, better yet, a newsletter editor who's only responsibility would be to gather information, and receive submissions from willing contributors? You might get lucky, and have someone in the organization that wants to do the newsletter, and is highly skilled and conscientious in that area. More likely, you'll wind up doing the job yourself. It will fall to you to come up with content and do all the writing, not to mention creating the layout, printing or having the piece printed, producing the mailing list and labels, and finally mailing each issue. Why does it fall to you? Because you are the Secretary, and in that position you are where the action is. You probably know more about what's going on than any other single officer or member of your organization.

"News-letter*"* is a misnomer. Much of the content will be about the organization and its mission, and related business details. However, most readers will not find that kind of information highly engaging. Successful newsletters capture the reader's interest with articles that are useful or entertaining. These should be the primary focus, and if done well, will carry all the more mundane content. What these articles are about depends upon what your organization is about.

For the example pictured above, the readers enjoy articles about the islands' more obscure, little known or poorly understood features, articles about historical aspects, biographical sketches on early settlers, or even members' island-related poetry and art. Articles about current activities are not as well received, but can be enhanced by concentrating on humorous or human-interest aspects. Praise and congratulations work to the extent that readers were associated with the activity. For example, if a small crew of volunteers accomplishes some wonderful organization-supported project, readers can be included in the warm fuzziness by emphasizing that the project was only possible because of the very generous contributions. Thus, the article becomes more of a thank you to everyone, rather than just praise and congratulations for a few.

Organizational newsletters are usually published quarterly or seasonally. So you have a long time in between issues to come up with ideas. Creative minds do not work well with schedules or deadlines. Keep the newsletter in the back of your mind, and you'll come up with good ideas while on the golf course, at dinner, while driving in freeway traffic, or in the shower. Create a folder on your computer for the next newsletter, open your text editor and make a document named "topics.txt". Every time inspiration strikes, make a note of it, and transcribe that to "topics.txt". If you're inspired to begin working on a draft of an article, perhaps collecting background material and prospective photographs or other illustrations, create an appropriately named subfolder for those files. Others might occasionally submit or recommend content. Add that to your list, and save the information in a special sub-folder. When the time comes to turn your attention to getting out the next newsletter (about six weeks prior to the desired mailing date), you'll probably have more potential content that you have space!

General Layout - Look and Feel

Look at any magazine or newspaper, and you'll see how to design the newsletter. Use two or three columns on an 8-1/2" x 11" page, in portrait orientation; three to four columns in landscape. Using a single, page-wide column almost never works.

White space (empty space on the page) will make the newsletter look open and clean, easy to read and digest. Crowding has the opposite effect. Attempting to pack something into every available square inch will give the piece a "hard work" look, giving prospective readers the feeling that this is something to be studied later, rather than enjoyed now. And later will probably never come. Generous margins all around are therefore appropriate, as is liberal spacing between text and pictures, and between articles. Thinking about packing in a little more content by reducing the font size or the line spacing? That's never a good idea!

Illustrations add interest. Pictures can also often provide more information than hundreds of words of descriptive text. Inserting illustrations in paragraphs breaks up the monotony of columnar text, and makes the piece easy to read. Images can be photographs directly related to the adjacent subject matter, or drawings such as charts and graphs. Avoid stock clip art, such as that supplied with Microsoft Office. Clip art is usually not appropriate for this purpose, since it will look like gratuitous fluff or filler. On-topic cartoons, on the other hand, are sometime fun, even though not directly connected to the organization, people or project being discussed.

The tabloid format usually works out best for newsletters of four, six or eight pages. The copy is printed on 11" x 17" sheets, which are then folded in the middle to become standard 8-1/2" x 11" documents. These are easy to mockup, can be produced by standard printers and copiers, handily fit standard envelopes and file folders, stack well with other documents, and can be mailed at regular first class rates.

Proof Reading

Never proof read your own work!

That's not possible, of course. Naturally you'll have to proof read your own work. The comment was made to get your attention, and hopefully imprint that idea on your mind.

Ever hear of the paradigm principle? – *"The mind modifies the data to confirm the reality it knows to be true."*

When you try to proof read your own work, your mind knows what you were trying to say, so doesn't bother with minor details. It'll skip right over typos, spelling and grammar errors that would be glaringly obvious to anyone else. At best, wait several hours or a couple of days before reviewing your own work. Then have someone else proof read it before submitting the draft for final approval, where concern should only be with content; not with spelling and grammar.

Word's spell-checker is useful, but do not rely on that. You've probably seen this somewhere –

"My Spell Checker: The checker pours ore every word
To cheque sum spelling rule. Be fore a veiling
checkers, Hour spelling mite decline ..."

Editorial Control

It's never a good idea to publish a newsletter without someone else's critical review and approval.

You can't think of everything. Seemingly innocuous remarks, innocently written or included with the best of intentions, sometimes have the potential of adverse interpretations. In other cases, your exuberance or pessimism might sneak into something you write. These potentially embarrassing situations need to be caught and corrected before the newsletter mails. Knowing that someone else will be reviewing the content, with the prerogative of requiring a re-write, often keeps these things from sneaking into the newsletter in the first place.

Who should have this editorial control?

Do not submit the draft newsletter to a committee! *The Buck Stops Here* should be the chief executive's philosophy (as is probably established by the organization's bylaws). That person, who is usually called the president or executive director, will be responsible for the newsletter, and should be the only person with editorial control. The reasons are two.

First, newsletters are essentially creative works and as such are open to subjective criticism. If ten people are polled, there will very likely be ten different opinions. People are often moved to offer suggestions just for the sake of having some input, or feeling that they have a share in the process. Suggestions come easy to people who won't have to roll up their sleeves and do the rework. If you submit the draft to several people for critical review, you will receive lots of suggestions and comments from those who respond.

And that brings up the second issue – the timeliness of their response. Newsletters usually run into deadlines. The chances are good that the draft will not be finished until sometime very near, or just past, the intended mailing date. Requiring that the draft be approved by several people is a good way to ensure that newsletters will always be late, since many will consistently have trouble getting around to it.

If the matter is left exclusively up to the chief executive, a speedy approval with suggestions regarding only the most salient flaws and necessary revisions will be the likely result. Why? Because that person understands the mission, has a full agenda, appreciates the amount of time and effort already put into the project, and will not be interested in spending a lot of time nitpicking.

Production and Mailing

If you have a printer that supports the 11" x 17" tabloid or A3 size, Microsoft Word will offer that option in the *File|Page Setup...* dialog box. However, for draft purposes it is usually more convenient to work with standard letter size pages. When you've made all the necessary corrections and revisions, are satisfied with the piece and are ready to publish, simply copy and paste these pages into a tabloid-size document.

Your printer probably will not print on 11" x 17" paper, so you won't have that option. If you are mailing only a few newsletters, the most practical approach is photocopying. Make originals for each 11" x 17" side by printing on 8-1/2" x 11" and taping two pages together, side-by-side using regular *Scotch® Matte Finish Magic Tape* (tape on the back side), as follows:

Four Page Newsletter

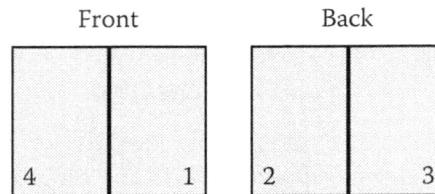

Front	Back
4 1	2 3

Six Page Newsletter

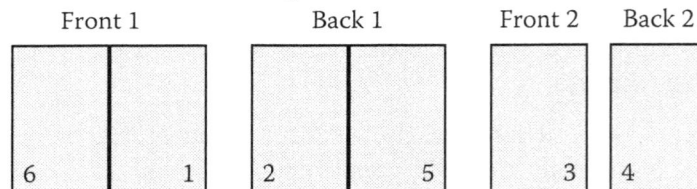

Front 1	Back 1	Front 2	Back 2
6 1	2 5	3	4

Eight Page Newsletter

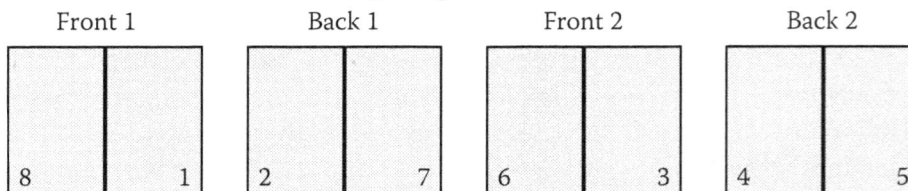

Front 1	Back 1	Front 2	Back 2
8 1	2 7	6 3	4 5

If your mailing list contains hundreds, rather than tens, of names, printing will be much cheaper than photocopying. In fact, the printing might actually be done by a laser printer such as a Xerox DocuTech. These are similar to a photocopier; however the input will be your digital file, rather than a paper original.

Most vendors will be able to accept your MS-Word files; however Word files may not look the same when opened on a system other than the one that produced them, because the *normal.dot* template will not be the same, and the target system might not have all the fonts used in the original document. Because of this, most vendors prefer files in the Adobe PDF format. You can easily convert your individual MS-Word "doc" pages to PDF, using Adobe's Acrobat Distiller (comes with the Adobe Acrobat program). This ensures that mechanical aspects will be maintained and all fonts will be faithfully reproduced:

1. Select *File|Print (or Ctrl+P)*
2. Select *Printer-Name: Acrobat Distiller*
3. Check *Print to File*
4. Click *OK*
5. The *Print to file* dialog box appears.
6. Navigate to *C:\Program Files\Adobe\ Acrobat\Distillr\In.* (If the *Distillr* folder doesn't contain an *In* folder and an *Out* folder, create these two folders.)
7. Provide a name for your print file in the *In* folder.
8. Click *OK*
9. Select *Start|Programs|Acrobat Distiller*
10. When Distiller starts, it will search the *In* folder for *.prn* files, convert whatever it finds to PDF format and save them in the *Out* folder.
11. Open the files found in C:\Program Files\Adobe\Acrobat\ Distillr\Out using Acrobat or the Adobe Reader, and inspect them carefully to ensure that your documents have been faithfully converted.
12. These two files can be transmitted to the printer electronically or on disk.

Otherwise, several alternative tools are now available. Click-to-Convert is recommended. A less expensive choice is available at www.pdfonline.com, where you can convert your documents for free online (results are sent to your email address as a file attachment), or purchase a print driver for only $14.95 and do the same thing on your desktop. Unless otherwise instructed, provide your printer with PDF files for individual pages, rather than combining pages in tabloid form. They'll combine the pages as necessary using whatever software is appropriate for their system.

A six page newsletter printed on 20# stock will usually come in under one ounce, and when folded to 5-1/2" x 8-1/2" can be mailed at the basic first-class rate. An eight-page production will usually require second-ounce postage.

Bulk mailing permits are not usually practical until your mailing list exceeds seven-hundred pieces. This results from the fact that there is a $160 fee for the permit. The basic nonprofit presorted first-class rate is 17-cents vs. 39-cents, so the break even point is about 730 pieces.

Other restrictions apply, such as one requiring your bulk mailings to be sent from the post office originally issuing the permit, which might not prove practical or convenient if your organization does not operate from a permanently located office. Furthermore, you must prove to the postal service that you qualify for nonprofit mailing privileges. Your conformed articles of incorporation and 501(c)3 letter of determination can be provided as evidence, but the postal service makes its own determination. In view of all this, you will probably opt to not bother with a bulk mailing permit application until your mailing volume is well beyond the break even point.

As an alternative, printers often offer complete printing, folding, labeling and mailing services. Some are willing to quote a full-service price, which includes mailing at bulk rates using their own permit.

— ❧ —

Other Projects

The Annual Report – and other opportunities

It's always worth repeating – *People will often know your organization only through the printed material you distribute.*

The theme of this book is *"... how to build a first class image on a third rate budget."* The reason you want to develop a reasonably proficient desktop publishing capability is just that – so that you'll look good, and your organization will look good. Remember the discussion in Section 2 about image and brand, and how those things are related to success? Looking good would be easy if you had the money to buy it. But this book is written for secretaries of small NPOs; by definition, you won't have that kind of money. As you've seen however, the quality of the information you publish isn't determined by the size of your bank account. It's a function only of your personal creativity, ingenuity and care.

When you have information your organization needs to publish or share, think about ways to make that document or publication work for you; not by its informational content, but by the quality and class of the piece you create to present it.

Consider the annual report discussed in Section 3, an example of which you can find on the *SfS* website. The information included in the annual report is often otherwise passed out at annual meetings as separate documents, usually created by different people. The pages therefore usually differ in design and layout, having the look and feel of an obligatory and hurriedly prepared handout of photocopy quality. Sometimes the information isn't committed to print at all, being shared only verbally at the meeting, being thereafter forever lost as the sound waves wane beyond the last row of chairs. What a great opportunity to compile that same information into a presentation piece that can work for you not only at the annual meeting, but also all during the twelve months leading up to the next gathering!

In your role as Secretary, you are in a powerful position with respect to your organization's public image. You can, if you want to, single-handedly do more to make your organization look great than any other individual board member, and probably more than all the others combined.

— ❧ —

6

Graphic Arts

Graphic arts originated in southern Germany in the early 15th century, where woodcuts were used to produce the first images on paper.

— ❧ —

6
Graphic Arts

Resourcefulness

... the art of getting things done using what's at hand...
(... or "This ain't Kansas anymore Toto!")

If you're a degreed specialist who is used to working in an established commercial or institutional setting, this section of the book might seem provincially amateurish and penny wise. It's about things you've always ordered out, but will now have to do for yourself. In the big time, perhaps you were always able to dismiss the make or buy decision by employing the conjecture about purchase costs probably being much less than the cost of in-house do-it-yourself man-hours. Or perhaps you worked with expertise snobs ("You don't invade my area of expertise, and I won't encroach upon yours.")

"This ain't Kansas anymore." If you're not used to having to be resourceful, change your mind and have some fun. With your desktop computer system and ink-jet printer, you can easily create business essentials such as these:

- letterheads
- envelopes
- business cards
- membership cards

You'll also be able to provide specialty items such as:

- contribution acknowledgement cards
- personalized note stationery
- simple paper boxes
- reply envelopes
- fancy certificates

You might even find yourself coming up with nifty, low-cost handouts and fundraising items, like these:

- bookmarks
- memorial contribution kits
- monogram license plates

Where does it say that the Secretary's job has to be all work, and no play? Where does it say the Secretary is supposed to be all business; not artistic and creative? A lot of the work you have to do isn't particularly challenging or rewarding in any other way, so you deserve to treat yourself to some projects that are.

If you don't have the time, or the interest, that's okay. In that case, the possibilities described in the following pages make great opportunities for volunteers who do to participate in meaningful ways.

Mission Statement, Logos & Tag Lines

You'll want to use various versions of your logo in most of these projects. Some also provide opportunities for you to use your mission statement or tag lines. If these are available in advance, you'll be able to easily walk right through the needed customizations. If these items are not yet available, revisit that part of Section 2 before going further into this Section.

— ❧ —

Letterheads and Envelopes

Letters written on behalf of your organization should always be printed on your organization's own letterhead. Officers, directors and staff should understand this essential component of the organization's effort to create a positive image and respected brand. People are otherwise apt to use personal stationery or, worse yet, lined three-ring notebook paper, yellow lined sheets from legal pads, or sheets ripped out of a spiral-bound composition or a stenographer's tablet. To discourage that:

- Make personalized letterheads available for each person.
- Provide convenient secretarial services for your board and staff.

Your letterhead should have these components:

- Your logo.
- Your organization name, mailing address and phone number.
- The writer's name, mailing address, and email address.
- Your organization's web address.

Your official correspondence should be mailed in regular business size (No. 10) envelopes. A template letterhead with matching envelope is available on the *SfS* website. Customize these as you wish, or use them as an example when creating your own design.

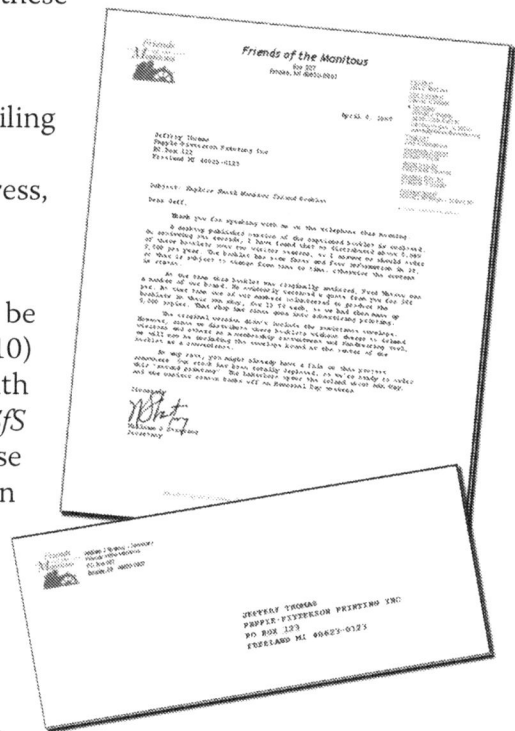

Customizing the Letterhead

1. Replace the *Friends* logo with your own. Use the 1-1/4" 300 dpi version (see Section 2). If your logo is in color, that's fine, otherwise convert it to grayscale if you prefer.

2. Replace the *Friends* header with your own name and address.

3. Edit the information in the officers, directors and staff text box on the right side of the page. Full contact information is provided for the person signing the letter. For all others provide title and name only.

4. Practice your signature in dark blue or black ink on a white background. Scan it at 300 dpi, scaling its height for 1" to 1-1/4", then save it as a transparent PNG image.

> ❧ Help: Using IrfanView, select from the menu *File|Acquire/Batch Scanning...* or touch [Ctrl+Shift+A]. After scanning the signature, do this:
>
> - Crop it as needed to eliminate any peripheral white space by clicking in the upper left corner, dragging to the lower right corner, then select *Edit|Crop selection* or touch [Ctrl+Y].
> - Click *Image|Convert to Grayscale*. This will result in a black and white image, which usually works best because of the desired transparent background.
> - Click *Image|Decrease Color Depth...|2 Colors*.
> - Click *Image|Resize/Resample...* or touch [Ctrl+R]. Choose *Set new size* and set *Height:* at 1 to 1.25 *inches*, and *DPI* to 300, then click *OK*.
> - Click *File/Save as...* or touch [S]. Choose an appropriate *Save in:* location, enter an appropriate *File name:*, then set *Save as type:* to *PNG – Portable Network Graphics*. The *PNG save options* box appears; accept the default compression level, check the *Save transparent color* box, then click the *Save* button.
> - The *Choose transparent color* box appears. Click anywhere in the white background to complete the process, then dismiss IrfanView.

5. Revise the signer's name and title, then import their scanned signature. The signature will look most realistic if it slightly overlaps the complimentary close ("Sincerely") and the signer's typed name, with these lines showing through its transparent background.

> ❧ Note: Since you will be preparing documents for your organization's President, it will be very helpful for you to have a scan of their signature too. If you will be preparing letters for other officers, directors and staff, they may also wish to take advantage of this convenience. Some may object, but there's really little reason since signatures can so easily be lifted by anyone from signed documents, credit card terminals, and so on.

6. Revise the footer to show your organization's own tagline and web address.

7. Save your personalized template for future use. Using Windows Explorer, find your template, right-click the file and choose *Properties*, then check the *Read-only* box. This will prevent you or anyone else from inadvertently changing it. Whenever you use the template, save the letter you are working on using a different filename.

The Envelope Template

Prepare a matching envelope for each personalized letterhead. To customize your envelope template:

8. Change the logo to your own, use the 1" 300 dpi version that you rotated to 90-degrees.

9. Revise the return address in the adjacent text box. The name, title and return address on the envelope should match that on its associated letterhead.

Using Your Stationary Effectively

Regardless of the design of your letterhead, always use a monospace (typewriter-like) font such as courier new in the body of your letter, left aligned with single spacing. Double-spacing is never appropriate for correspondence. The use of proportional fronts and justified lines result in a form letter look. Offer a generous amount of white space to avoid a busy look and to make your letter easy on the eyes. Before printing it, check its appearance in full page view and center the body as necessary to balance the look of the page. Letters should ordinarily be printed single-sided to avoid the form letter look. A quality white paper, 24 lb/97 bright, is recommended (regular copy paper is 20 lb/80 bright).

Although the address field in the letterhead can be set up for window envelopes, always use plain #10 business envelopes for general correspondence. The template provided will print correctly for envelopes fed through the regular paper tray. Envelopes feed better and are less likely to be wrinkled by the paper transport mechanism when passed through the printer with the flap open.

> ❧ Hint: When you do have an occasion to use window envelopes, the letterhead template will work perfectly if you adjust the position of the address field so that the top of its first line is two-inches from the top edge of the paper.

— ❧ —

Business Cards

Business cards represent a tradition that began over 400 years ago. First appearing as calling cards in China in the 1600's, then in Europe 200 years later, cards were originally used by the footmen of royalty and aristocrats to announce their arrival to the servants of their host. They became an indispensable tool of etiquette, an essential accessory for any lady or gentleman. Trade cards first became popular in London during the early 1600's, as advertising giving directions to business places, since at that time London had no formal street numbering system. Cards became increasingly important to the growing group of private entrepreneurs during the Industrial Revolution, who had a constant need to exchange contact information.

The exchange of cards has become a common practice. Business cards are therefore an important component of your organization's image, and the brand you need to develop and maintain. They let people know that your organization takes itself seriously and observes respected business decorum. Cards should be provided for every titled position, which generally includes officers, directors and staff members. Also include these instructions regarding their use:

- Always keep your cards handy; in your pocket, purse, briefcase or wallet; on your desk and in the reception area at your office. Opportunities to give out a business card often happen unexpectedly.

- Include a business card with everything you mail. Recipients will variously value this gesture:

  - As a courtesy – convenient and comprehensive contact information.

  - As an invitation – a possible networking relationship.

  - As an advertisement – who you are and what you do.

- Use your card in support of introductions. Offer your card when introducing yourself, or when being introduced in a social setting.

- Use it as a calling card. Present your card to receptionists and secretaries when appearing for appointments and business meetings.

- Business cards are not costly or scarce. There is no need for frugality. Give them out to anyone who shows the slightest interest, including family and friends.

Business cards are very easy to come by. You can design and order cards online in minutes, using services whose charges, even in low quantities, are very reasonable. For example, at 123Print you can create and order a card in about ten minutes. One hundred to 2,000 cards cost about six cents each, with seven day service. Although inexpensive and quick, these sources usually offer only very limited customization options. For example, this one offers only a few canned options for the back of the card, none of which enables you to provide a message of your own.

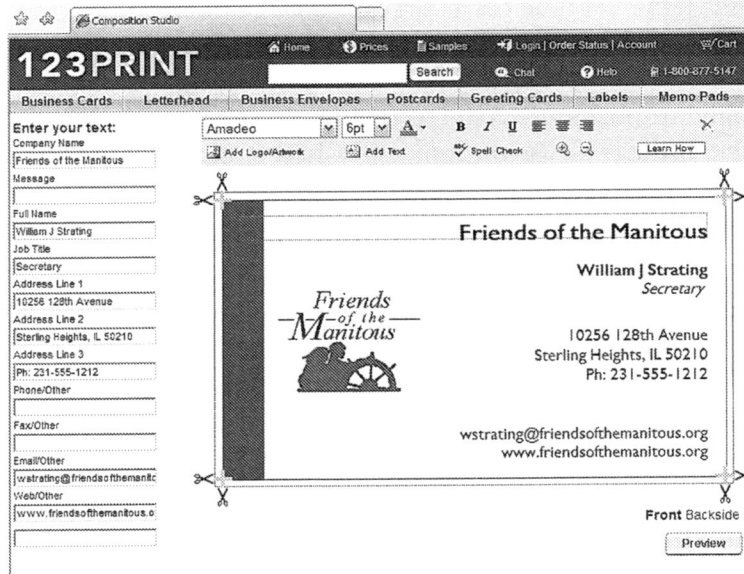

Alternatively, you can print cards of your own design for less than a penny a piece. Added advantages include your complete control over the design, and the ability to produce new cards or additional quantities on short notice and make them immediately available when needed.

Front and back templates for a simple but attractive business card are provided on the *SfS* website. You can easily customize these for your own organization, or use them as a guide for creating a design of your own. Standard American business cards are 2" x 3-1/2". The templates are set up to provide ten double-sided cards per sheet. Cards can be printed on standard 110#/90 brightness card stock, 67# cover stock, or any similar material of your choosing. The cards can be used as printed; however if printed on an ink jet printer, they will be somewhat susceptible to moisture, the ink running and smearing should it become wet (for example, as a result of perspiration if carried in your shirt pocket). To ensure against this, and to add a touch of class, you may

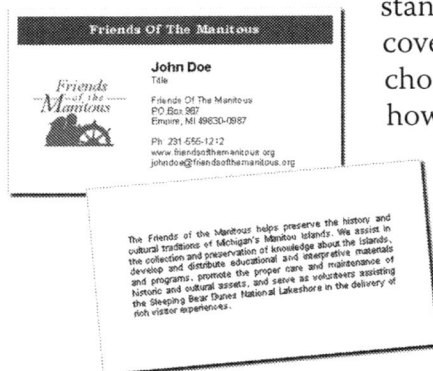

choose to apply a self-adhesive plastic laminating sheet to the front of your cards. That is easy to do, and only increases the cost by about three-cents per card.

Customizing the Front Side

1. Download and open the template "businesscard-front.doc".

2. Replace the *Friends* logo with your own. Use your 1" width 300 dpi version. If your logo is in color, that's great, otherwise grayscale is fine too.

3. Replace the *Friends* name in the dark blue banner text box. Select the text "Friends Of The Manitous" in the first frame, then type the name of your organization over the highlighted text. Select what you just typed and copy it to the clipboard [Ctrl+C], then select "Friends Of The Manitous" in each of the other nine frames and paste [Ctrl+V] your organization's name over the selected text.

4. If you wish to change the background color of the banner text box, select all ten by holding down the [Ctrl] key while clicking on boxes one through ten. With all ten text boxes selected, click on *Format|Text Box ...|Colors and Lines*, then choose whatever *Fill* color you wish. You'll probably also decide to set the *Line* color to match. Then click *OK* to change all the banner boxes at once.

5. Replace text items on the card by clicking anywhere in the white space on any card, then clicking *Table|Select|Table*. Bring up the *Find and Replace* dialog box by clicking *Edit|Replace...* or touching [Ctrl+H], and then –

    a. Check the *Match case* box. Type "Friends Of The Manitous" in the *Find what:* box, then the name of your organization in the *Replace with:* box. Click *Replace All* to provide ten replacements.

    b. Type "friendsofthemanitous" in the *Find what:* box, then your organization's domain name in the *Replace with:* box. Click *Replace All* to execute twenty replacements.

6. At this point, you have completed all of the changes needed to customize the template for your organization. Save it for future use in this configuration. Using Windows Explorer, find your template, right-click the file and choose *Properties*, then check the *Read-only* box. This will prevent you or anyone else from

inadvertently changing it. Whenever you use the template, save the card you are working on using a different filename.

Customizing the Back Side

7. Download and open the template "businesscard-back.doc".

    ❧ Note: If you have created a mission statement, this is a good place to use it. The existing statement includes 66 words, which involve 457 characters and spaces, and is rendered in 7pt Arial type. A larger typeface might be more appropriate for shorter statements. White space is important for an appropriate look and feel. If your statement is too long for use here, create an abridged version of it, or consider using a simple tag line instead.

8. To replace the *Friends* mission statement with your own, or your own tag line, you'll have to use the copy and paste method, since Word's find and replace function doesn't support more than 255 characters and spaces. Simply copy your own text to the clipboard, highlight the *Friends* text in the first frame and touch [Ctrl+V].

9. If necessary, readjust the font face, size and position. Choose horizontal centering in the usual way. To control vertical centering, select the entire table, and then click *Table|Table Properties ...|Cell|Center* and *OK*.

10. Copy the text in the first frame to the remaining nine frames.

11. Save your revised template for future use. Using Windows Explorer, find your template, right-click the file and choose *Properties*, then check the *Read-only* box. This will prevent inadvertent changes.

Personalizing and Printing the Cards

To quickly personalize the front side of your business card layout, use Word's search and replace function –

12. Retrieve your generic template for the front of the card, then save it using a new filename, such as "card-johndoe.doc".

13. Click anywhere in the white space of any frame, then click *Table|Select|Table*. Bring up the *Find and Replace* dialog box by clicking *Edit|Replace...* or touching [Ctrl+H], Then do this:

a.   Check the *Match case* box. Type "John Doe" in the *Find what:* box, then the name of the real person in the *Replace with:* box. Click *Replace All* to provide ten replacements.

b.   Type "Title" in the *Find what:* box, then the named person's title in the *Replace with:* box. Click *Replace All* to provide ten replacements.

c.   Type "PO Box 987" in the *Find what:* box, then the named person's mailing address in the *Replace with:* box. Click *Replace All* to provide ten replacements.

d.   Type "Empire, MI 49630-0987" in the *Find what:* box, then the named person's city, state and zip code in the *Replace with:* box. Click *Replace All* to provide ten replacements.

e.   Type "231-555-1212" in the *Find what:* box, then the named person's telephone number in the *Replace with:* box. Click *Replace All* to provide ten replacements.

f.   Type "johndoe" in the *Find what:* box, then the named person's email handle in the *Replace with:* box. Click *Replace All* to provide ten replacements.

14.   Save the finished personalized layout.

For best results, print the cards on premium card stock (extra-heavy 145# coated card stock, such as ProJet Part No. JANUSMDC08511 from www.adorama.com is ideal, although much more expensive); most regular card stock is porous enough to blotch the ink and smudge fine print. Print the front side of the card, then flip the page, inserting the same leading edge into the feed tray and print the back in a second pass. Depending upon the title, twenty to fifty cards is usually sufficient. It's always easy to provide additional quantities as needed.

If you are going to use the plastic laminate (e.g., C-Line No. 65001 Cleer Adheer®, or Avery No. 73601 Self-Adhesive Laminating Sheets), apply that prior to cutting the cards. Strip the backing from the laminate. To keep static electricity from interfering with the process, use tabs of masking tape to affix it to a flat surface, adhesive side up. Then, beginning at one end, carefully roll the front side of the sheet of cards onto the adhesive, being careful to avoid air bubbles.

> ⚜ Hint: Laminate is recommended only for the face of the card. Applying the film to both sides give the card an inappropriate hammy look.

The front side of the sheet is printed with faint 2" x 3-1/2" outlines. Using your paper cutter, trim 1/4" off the top of the sheet, then 3/4" off the bottom.

✤ Hint: A light source under the edge of the paper cutter is a big help at this point. A small 12" fluorescent lamp is ideal, but a flashlight will also do.

Next trim the sides of the block of ten cards, then cut down the middle to provide two rows of five cards, each exactly 10" long. Using the ruler on your paper cutter, trim the cards by cutting these strips at 8", 6", 4" and 2".

When presenting newly printed business cards to a new member of your board or staff, including a wallet will help ensure that the cards will be neatly maintained, carried and appropriately used. Simple, inexpensive but attractive wallets are available from office supply stores (for example, Buxton Style No. ST10-939, price about $2.98). Attractive plastic business card holders for service counters or receptionist desks are also available for as little as $1.59.

Don't forget to include instructions! Not everyone is use to having personal calling cards, so a few hints are often appreciated. Download and print "businesscard-hints.pdf", and insert a copy with each set of cards.

— ✤ —

Membership Cards

Every organization should have a membership card.

- People like the feeling of belonging, and a membership card in their purse or wallet promotes that feeling every time they see it.

- Members need recognition when paying dues or otherwise giving money. A new membership card is always an appreciated thank you.

- Membership cards are essentially ID cards, and can be useful as a way to qualify members for admission to meetings or special events, special prices for fundraising merchandise, or for discounted prices from cooperating merchants or at ticketed events.

- When retained in purses or wallets with credit cards, the driver's license, and other cards, membership cards serve as a valuable membership retention tool in the same way that advertising billboards work. By keeping your name and imagery in front of the member, you keep your organization and its agenda near the front of the member's mind. People become comfortable with familiar things, and naturally resist change, so the continuing presence of the card can make the difference when it comes time for people to renew their membership.

- Membership cards help promote direct participation by boosting members' confidence that they will be accepted on an equal basis with everyone else in the group.

There are lots of online sources for membership cards; however these are not usually timely or cost effective for small groups. This doesn't mean you have to settle for less. You can create your own professional-looking and attractive cards, and the fact that they're actually being made by hand in your office will make them more special to many of your members than a highly engineered machine-embossed piece of plastic with a multiple-digit member number and a magnetic strip on the back.

Here are some suggestions:

- Your cards should be standard credit card size, which is 2-1/8" x 3-3/8".

- Laminate them with protective plastic film on both sides.

- The card should show the member's name, and their title (within your organization).

- The date of issue and (possibly only by inference) the date of expiration should be included on the card.

- Your organization's logo, contact information and web address should be prominently featured.

- Your mission statement or other useful information should be printed on the back side of the card.

- Make your cards visually attractive, so that members will be sure to carry them and proud to show them off.

You'll find templates for a card like this on the *SfS* website. Separate front and back templates are provided, with a trim size of 1.925" x 3.175", which allows 1/10" (0.1") all around for laminate overlap, providing a finished product of credit card size, 2-1/8" x 3-3/8".

You can use these templates as is, or as a guide for creating a custom design of your own.

Customizing the Front Side

To customize the front side of the membership card template, do this:

1. Replace "Friends of the Manitous" with your organization's name, and friendsofthemanitous.org with your organizations domain name.

2. Replace the contact information in the lower left-hand corner with your own information.

> ♨ Note: to add or delete lines, be aware that the vertical position of these lines is controlled by the top address line. To adjust the vertical position of the contact information lines, highlight the top line, then click *Format|Paragraph...* and change *Indents and Spacing|Spacing|Before:* as needed.

3. Replace the *Friends* logo with the 0.625" 300 dpi version of your logo. If your logo is in color, that's fine, otherwise grayscale works well here.

4. The brick brown and navy blue text box background colors can be change by double-clicking the boxes' borders, then choosing whatever *Fill* color you like. Ordinarily, set the *Line* color to match, or select *No Line*.

5. Save your revised template for future use. Using Windows Explorer, find your template, right-click the file and choose *Properties*, then check the *Read-only* box. This will prevent inadvertent changes.

Customizing the Back Side

To customize the back side of the business card template –

6. Replace the *Friends* mission statement with your own, or your own tag line.

> ❧ Note: If you have created a mission statement, this is a good place to use it. The existing statement includes 66 words, which involve 457 characters and spaces, and is rendered in 7pt Arial type. A larger typeface might be more appropriate for shorter statements. Remember, being generous with white space will give your cards a professional look and feel. If your statement is too long for use here, create an abridged version of it, or consider using a simple tag line instead.

7. If necessary, readjust the font face, size and position. To adjust the width and position of the text, click anywhere within the text box, then select *Format|Text Box...* , select the *Text Box* tab and set the margins as needed to center the text vertically and horizontally.

8. Save your revised template for future use. Using Windows Explorer, find your template, right-click the file and choose *Properties*, then check the *Read-only* box. This will prevent inadvertent changes.

To quickly personalize the front side of your business card layout –

9. Retrieve your generic template for the front of the membership card, then save it using a new filename, such as "membershipcard-temp.doc".

10. Replace "John Doe" with the member's name. If the person has a special title, you may wish to indicate that by changing

"Member" to "Charter Member," "President," "Media Director," or as appropriate.

Membership cards are easily printed and finished. Here's how:

15. Membership cards are usually printed individually as needed rather than as a batch. To simplify the application of laminating sheets, the template is set up for one card per sheet. Use premium card stock (such as ProJet Part No. JANUSMDC08511); since most regular card stock is porous enough to blotch the ink, smudging fine print and permitting colored backgrounds to bleed into the edges of the white lettering. Print the back of the card first because it's less ink intensive and dries almost instantly. Then flip the sheet and print the front side.

16. The front side of the sheet is printed with faint trim lines around the perimeter. Use your paper to trim the card to 1/10" less than credit card size by trimming exactly on these lines.

    ❧ Hint: A light source under the edge of the paper cutter is a big help at this point. A small 12" fluorescent lamp is ideal, but a flashlight will also do.

17. Apply a 3" x 4-1/2" sheet of plastic laminate to the face of the card, smoothing it out to promote adherence over the entire face of the card without any entrapped air bubbles.

    ❧ Note: The laminate comes in 9" x 12" sheets. Cut each sheet using your paper cutter to provide eight 3" x 4-1/2" pieces.

18. Turn the card over and apply an identical piece of laminate to the back side. Use a burnishing tool to seal the laminate sheets to each other around the edges of the encapsulated card stock. A small common screwdriver works well, drawing its flat blade over the laminate along the edge of the card while exerting a little downward pressure.

19. Using the paper cutter, trim the card to 2-1/8" x 3-3/8", leaving a .1" perimeter of laminate all around the paper card.

    ❧ Hint: 1/10th of an inch is just slightly less than 1/8th (0.100" vs. 0.125"). With a little practice, you'll be easily able to eyeball this without having to measure anything or use any sort of guide. Until then, you can measure while making the first cut, and then cut the other three sides so that the perimeter is more or less equal all around.

20. Rounded corners will give your cards a more professional look, and make them easier to insert in wallets. A fingernail clipper is an ideal tool for rounding the corners of the laminate.

— ❧ —

Contribution Acknowledgement Cards

Contributions to your small organization *must be* acknowledged immediately, directly and personally. Never use a form letter. Never let it go until late. Have a system for acknowledging donations, and do it immediately.

You'll find a template for a French folded 4-1/4" x 5-1/2" card on the *SfS* website. These professional-looking, keepsake quality cards are easy to personalize and print, and will fit standard A2 size (4-3/8" x 5-3/4") card envelopes. Although the card requires three passes through the printer, two of these can be done in advance to create a stock of ready-to-go blanks. You can then print the final personalized message as each card is needed, and a matching envelope, which takes only a few moments.

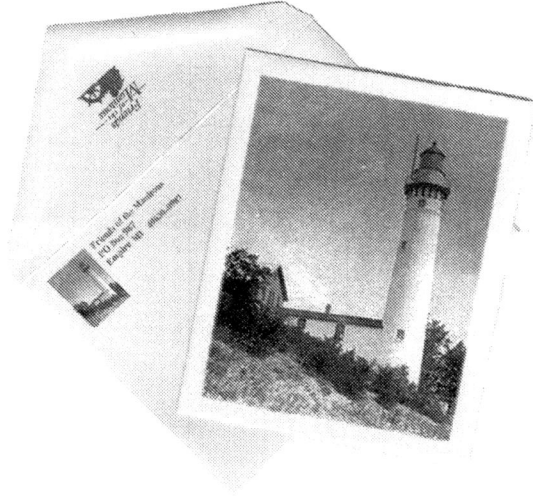

To create appropriate cards for your organization, download all four template files from the *SfS* website:

- contribackcard-front.doc
- contribackcard-back.doc
- contribackcard-inside.doc
- contribackcard-envelope.doc

Customizing contribackcard-front.doc

This is the front panel of the card, which, in the case of the template, is an image. The front panel will be 1/4 of a standard 8-1/2" x 11" size sheet of paper, or 4-1/4" x 5-1/2". A 1/4" border is provided all around the image, so the image size is 3-3/4" x 5". Since most inkjet printers require a 1/2" margin at the bottom of the page, the image must be positioned upside down in the top left corner of the page.

Choose an image appropriate for your organization. Crop and resize it as necessary to provide a 300 dpi (dots per inch) version measuring exactly 3-3/4" x 5". Save your image in JPG or PNG format, then insert it on a blank page, positioned exactly 0.25" from the page's top and left edges.

If you feel that text would make for a more appropriate front panel than a picture or other graphic, you'll need to create the text message as a graphic and invert it. Word ordinarily has no means of inverting text. However, if using a version of Word 2002 or higher, you can try this:

1. Create a 3-3/4" x 5" text box on a blank page.

2. Enter the desired text and format it as you want it to look.

3. Select the desired text box line and background properties.

4. Select the text box and touch [Ctrl+X] to cut it to the clipboard.

5. Select *Edit|Paste Special...* and choose *Picture (PNG)* .

6. Select the green handle on the inserted picture and rotate the image 180-degrees.

7. Select *Format|Picture...|Layout|Advanced...* and position the image 0.25" from the top and 0.25" from the left edge of the page.

8. Save your finished version as contribackcard-front.doc.

If using an older version of Word, do steps 1 through 4, then do this:

9. Paste the clipboard into IrfanView or PaintShop Pro.

10. Check the images properties to make sure its still 3-3/4" x 5" at 300 dpi, and if not resize or resample it to provide those attributes.

11. Use the program's *Mirror* and *Flip* functions to invert the text box.

12. Save the inverted text box as a PNG file.

13. Using Words *Insert Picture* function, find the inverted text box and insert it on a blank page.

14. Select *Format|Picture...|Layout|Advanced...* and position the inserted image 0.25" from the top and 0.25" from the left edge of the page.

15. Save your finished version as "contribackcard-front.doc".

Customizing contribackcard-back.doc

This is the layout for the left-hand inside panel, and the back of the card. To customize this layout for your organization, do this:

1. The text in the box at the bottom left corner of the page includes 80 words, 527 characters and spaces in 6 pt Times New Roman. In this case, the text provides information about the image used on the front of the card. Depending upon what you use for the front of your card, you may wish to provide similar comments about your image. Otherwise, this is a good place for your mission statement or tag line. You can increase or decrease the height of the box, as needed.

2. Replace the *Friends* logo with your own, using your 1" 300 dpi version.

3. Revise the information in the copyright box with your own. You can copyright something merely by making this statement. There is no formal registration process. Be sure to name your organization as the copyright owner. Naming an individual will conflict with IRS rules regarding your exemption status.

4. Save this page as your finished version of "contribackcard-back.doc".

Customizing contribackcard-inside.doc

This is the layout for the inside, right-hand panel of the card, which contains a personalized acknowledgement and thank you note. On inspection, you'll see this document is set up as a simple Word form. When creating these cards, you need only enter a salutation and dollar amount. The date will be entered automatically by Word.

> Note: Besides being an acknowledgement and thank you, this card also serves as an official receipt. Although receipts are not required for small donations to be legally deductible, including the amount of the gift in the acknowledgement signals that the amount given was considered significant and was officially noted. For large gifts, this will be taken as a gesture of appreciation. For smallish donations, spotlighting the amount in this way might prompt, in a tasteful *res ipsa loquitur* manner, greater future generosity.

The form is protected (locked), with the form fields shaded. Use the Tab or up and down keys to move from one field to another. The field shading is provided for your benefit only, and will not be printed. To revise text on this page –

1. Unprotect the form by clicking *Tools|Unprotect Document.*

2. Change the name "William Strating" to your name, or the name of the officer your organization wishes to use for this purpose.

3. Change the title "Secretary" to the title of the above named person.

4. The text of the message will also be editable now; change it if you wish.

5. To change the default text in the form fields, double-click the field and edit contents of the *Default text* box.

6. When finished, lock the form by clicking *Tools|Protect Document*. The *Protect Document* box appears; click the *Forms* button, do not enter a password, then click *OK* to dismiss the dialog.

Customizing contribackcard-envelope.doc

Use this template to print envelopes for your gift donation cards. This template is set up for standard A2 size (4-3/8" x 5-3/4") card envelopes, which are commonly available at office supply stores. Here's how to customize this template for your organization:

1. Create a miniature of the image you used for the front of your card. Rotate it 90-degrees right (assuming it's upside down to begin with), then reduce the image to 20% (300 dpi) of its original size. Use this image to replace the small lighthouse picture.

2. Enter your organization's return address in the adjacent text box.

3. Replace the *Friends* logo with the 1", 180-degree version of your own (refer back to the *"Stock Logos"* discussion in Section 2, if needed).

> ❧ Note: Your logo must be carefully positioned so that it'll be properly centered on the back flap of the envelope. Select your logo, then click on *Format|Picture...|Layout|Advanced...* and adjust its horizontal and vertical position with respect to the left and top edged of the *Page*.

> ❧ Hint: Word's positioning works with respect to the image's upper left-hand corner. Using Word's dialog, place your 1" image 5.0" to the right of the page. Its correct vertical position will be half the envelope width less half the image width, or (2.875"- 0.5" = 2.375"). Therefore set the vertical position to 2.375" from the top of the page.

4. Save your finished version as "contribackcard-front.doc".

5. To protect your work from inadvertent changes, select all four customized templates in Windows Explorer, right-click, then check their *Read-only* attribute.

Printing Acknowledgement Cards and Envelopes

You can prepare a handy stock of blank cards by printing the fronts and backs in quantity in advance. Print the fronts (*contribackcard-front.doc*) first. Then flip the page (the last edge out when printing fronts is the first edge in to print backs), and print the backs (*contribackcard-back.doc*) on the same side of the sheet.

As you need cards –

1. Print the inside (contribackcard-inside.doc) on the same side as the front and back, feeding the pre-printed sheets into the printer image end first.

2. Print a corresponding envelope, feeding the A2 card envelope into the printer with its flap open.

   > ❦ Hint: Rather than trying to type the address sidewise, it's easy to import it from your database to NotePad or Word, else just type it on a blank page, then cut it to the clipboard and paste it into the delivery address text box. (If the *Paste Options* box appears, choose *Match Destination Formatting*).

3. The four diagonal lines left of the front panel are a provision for membership cards. If sending new membership cards with your contribution acknowledgements, cut on these lines with an Exacto blade or small snap-off blade box cutter to provide a nifty card holder.

4. Fold the sheet in half to 5-1/2" x 8-1/2", and then fold again to provide the finished 4-1/4" x 5-1/2" card. Insert the new membership card(s), if applicable, and then insert the card in its corresponding envelope.

   > ❦ Caution: Getting cards mixed up and sending them to the wrong people results in moments that are awkward and embarrassing. Such mix-ups are easy, especially when you're in a hurry. When doing two or more acknowledgements at a time, lay all the components out together, assuring that they are properly matched up before stuffing and sealing envelopes.

— ❧ —

Personalized Note Stationery

Letter writing seems to have become a thing of the past with the advent of email, instant messaging and low cost long distant telephone service. Custom note stationary is therefore less productive as a fundraising item than in times past. On the other hand, you can produce it very easily and inexpensively with your desktop system, and even personalize it with individual names and addresses. Appropriate uses include holiday greetings, personal sympathy notes, RSVP responses and special thank you notes.

You can leverage your acknowledgement card design to easily create note stationery. Just erase the membership card slot marks from the *contribackcard-back.doc* template, and then print the front and back, omitting the inside template. Delete the address text boxes from the envelope template to provide blank matching envelopes.

For a somewhat more attractive and appropriate design, use the templates for personalized note stationery provided on the *SfS* website. This design has the added advantage of single-pass printing. The files are:

- persnotecard.doc
- notecardenvelope.doc

Customizing persnotecard.doc

This is the front panel of the card. The template uses the same image as the contribution acknowledgement card, except that it is cropped and resized to suite this format. The front panel is again 1/4 of a standard 8-1/2" x 11" size sheet of paper, but in this case is oriented horizontally, or 5-1/2" x 4-1/4". A 1/2" border is provided all around the image, so the image size is 4-1/2" x 3-1/4". The 1/2" border is necessary because most inkjet printers require a 1/2" margin at the bottom of the page. In this case, the edges of the image are feathered somewhat to soften the picture.

Choose an image appropriate for your organization. Rotate, crop and resize it as necessary to provide a 300 dpi (dots per inch) version measuring exactly 4-1/2" high x 3-1/4" wide. Save your image in JPG or PNG format, then insert it on a blank page, positioned exactly 0.5" from the page's top and left edges.

If you want to feather the image's edges, try this:

1. Open the 4.5"x 3.25" 300 dpi image in PaintShop Pro.

2. Click on *Image|Add Borders...* , then check *Symmetric,* adjust the border size to about 20 pixels, choose white as the border color and click *OK.*

3. In the *Materials* palette, set both foreground and background colors to white.

4. Select the *Magic Wand Tool:*

   a. For images with well-defined edges, set *Tolerance:* at zero.

   b. Set *Feather:* equal to about 10% of the images width in pixels, which will be about 3.23 x 300 x .1 = 98, then click anywhere within the white border.

5. Select the *Flood Fill Tool,* then click anywhere within the white border to apply the effect. Click as many times as needed to produce the desired degree of feathering.

6. Click *Selections|Select None* to remove the selection marquee.

7. Your image is now oversize because of the borders you added. Click the *Crop Tool,* adjust the selection rectangle to the original 4.5" x 3.25" size, then click *Apply.*

8. Save your image in PNG or JPG format.

   a. To provide a miniature version for your envelope, resample or resize this image to about 20% of its original size, or about 0.9" x 0.65" x 300 dpi. Save this image also in PNG or JPG format.

Next, to customize the template for your organization's use, do this:

9. Replace the lighthouse image on the template with your own. Adjust its position to exactly 0.5" from the left edge of the page, and 6" from the top edge of the page.

10. The text in the box at the bottom left corner of the page includes 80 words, 527 characters and spaces in 6 pt Times New Roman. In this case, the text provides information about the image used on the front of the card. Depending upon what

you use for the front of your card, you may wish to provide similar comments about your image. Otherwise, this is a good place for your mission statement or tag line. You can increase or decrease the height of the box, as needed.

16. Replace the *Friends* logo with your own, using your 1" 300 dpi version.

17. Revise the information in the copyright box with your own. You can copyright something merely by making this statement. There is no formal registration process. Be sure to name your organization as the copyright owner. Naming an individual will conflict with IRS rules regarding your exemption status.

18. Save this page as your finished version of "persnotecard.doc" template.

Customizing notecardenvelope.doc

Use this template to print envelopes for your gift donation cards. This template is set up for standard A2 size (4-3/8" x 5-3/4") card envelopes, which are commonly available at office supply stores. To customize this template for your organization —

1. If you have not already done so, create a miniature of the image you used for the front of your card. Reduce the image to 20% (300 dpi) of its original size. Use this image to replace the small lighthouse picture.

2. Replace the *Friends* logo with the 1", 180-degree version of your own (refer back to the "Stock Logos" discussion in Section 2, if needed).

    ❧ Note: Your logo must be carefully positioned so that it'll be properly centered on the back flap of the envelope. Select your logo, then click on *Format|Picture...|Layout|Advanced...* and adjust its horizontal and vertical position with respect to the left and top edged of the *Page*.

    ❧ Hint: Word's positioning works with respect to the image's upper left-hand corner. Using Word's dialog, place your 1" image 5.0" to the right of the page. Its correct vertical position will be half the envelope width less half the image width, or (2.875"- 0.5" = 2.375"). Therefore set the vertical position to 2.375" from the top of the page.

3. Save your finished template as "notecardenvelope.doc"

4. To protect your work from inadvertent changes, select the customized note card and envelope templates in Windows Explorer, right-click, then check their *Read-only* attribute.

Printing Personalized Note Cards and Envelopes

As you need cards and envelopes, simply change the generic contact information and print sets; usually a dozen of each.

> ✤ Hint: Rather than trying to type the address sidewise, it's easy to import it from your database to NotePad or Word, else just type it on a blank page, then cut it to the clipboard and paste it into the delivery address text box. (If the *Paste Options* box appears, choose *Match Destination Formatting*).

Cut the sheets in half to 5-1/2" x 8-1/2", and then fold them to provide the finished 4-1/4" x 5-1/2" card. Tuck a card under the flap of each envelope.

> ✤ Packaging Suggestion: 6" x 6" crystal clear PVC shrink bags (www.papermart.com item 3636066) provide an attractive package for a little over a penny. These packets will fit nicely in a 6" x 4-1/2" x 1" box, which you can also make. Attach your own customized "notecardlable.doc" to complete a professional-looking package.

— ✤ —

How to Make Simple Boxes

Seems like you always need a little box for something, and you can never find anything at the store that's really suitable. Personalized note cards are an example. You could just stick 'em in a large manila envelope, of course. But as they say downtown, "presentation is everything." A little box would be really nice. Use the pattern below to make any size box.

Here's how to make a simple but attractive 6" x 4-1/2" x 1" box for note cards:

1. Cut two 8" x 6-1/2" pieces of regular 1 lb. glossy poster board (staples.com item 247403) or .022" chipboard (uline.com item S-6419).

2. Using the edge of your paper cutter, bend down 1" flaps all around on one piece, which will become the bottom. To make the top slightly larger for a nice fit, bend 15/16" flaps all around on the second piece.

3. Use your snap blade box cutter to make 1" cuts (dashed lines) at the bend on either end of both pieces to provide 1" x 1" tabs (gray areas) for stapling.

4. To finish the box, bend the flaps up with the tabs in, and then staple the tabs to the adjacent flaps using your flat clinch stapler.

For a nice finished appearance, create a simple 5-1/2" x 4" label, print it on regular paper, cut it to size, tack it to the cover using your handy glue stick, and then seal your package in a crystal-clear shrink bag. You can find inexpensive shrink bags in a variety of sizes at www.papermart.com. For this project, their 8" x 12" PVC bag, Item No. 36360812, works fine ($15 per box of 500). Simply cut off the excess length, insert your box, and then use a heat gun or your regular hair drier to shrink the wrapper. You'll have a nifty little package you'll be proud to present to anyone!

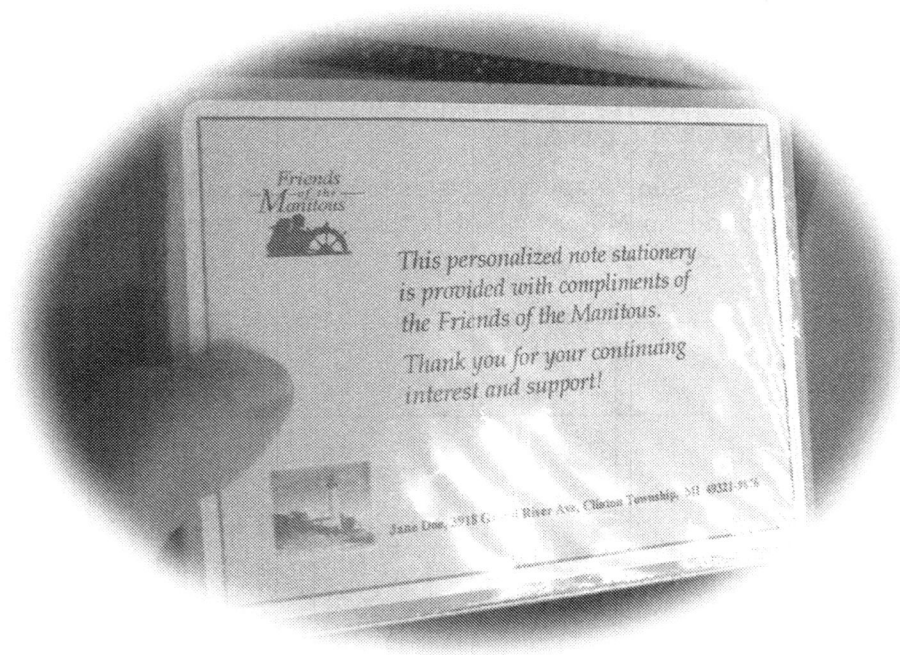

Reply Envelopes

In Section 7 you'll read, "Never overlook an opportunity to ask for support. If you hear people joke (or complain) that you are always looking for a handout, you'll know you're doing it right." Reply envelopes, otherwise known as *remittance envelopes* are therefore a must have item. When you distribute brochures, newsletters, fundraising items or handouts, they should always be accompanied by a remittance envelope.

Find these templates for No. 6-3/4 remittance envelopes on the *SfS* website:

- replyenvelopemodel.doc
- replyenvelopemodel-msg.doc

This is a standard envelope, sized to accommodate U.S. currency or a standard personal check. These two templates make it easy for you to design and fabricate a hand-made model of remittance envelopes you wish to print in quantity (e.g., an envelope to accompany your newsletter or a special mass mailing). This kind of mock-up is very useful in preventing misunderstandings, assuring that the printer will produce exactly what you had in mind.

Customizing replyenvelopemodel.doc

The design, printing and fabrication of remittance envelopes is more highly mechanical that most other projects. To customize these templates for your own use, follow these instructions carefully:

1. Notice the dimensions and instructions on the left edge of the page. Use these to fabricate the envelope after printing. They need not be deleted before printing.

2. The text box at the top of the page contains a form to capture payee information. You may change the form as appropriate for your situation. However, this box corresponds to the inside panel of the remittance envelope. Its size is 3.375" x 6.5", and it

is carefully positioned at 1.25" from the left edge of the page, and 0" from the top edge. Do not change its size or position.

> ❧ Fundraising 101: The contribution check boxes are a way of suggesting levels of giving that are considered appropriate and customary. Keep in mind that people will give you what you ask for. If you personally feel that $100 is as much as you dare suggest, chances are good you'll never receive a check for more than that amount.

3. Revise the note under the form. Change "Friends" to the name of your organization, and "friendsofthemanitous" to your domain name. If you have not yet received recognition from IRS, change "is a 501(c)3" to "operates as a 501(c)3" (permitted under the current law so long as your average annual receipts do not exceed $25,000).

> ❧ Note: When the envelope is used, the glue strip from the sealing flap will be stuck to the bottom 5/8" of this box. Keep that area clear of information you wish to retrieve when the envelope is opened.

4. Notice the tiny "Tracking Ref" text box at the right side of the form. It is often interesting or helpful to know what prompted the remittance. For example, if you are sending out this particular envelope with your "Fall/Winter 2007" newsletter (Vol 2, No. 3), you might identify these envelopes by replacing "Tracking Ref" with the code "NL-V2N3".

5. Replace the *Friends* remittance address with your own. This text is inverted using Word's WordArt feature. Select the address box by clicking anywhere within address, then right-click and choose *Edit Text...* Make your changes in the *Edit WordArt Text* box, and then click *OK*.

> ❧ Check the Position of the Box: Since the width of the address box does not change, you'll probably see that the new address is undesirably compressed or extended. Use the handles on the WordArt box and readjust its width so that the text looks normal again. You must then readjust the horizontal position of the WordArt box. The correct position from the left edge of the page is ...
>
> $$h = 8.5" - (w + 3")$$
>
> ... where "w" is the new width of the WordArt box. Before you changed anything, the width of the box was 2.5", so its horizontal position was 3" from the left edge of the page. Its height was 0.5", and its vertical position was 4.25" below the top edge of the page. Unless you change the font size, these parameters will not change.

Select the address box again, right click and choose *Format WordArt*, then:

a. Use the *Colors and Lines* tab to set the *Line Weight* to "0 pt".

    b.   Use *Layout|Advanced...|Picture Position* to adjust the exact position of the box with respect to the edges of the page.

6.   The 3.5" x 6.5" text box at the bottom of the page (positioned at 1.25" from the left edge of the page and 7.0" below the top edge) represents the sealing flap of the envelope. Replace the *Friends* logo with your own, using your 1", 300 dpi version. Replace the text beneath the logo with your condensed mission statement or tag line.

> ❧ Hint: Your logo should be more or less at the vertical center of the 3.5" x 6.5" text box, with your text just below that. To easily center these items horizontally, select *Line* from Word's Drawing Toolbar and draw temporary vertical and horizontal lines across center handles of the sealing flap text box. Move the logo as needed to position its center handles on these lines. Use the *Internal Margin* settings to position your message vertically and horizontally using within its small text box *(Format|Text Box|Text Box)*. Do not use spaces or line feeds.

Customizing replyenvelopemodel-msg.doc

This message will be printed on the inside of the envelope's sealing flap, which will give your envelope a more finished and professional appearance. To customize this template, do this:

1.   The 3.5" x 6.5" text box at the top of this page (positioned at 1.25" from the left edge of the page and 0.5" below the top edge) represents the inside face of the envelope's sealing flap. Do not change the size or position of this text box.

2.   Replace the *Friends* logo with your own, using your 1", 300 dpi version. Position your logo 1.63" from the left edge of the page and 1" below its top edge.

3.   Replace the message inside the text box with one appropriate for your situation, limiting yourself to the available space within the text box. Use the *Internal Margin* settings to position your message vertically and horizontally using within the text box *(Format|Text Box|Text Box)*. Do not use spaces or line feeds.

> ❧ Note: Commercial envelopes have an adhesive strip along the top 1/2" of the sealing flap. Therefore avoid placing content closer than that to the top of this text box.

Printing and Fabricating Model Reply Envelopes

1. Print your envelope on 24# white paper. Print "replyenvelope-model.doc" first. Then flip the paper over, feeding the end with the logo in first to print "replyenvelopemodel-msg.doc" on the other side.

2. Follow the instructions on the left edge of the paper:

   a. Trim 1/2" off the bottom edge.

   b. Fold at 3-1/2" and 6-5/8", as marked.

   c. Trim 1/2" off the left side of the folded paper.

   d. Fold 3/4" down on both the left and right sides, providing a 6-1/2" body.

   e. Trim the 3/4" x 3-1/2" tabs off the sealing flap section, and the 3/4" x 3-3/8" tabs off the bottom (form) section, leaving 3/4" x 3-5/8" gluing tabs on the middle section.

   f. Fold the middle section's tabs in, then rub the glue stick across the left and right edges on the underside of the bottom (form) section and fold up onto the tabs.

   > ❧ Hint: You can make your mock-up sealable if you wish by running your glue stick across the top edge of the envelope's sealing flap. Mask it with a piece of paper to do it neatly, making a 1/2" strip, then permit it to dry thoroughly. When moistened in the usual manner, the glue will work just like the gummed strip ordinarily used on envelopes.

Once you're satisfied with your mockup, you can also cut and paste its components into layouts that will enable you to print commercially made envelopes using your desktop printer, or which you can provide to the print shop for the production of larger quantities.

Printing Commercially-Made Reply Envelopes

Once you're satisfied with your mockup, you can cut and paste its components into layouts that will enable you to print commercially made envelopes using your desktop printer, or which you can provide to a print shop for the production of larger quantities.

Since Word documents are somewhat machine-dependant and may not be rendered correctly on a machine other than the one on which they were originally created, print shops prefer to have work submitted as PDF files, with all fonts, graphics and images embedded. Furthermore, printing envelopes on your desktop requires that some of the text box panels be inverted, so that you can feed the envelope into your printer body-first, rather than flap-first. Converting these features to images, which can easily be rotated 180-degrees, yields marginal results, because of resolution limitations. A better solution is to convert the documents to PDF, then use Adobe Acrobat to rotate the entire page. Here's how you can do that.

To make a layout for the inside of the envelope, do this:

1. Open the file "replyenvelopemodel.doc" and a new blank document.

2. Select the text box containing the form on "replyenvelopemodel.doc" and select *Edit|Copy* to copy it to the clipboard.

3. Switch to the blank document and select *Edit|Paste.*

4. Position this 3.375" x 6.5" text box 2.0" from the left edge of the page, and 7.625" below the top edge of the page.

5. Open the file "replyenvelopemodel-msg.doc".

6. Hold down the [Ctrl] key to select both the text box and your logo within the text box. Select *Edit|Copy* to copy both to the clipboard.

7. Switch to the blank document and select *Edit|Paste.*

8. Position this 3.5" x 6.5" text box 2.0" from the left edge of the page, and 3.875" below the top edge of the page. Reposition your logo within the text box as desired (probably 2.375" from the left edge of the page and 4.5" below the top of the page).

9. Save the new page as "replyenvelope-inside.doc", or any more meaningful name of your choosing.

Next, to make a similar layout for the outside of the envelope, do this:

10. Open a new blank document.

11. Select the WordArt address block on "replyenvelopemodel.doc" and select *Edit|Copy* to copy it to the clipboard.

12. Switch to the new blank document and select *Edit|Paste.*

13. The ideal position for the address box is 0.75" below the top edge of the page, and 2.5" from its right edge. To achieve this, check the width of your address box, then calculate the distance from the left edge of the page as h = 8.5" − (w + 2.5").

   ❦ Example: the *Friends* address box is 2.5" wide, so its correct horizontal position would be 3.5" from the left edge of the page.

14. Returning to "replyenvelopemodel.doc", hold down the [Ctrl] key to select both the text box at the bottom of the page and your logo within the text box. Select *Edit|Copy* to copy it to the clipboard.

15. Switch to the blank document and select *Edit|Paste*.

16. Position this 3.5" x 6.5" text box 0" from the left edge of the page, and 3.625" below the top edge of the page. Reposition your logo as appropriate, or draw temporary centering lines though the middle vertical and horizontal handles of the text box to use for its exact centering.

17. Save the new page as "replyenvelope-outside.doc", or any more meaningful name of your choosing.

Converting Your Files to PDF

Check your layouts by printing these two files on regular paper, then comparing them for size and layout with a blank No. 6-3/4 remittance envelope (e.g., www.actionenvelope.com item number 17889). When satisfied with your layouts, convert them to PDF using the Acrobat Distiller printer, a companion utility of Adobe Acrobat:

18. Open "replyenvelope-inside.doc".

19. Select *File|Print...* In the *Print* dialog box, select *Name: Acrobat Distiller* and check the *Print to file* checkbox.

    a. Click the *Properties* button, then choose the *Adobe PDF Settings* tab and select *Press*, then click *OK*.

20. In the *Print to file* box, set *Save in:* to the "in" subfolder under the Acrobat Distiller folder (e.g., C:\Program Files\Adobe\Acrobat 5.0\Distillr\in).

    ❧ Note: "In" and "Out" subfolders are not created by default when Acrobat is installed. If they do not exist, create them at this location.

21. Enter a *File name:* then click *OK*.

22. Next, open "replyenvelope-outside.doc".

23. Again select *File|Print...* In the *Print* dialog box, select *Name: Acrobat Distiller* and check the *Print to file* checkbox.

24. In the *Print to file* box, set *Save in:* to the "in" folder under the Acrobat Distiller folder.

25. When you run Acrobat Distiller, the utility will check for print files in its "in" subfolder. If it finds any it produces PDF

versions of those files and moves them to its "out" subfolder. Therefore run Distiller now to convert your layouts to PDF, and then retrieve them from Distiller's "out" subfolder.

> ❧ Note: Distiller may also create ".log" files in the "out" subfolder. These and the original ".prn" print files may be deleted. Save only the PDF files.

Printing Envelopes Manually

Open your files in Adobe Acrobat. "replyenvelope-outside.pdf" may be printed as is, feeding the bottom of the envelope first. To print the inside –

26. Open "replyenvelope-inside.pdf" in Adobe Acrobat (or Reader)

27. Rotate the inside layout by selecting *Document|Rotate Pages...|180 degrees* and click *OK* (or touch [Shift+Ctrl+Plus] two times if using the free Adobe Reader)

28. Select *File|Print...* The Acrobat *Print* dialog box will appear.

   a. Deselect any checkbox options that instruct Acrobat to resize or reposition your layout in any way.

   b. Select the number of envelopes to print, then click *OK*, being prepared to manually feed envelopes at your printer.

   > ❧ Note: Check for proper centering. Acrobat might automatically position your layouts according to your printer's minimum margin specifications. Newer versions of Acrobat enable you to uncheck this option. Otherwise print your envelopes with the latest version of Adobe Reader.

Fancy Certificates

There are lots of occasions to honor people by awarding a fancy certificate that they can proudly display in their home or on their office wall. You'll find several certificate templates on the *SfS* website:

- membership certificate
- membership certificate – charter member
- membership certificate – family membership
- special achievement certificate
- volunteer recognition certificate
- certificate of appreciation
- certificate mailing label

These layouts will print on 8-1/2" x 11" certificate forms, a variety of which you'll find at any office supply, or online (e.g., www.baudville.com, www.geographics.com). The Geographics "Conventional Blue" style (Item 20008) is shown here. These fine linen or parchment forms are suitable for laser or ink jet printing and cost less than 20-cents each in packs of 25 or 50.

The small assortment of templates can be used as a design guide, or you may find them suitable as is, and customize them for your organization. The content is simple enough that you can see what changes are needed simply by inspecting the form. To make sure you don't miss any of the fine print:

- Use Word's search and replace function to change "Friends of the Manitous" with the name of your own organization.
- Use the search and replace function to also change "friendsofthemanitous" to your organization's domain name.

The signatures shown on these templates were produced by scanning. For this purpose, the signatures can be faked if signers object to providing a scanned image of their actual signature. Signatures look most realistic when they slightly overlap the signer's printed name, with those lines showing through the signature's transparent background. See the previous section on customizing letterheads for instructions on scanning and touching up signatures.

When presenting certificates at meetings, consider framing them. Certificate frames are inexpensive, commonly less than $3.00 and sometimes found in dollar stores for much less. When presenting several certificates at once, embossed paper certificate holders are a nice touch and take up less space; usually about $1.50 each (e.g., Gartner Studios Item # 35007).

Bookmarks

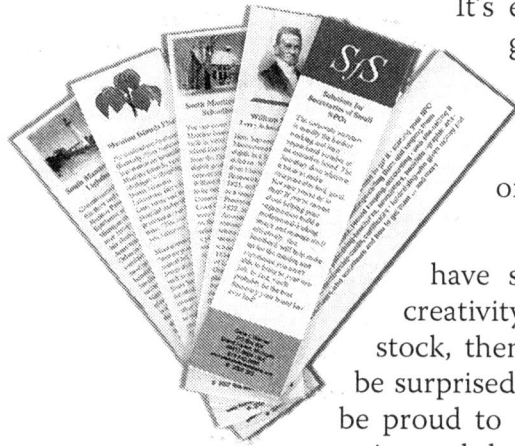

It's easy to make bookmarks that look as good as those sold in stores, and which are just as durable and useful. Moreover, you can design them with themes that promote your organization or a special event.

This project gives you a chance to have some fun while exhibiting your own creativity. The bookmarks are printed on card stock, then laminated in plastic. You'll probably be surprised at the quality of the results, and you'll be proud to offer this handout to anyone. They're attractive and durable, so are likely to be kept and used over and over again. If you use them to promote your organization, they'll keep your message in front of whomever you give them to for a long time.

The templates provided on the *SfS* website are:

- bookmarkback.doc
- lighthousebookmark.doc
- poisonivybookmark.doc
- schoolhousebookmark.doc
- sfsbackbookmark.doc
- sfsbookmark.doc
- laminatingtemplate.doc
- bookmarkwallet.doc

These examples will give you ideas for your own designs. As a starter, modify one of these designs to make a bookmark representing your organization. They're laid out using a Word table and this project will show you how to work within that paradigm. We'll use the first two examples.

Please download "lighthousebookmark.doc" and open it in Microsoft Word. The file provides six identical bookmarks, arranged in a 6-column x 3-row table, as shown here:

Customizing the Bookmark's Front Side

Click anywhere within this table, then select *Table Properties...* from the popup menu. Inspecting the *Table Properties* dialog box, you can see that this is where you can control various aspects of the table, its rows and columns, and individual cells. The bookmark tables are set up with three rows; 1", 4" and 1" respectively. The table height is therefore 6". The table's six columns are set at exactly 1-1/2". The printed bookmarks are therefore 1-1/2" by 6".

Let's modify lighthousebookmark.doc:

1. First, save this file with a different filename, such as "myfirstbookmark.doc"

2. Prepare an image that will fit within the 1" x 1-1/2" top cells of each column. Load up IrfanView or PaintShop Pro:

   a. Select an image you think might work.

   b. Crop it with an aspect ratio of 1:1.5 .

   c. Resample or resize it to about 0.95" x 1.425" at 300 dpi.

   d. Save it as a PNG for JPG file.

3. Select the six lighthouse photos and delete them.

4. Insert the image you prepared in the top cell of each column. For easy centering;

   a. Hold the [Ctrl] key down while selecting all six images.

   b. Click the *Format Picture* icon on the *Picture* toolbar, then choose *Layout* and click the *In front of text* wrapping style.

c. Zoom your document up to 200%, then click each image individually and center it within the cell using the arrow keys. Hold down [Ctrl] while using the arrow keys for fine adjustment.

5. Compose some text for the 4" body of the bookmark. The cell will accommodate about 625 characters and spaces, not including the title line. You'll also have an opportunity to compose something for the back of your bookmark. That's a good place for your mission statement. It's nice to coordinate this text to the picture on this side. But feel free to compose what you will.

a. Select the middle cells by clicking outside the table just to the left of the first middle cell. With all of the middle cells highlighted, touch the [Delete] button.

b. Select the first 4" cell, then copy and paste the text you've composed into that cell to try it for size. Edit your comments and/or adjust the font size to provide a nice fit.

c. When satisfied, select what you have in the first cell, copy it to the clipboard, and then paste it into the other five 4" cells.

6. The little blue helmsmen logo is 0.35" x 0.7" (1:2 aspect ratio). If you have an appropriate logo of your own, use your image processing program to provide a 300 dpi version of the appropriate size. Otherwise just delete these.

7. Revise the details in the bottom 1" cells as appropriate for your organization. When satisfied with the first cell, just copy and paste its contents over the remaining five cells.

   ⚜ Hint: Word's find and replace function also works nicely in tables. For example, you could find "Friends of the Manitous" and replace all six instances with "My Organization".

8. Save your file.

Modify the Bookmark's Back Side

The back side of the bookmark is a good place to use your mission statement, or a condensed version of it. Otherwise compose whatever you feel might be appropriate or useful for the back of your bookmarks, and insert it as follows:

9. Load the file "bookmarkback.doc" and save it with a different name, such as "myfirstbookmark-back.doc".

10. Notice this layout consists of a similar 6 x 3 table, with text centered vertically and horizontally in the middle cells.

11. Select all the middle cells by clicking outside the table just to the left of the first cell, then touch *Delete*.

12. Copy and paste your text into the middle cells of the first column. The existing text had about 460 characters and spaces formatted in 7pt Arial. Feel free to adjust the height of the top and bottom rows as needed to provide the needed space and desired formatting for your text. Use the *Table|Table Properties...* functions to position it as desired within the cell.

13. When satisfied with your text, copy and paste it into each of the other five middle cells.

14. Save your file.

Printing, Laminating and Trimming the Bookmarks

Print your bookmarks on premium grade 110# card stock or 67# cover stock.

15. Print "myfirstbookmark.doc" first, then feed the same pages into your printer to print "myfirstbookmark-back.doc" on the opposite side. Since the table layouts are centered on the page, the back of the bookmark should print exactly centered with respect to the front side.

   ❧ Hint: For best results when printing very small font sizes, select your printers top quality mode, usually by selecting *Properties* in the *Print* dialog mode, then "Best," "Highest," or whatever the highest resolution mode is called on your printer.

16. To cut them out –

   a. Use the trim lines at the bottom edge of your bookmarks to trim that edge first using your paper cutter.

   b. Use the trim mark on the left edge of the left-most bookmark to trim that side, squaring it up on the bottom edge which you just cut.

   c. Trim the remaining two sides to provide a 6" x 9" rectangle, and then trim off the six bookmarks by slipping the sheet along the paper cutter's ruled edge and cutting at 7-1/2", 6", 4-1/2" and 3".

Now for the finishing touch – applying the plastic laminate to both sides and trimming to the finished size.

17. Download and print the file "laminatingtemplate.doc".

18. 9" x 12" sheets of laminate (C-Line No. 65001 Cleer Adheer®, or Avery No. 73601 Self-Adhesive Laminating Sheets) have space for seven bookmarks. This template will help you position your 1-1/2" x 6" bookmarks to make final trimming easy. Here's how:

    a. Tape this template to your work surface.

    b. Remove the backing paper from one sheet of laminating film, and tape it over this template, adhesive side up.

    c. Carefully position seven of your printed 1-1/2" x 3" bookmarks on the laminate, within the rectangles showing through.

    d. Apply the second film of laminate, adhesive side down, starting from one edge and laying it down carefully to avoid air bubbles.

    e. Press down all over to fix the laminate and remove air bubbles.

        ❧ Note: residual air bubbles are more easily removed after having trimmed the laminated bookmarks.

    f. Use your paper cutter to trim the 9" x 12" sheets of laminated bookmarks. Trim exactly between the edges of the paper to provide a 1/8" sealing margin all around.

    g. Finished bookmarks are 1-3/4" x 6-1/4".

Bookmark Packaging and Distribution Ideas

These bookmarks cost about 12-cents each. If your organization sells books related to whatever it is you do, they're a perfect toss-in item. When you exhibit at public events, they make a nice, and probably valued, give-away item for your table.

Do you serve other organizations that have book stores or offer books for sale online? Your partner organization might be quite willing to help promote your organization by including one of your bookmarks with each item they sell. Provide small packets in neat little wallets made using the same card stock (a template for which you'll also find on the *SfS* website.)

Making bookmarks is a useful and enjoyable time-filler when things are slow; when you or your volunteers are becoming restless. A shelf stock is well advised since opportunities to exploit these promotional items often arise suddenly, and without much notice.

— ❧ —

Memorial Contribution Kits

"In lieu of flowers ..."?

Flowers are a metaphor for life. Sending flowers has a long tradition as symbolic of sympathy. Nevertheless, obituaries and death notices these days often ask the friends and family of the deceased to make contributions to a specified charity or organization instead of sending flowers.

Funeral homes report fewer flowers at funerals, and an increase in notices suggesting contributions. Many people think flowers are a waste of money. Living plants are often sent instead, because they keep while cut flowers die quickly. The increase in graveside funerals is another factor that makes flowers less practical. Meanwhile, certain religions also observe traditional practices in which flowers are discouraged.

The phrase "in lieu of flowers," doesn't mean not to send flowers. It just means that donations are another option. ("Please omit flowers" is the proper protocol for those not wanting flowers sent.) Some families choose to say nothing, leaving it up to individuals to decide how best to express their sympathy. Otherwise, families usually suggest donations as a way of providing guidance as to what might be most appropriate.

Memorial gifts are frequently earmarked for a favorite cause or concern of the deceased. Memorials are often to a church, a school or favorite charity, and are valued as a gift that will keep on giving long after the burial, or as a final legacy from the deceased. The only reason your organization would be designated as an appropriate recipient of such gifts is because it played a special role in the deceased's life, or was otherwise dear to their heart for some reason. The mere fact of someone having been a member or participant is usually not sufficient to prompt such final wishes.

While you can't do much to promote this sort of giving assertively, you can make it known that your organization has provisions for accepting and properly acknowledging memorial gifts. Mention that in your newsletters and membership materials, on your website and at annual meetings. Then be prepared to make donor designation cards and envelopes available to funeral directors, and to acknowledge such gifts to the donors and the deceased's designated next of kin.

Templates for these materials are provided on the *SfS* website. They are:

- giftdesignationcard.doc
- no6.75remittanceenvelope.doc
- acknowledgementcard-inside.doc

- acknowledgementcard-outside.doc
- acknowledgementenvelope-back.doc
- acknowledgementenvelope-front.doc

The gift designation cards are simple forms printed on 110# card stock. They provide a brief explanation of who you are and your organization's purposes. Spaces are also provided to allow donors to give their name and address, and to designate who should receive a card giving notice of their memorial contribution. Matching size 6-3/4 regular gummed flap business envelopes are provided with these cards. Ordinarily, packets of these cards and envelopes should be provided to the funeral director, who will make them available during visitation hours and also after the funeral, usually with an appropriate comment offered with other closing announcements.

Customizing the Gift Designation Cards

1. Open "giftdesignationcard.doc" in Word. This layout provides for three cards per 8-1/2" x 11" sheet.

2. Replace the *Friends* logo with the 0.625", 300 dpi version of your own.

3. The text beneath the logo is captured in a text box, which will accommodate about 565 characters and spaces. Use the existing text as a guide for composing appropriate content of your own. Then delete the existing text and paste your own in its place.

   ᭞ Note: The existing text is formatted in 7pt Times New Roman. This is not one of Words pre-selected sizes, so just select your text by clicking anywhere within the text box and touching [Ctrl+A], then enter the number "7" in the *Font Size* box on the formatting toolbar and press [Enter].

4. Save your customized gift designation card file.

5. Optional – These cards can be prepared in advance so they can be made immediately available when needed. Alternatively, if time permits you can pre-print the "In Memory of" line, and the "Send Card to" information, if known.

Customize the Matching Envelopes

6. Open "no6.75remittanceenvelope.doc".

7. Replace the *Friends* logo with your own 1.0" 300 dpi 180-degree rotated version.

> ❧ Hint: To easily center your logo, draw a temporary horizontal line positioned vertically at 3.25" from the edge of the page, and a temporary vertical line positioned horizontally at 4.375". Then position your logo exactly on these crosshairs. Commercial envelopes vary somewhat in width, so check your logo's position by printing on plain paper and comparing to the envelopes you have, tweaking the positioning if needed.

8. Replace the *Friends* mailing address with your own.

> ❧ Note: Memorial gifts are actually seldom mailed. They're more often left with the funeral director, or a family member.

9. Save your customized return envelope.

Printing and Packaging Your Memorial Gift Kits

10. Print your cards on regular 110# card stock. Trim 1/8" outside the border rectangle all around to produce cards of 3-1/2" x 6". Use the outline marks provided to cut the cards accurately using your paper cutter.

11. Print your envelopes one at a time with the flap open. If uncertain about the correct orientation, print a regular sheet of paper first, and then orient the envelopes in the printer's feed tray accordingly.

12. These sets of envelopes and cards will fit nicely in a 6-3/4"" x 3-3/4" x 1" box, which you can also make, and which will hold about 24 sets. See the previous item, "How to Make Simple Boxes."

Gift Acknowledgement Cards

Memorial contributions should be acknowledged immediately as they are received. Two acknowledgements are mailed for each gift; one to the designated surviving member of the deceased's family, and one to the donor. A simple, but tasteful keepsake-quality card is available for this purpose.

These cards can be printed on Avery 3259 ivory embossed note cards, which come with matching envelopes. Each 8-1/2" x 11" sheet provides two cards, which makes it easy to print the required pair. As a less expensive alternative, the cards can be printed with artificial embossing on 32# ivory resume paper (Southworth 80720), with envelopes handmade using the same material (a good project for a volunteer). Alternatively, envelopes in the appropriate size and color are commonly available.

Customizing the Acknowledgement Cards

1. Open "acknowledgementcard-inside.doc" in Word. This layout provides for two cards per 8-1/2" x 11" sheet. The mechanical layout is designed to suit the 3-1/4" x 4-1/2" embossed rectangle of the Avery cards using carefully positioned content.

2. Light border lines have been added to simulate the embossing of the Avery cards when using a fine paper instead if the cards. If using the Avery cards, you may remove these border lines. Simply select and delete them.

3. The words *"In Memory of"* may not be rendered in the fancy script shown here because they are formatted in the TrueType font "Shelley Allegro BT," which is commonly distributed with graphics software but which might not be installed on your system, If needed, download this font and install it.

4. Replace "The Friends of the Manitous" with the name of your organization on both cards.

5. Save your changes and close the file.

6. Open and inspect "acknowledgementcard-outside.doc". The layout is the same as above, representing the outside of the embossed cards. An appropriate picture is printed inside the embossed area on the front of the card. The back side includes an appropriate thought, and identifies your organization. (The image on the front side is inverted because it is easier to invert images than text.)

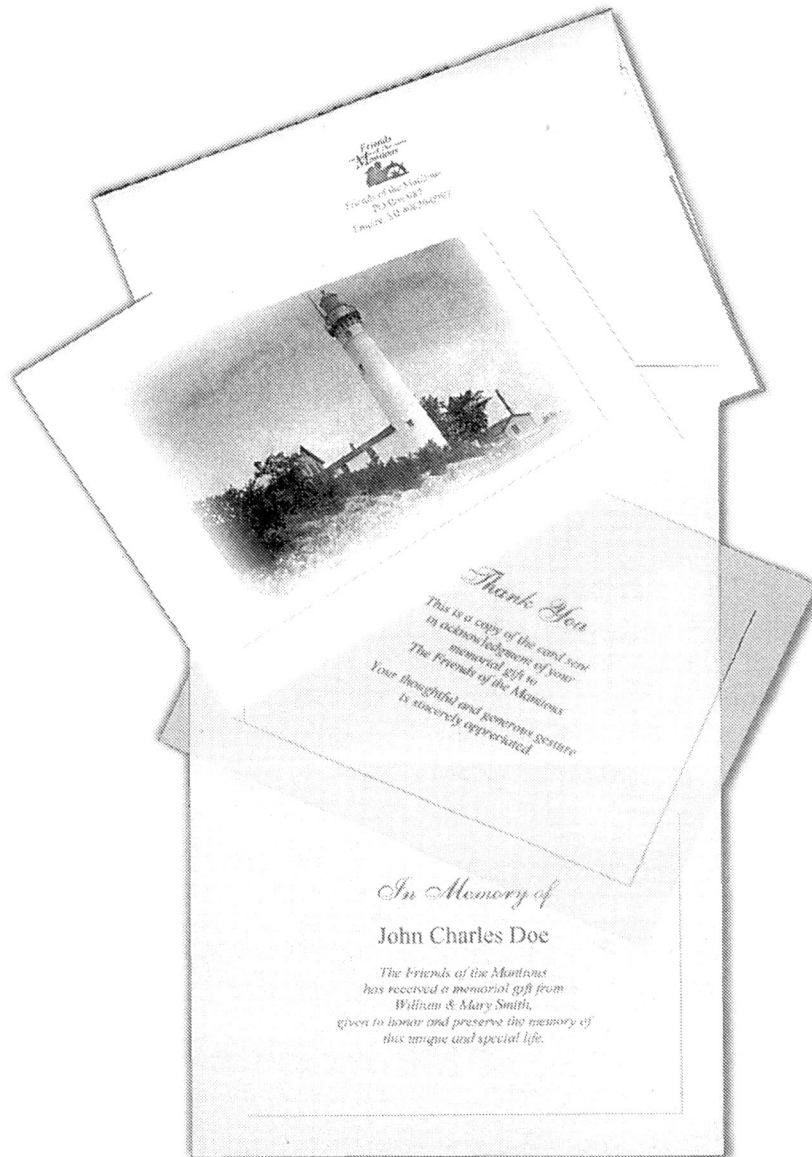

7. You'll no doubt wish to replace the images with something more appropriate for your organization. The embossed panels on these cards (in landscape orientation) measure 4-1/2" wide by 3-1/4" high. Crop and resize your image to provide a margin of about 1/4" all around. For example, 4" x 2-3/4" would be ideal (the existing photo is 4" x 2-7/8").

8. On the back panel of the card –

   a. Replace the John Donne citation, if something else seems more appropriate for your situation.

b. Replace the *Friends* logo on the back panel of the card with the 0.625" 300 dpi version of your own logo.

c. Revise the contact and copyright information in the box beneath the logo for your organization.

> ❧ Hint: To make sure things are properly positioned, draw five temporary lines across the page, select your content item by item and nudge each one using [Ctrl] and the arrow keys as needed to position its center handles on these lines:
> - 2 vertical lines at 2.75" and 8.25"
> - 3 horizontal lines at 2.125", 5.75" and 7"

9. Save your changes and close the file.

Customizing the Matching Envelopes

The matching envelopes provided with the Avery cards are essentially common A2 size flat-flap announcement envelopes (5-3/4" x 4-3/8"). If you decide against using the Avery cards, envelopes of this size are commonly available in office supply stores in white and other colors. They're also very easy to make by hand using the same paper chosen for the cards.

To Make Your Own A2 Envelopes

1. Download the template "a2envelopemodel.doc".

2. Replace the *Friends* logo with your own 0.625" 300 dpi logo.

3. Revise the return address in the box under the logo with your organization's name and general mailing address.

4. Save your changes, and then print the envelope template on paper matching that used for your cards.

5. Follow the trimming and folding instructions printed on the template to assemble your envelopes.

To Use Ready-Made Envelopes

6. Open "acknowledgementenvelope-back.doc". This is a template for the envelope's sealing flap which in this case is printed in the closed position.

7. Replace the *Friends* logo with the 0.625 300 dpi version of your own logo.

    > ❧ Hint: To center your logo, draw a temporary vertical line at 2.875" from the left edge of the page, and a horizontal line 0.75" from the top of the page, then select your logo and center it on these lines by holding down the [Ctrl] key and using the arrow keys to nudge it into place.

8. Revise the return address in the box just beneath the logo with your organization's name and general mailing address.

9. Save your changes and close the file.

Customize the Thank You Insert

Donors are provided with an identical copy of the card sent to the family of the deceased. An insert is included with the copy sent to the donor explaining the card and thanking them for their generosity.

The template "acknowledgementcard-thankyounote.doc" matches the design of the cards, with four 4-1/4" x 5-1/2" inserts per sheet. To customize this template, you need only do this:

1. Replace "The Friends of the Manitous" with your organization's name.

    > ❧ Suggestion: Print these inserts on inkjet vellum (Staples Item No. 496755, or equal) to give the notes an appropriate look and feel, and a touch of class.

Preparing Acknowledgement Cards and Envelopes

Acknowledge memorial gifts immediately. Send a card to the family of the deceased, and an identical card with an explanatory note to the giver. To print these acknowledgement cards and envelopes:

1. Open "acknowledgementcard-inside.doc", change "John Charles Doe" to the name of the deceased, and then print this side.

2. Open "acknowledgementcard-outside.doc" and print this image on the opposite side of the same page.

3. Cut the printed page in half to provide two 5-1/2" x 8-1/2" sheets, and then fold these to provide two 4-1/4" x 5-1/2" cards.

4. If using commercially-made A2 envelopes, open your template "acknowledgementenvelope-back.doc" and print your logo and return address on the sealing flaps of two envelopes.

    ✤ Hint: To print the return address on the small A2 envelopes, hook the sealing flap over the right-hand edge of a sheet of regular 8-1/2" x 11" printer paper to facilitate feeding it through the printer.

5. Open "acknowledgementenvelope-front.doc". Type the mailing address of each recipient over the "Mary Doe" placeholder and print the face of each envelope.

6. Open "acknowledgementcard-thankyounote.doc" and print a vellum Thank You insert for the donor's card.

—— ✤ ——

Screen Printing Projects

Section 2 briefly discussed some marketing realities, including the necessity of actively promoting your organization to ensure its continuing growth and success. One of the most fundamental objectives of marketing is to get your brand out in front of people and keep it there. One way to do that is to put your name and logo on everyday things that people will be happy to use or display for you.

Many such items can be created by screen printing, which is an inexpensive process that is easy to do once you get the hang of it. Here are two easy projects that you or your volunteers will enjoy doing.

Monogram License Plates

Some states still require both front and back license plates, but many do not. Most vehicles therefore have provisions for front plates, offering special covers as an accessory for customers where front plates are not required. Those special covers, which usually feature the vehicle maker's name or logo, are expensive. Why pay big bucks to help promote their brand?

Buy aluminum license plate blanks from www.averyvinyl.com for only a dollar each and silk screen your name and logo on them, and many people will be willing to turn their front bumper into a billboard for your organization.

To print these plates you'll need these items:

- a silk screen, 16" x 20" x 200 mesh
- a 7" squeegee
- supplies
  - black ink – Nazdar 59-111

- white ink – Nazdar 59-112
- thinner – Nazdar 5560
- screen wash – Nazdar IMS-202

To buy ready-made screens with your artwork burned into them, check you local listings for silk screen service providers, or search for online sources such as www.screenprintingsupplies.com or www.standardscreen.com. Nazdar is sold online at www.sourceoneonline.com. If you want to do this for yourself, pre-stretched screens are commonly available online, and you'll also find lots of tutorial information showing how it's done.

Create your own artwork using Microsoft Word or PaintShop Pro. The layout for the plate shown above is available on the *SfS* website in Word format; "licenseplatelayout.doc". If submitting your layout electronically, refer to the instructions provided by the service you are using. If using a local service, print it on ink jet film using your printer's best quality mode.

Silk screening is not necessarily difficult or messy. To make the job easy, attach the silk screen to a piece of 3/4" plywood just a little larger than the screen itself, using ordinary hinges. Make a positioning jig for the blank plates by stapling strips of chipboard to the working surface of the plywood. This makes it easy to lift the screen to remove printed plates and insert another blank, guaranteeing that they will be properly positioned for the next impression. Screw a #8 sheet metal screw into the plywood and under the frame of the screen, as a spacer that will keep the screen from touching the plates – an tenth to an eighth of an inch is fine; the spacing isn't critical. Use masking tape and masking paper (available at Sherwin-Williams stores, The Home Depot, and similar outlets) to mask off everything but the image area of the screen to make cleanup easier when you're finished.

As for the task of screen printing itself, the trick is simply to move the squeegee smoothly but firmly across the image area, keeping the edge on the screen as shown here. Think about just squeegeeing the ink cleanly from one side of the image area to the other while pressing just firmly enough to cause contact with the plate beneath the screen. You don't need to think about forcing the ink through the screen. Pressing too hard or using the flat side of the squeegee is sure

to make a mess of things. Then lightly drag the squeegee back, bringing the ink back with it to flood the screen over the image area in preparation for the next impression. For practice, cut pieces of poster board and image them until you are confident you've gotten the hang of it.

Make 7" x 13" bags for your plates using a 15" x 15" piece of masking paper. As a courtesy, supply two No. 14 x 1/2" stainless slotted hex washer head sheet metal screws with your plates (available from www.mcmaster-carr.com in packs of 50; Item # 90286A310, $7.86)

Mouse Pads

Leverage your license plate silk screen by using it for mouse pads, a useful handout that'll keep your organization's brand in front of anyone who uses a computer frequently. Simply mask off everything but your logo and print it at the center of the pad in black, white or gray. Blank mouse pads are available in a choice of colors for as little as 69-cents from www.gocna.com.

Tee Shirts, Caps and Cups

It always happens; someone gets the idea that monogrammed tee shirts, baseball caps and coffee cups would be great fundraisers. As a general rule, don't expect to make big bucks selling monogrammed merchandise. People are usually somewhat reluctant to buy things they don't need, and if they do need these sorts of things they can buy them for a lot less at retail.

Nevertheless, there are occasions where items of this kind are appropriate. For example, for member events it might be fun and useful for participants to all wear monogrammed tee shirts and caps specially purchased for that occasion. Cups might be a nice take-home item if you offer seminars or similar special events, or even as part of the tableware when your organization hosts a banquet or has a potluck as part of the annual meeting.

It's easy to screen print flat things that are rigid enough to handle easily. Screening fabric and irregular surfaces is not so simple, and ordinarily require special jigs and fixtures to position and hold the items receiving the impression. Unless you will be doing a lot of that kind of work, it's probably better left to commercial silk screen services.

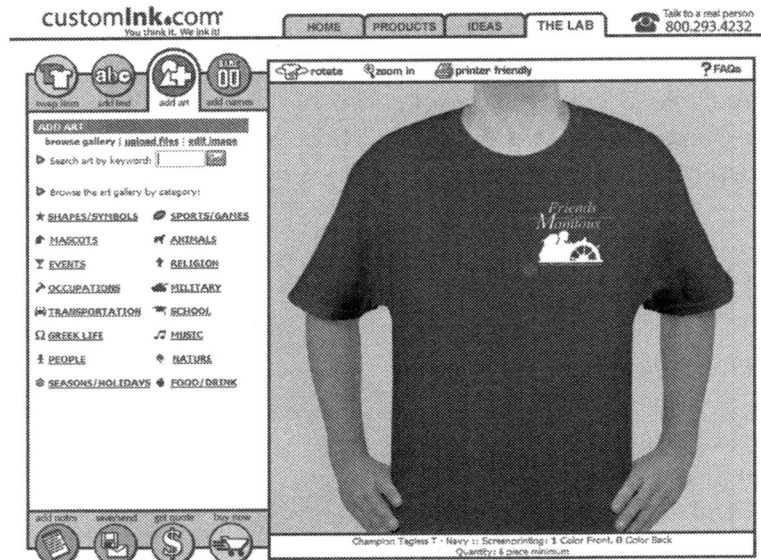

Local sources can usually be found by looking for silk screen services or businesses that offer advertising specialties. There are also lots of great online sources that are very easy to work with; some even offering totally automated ordering. You simply choose the item you wish to purchase from the variety of styles, qualities, colors and sizes, and then upload your artwork. You can also create artwork online. For example, you

can upload your organization's logo, and then add lines and text around it using a design utility provided on the vendor's web site. For example, visit www.customink.com, pick a tee shirt, mug or whatever, and the site will automatically take to the design creation utility. Try it; it's fun!

The Graphic Artist

Secretaries of small nonprofits wear many hats. Do you enjoy these kinds of projects?

The title "Graphic Arts" used to apply exclusively to the printing trade and vocational specialties involved in publishing. Today, the graphic designer is better described as anyone who uses images and type to create or enhance a wide array of works, including printed materials, advertising, product designs and online presentations, using a variety of sophisticated computer tools and relying upon their technical savvy, creativity and a good eye for design. Every business and organization has needs for this skill, yet the requirements are so diverse there is no well-defined career path. On average, graphic designers earn about $38,000 annually. Many work as free-lancers.

What you can achieve is limited only by your own technical savvy, creativity and good eye for design. You're sure to come up with some great ideas, and when you do, feel free to share them on the *SfS* website's reader forum.

7

Fundraising Basics

Why do these words begin with "fun" —
fungus, funk, funeral ... fundraising!

— ❧ —

7
Fundraising Basics

The Root of All Evil?

"For the love of money is the root of all evil."
— Timothy, 6:10.

... a familiar line from a letter written by Paul of Tarsus to his friend Timothy of Lystra about 1,900 years ago. Paul is often misquoted. He did not say money was evil. In fact, Paul was comparatively wealthy, and originally gained acceptance by his peers as a result of his being a great fundraiser. One might say that Paul, among other things, was Christianities first great fundraiser.

"Donors don't give to institutions. They invest in ideas and people in whom they believe." — G.T. Smith

This quotation, often referred to as *the first principle of fundraising,* is quoted hundreds of times on the Internet. But just who is G. T. Smith?

Dr. G. T. "Buck" Smith, listed in *Who's Who in America* for over thirty years, has served as President of California's Chapman University and West Virginia's Bethany College. But more to the point, he has also been active as an executive in philanthropies, his energies being directed toward helping strengthen the management of American and international non-profit organizations. A present-day apostle of philanthropy, one might say.

In the philanthropic vernacular, one could quite rightly assert, "Money is the root of all good." No matter what your purpose, it's not likely that you'll be able to achieve much without some generous financial support. If you're temperamentally disposed to look upon fundraising as begging or money grubbing, as many are, it's time to *check your premises*, because you will not be able to achieve what your mind cannot believe.

— ❧ —

The Mission Plan

A business plan is fundamentally a plan for making money, which is the main motive for doing business. The plan describes –

- the product and its merits,
- the prospective customers and their needs, and
- how the business thinks it can bring these two elements together in a profitable way.

Sometimes the business plan is carefully developed and published as a formal document. Sometimes it exists only as a set of notions in the mind of the businessperson.

The fundamental concerns of nonprofits are very similar. At some point, someone sat down and thought about –

- what service the organization performs,
- how that would be helpful to someone, and
- how it could come up with enough money to carry on that work.

In small NPOs, these ideas find their way into the articles of incorporation, bylaws and applications for recognition of exemption, but a carefully prepared and clearly written business plan is not often seen. As a consequence, groups wrangle over conflicting agendas and struggle with funding limitations and uncertainties.

Since making money is not the goal of nonprofit organizations, the plan is about the *mission*, rather than the *business*. Nevertheless, making money is just as essential to nonprofits as it is for any successful business enterprise. Businesses must have earnings. The first concern of people who start businesses is, "How much money would I be able to make doing this?" The burden of the business plan is to show how earnings will be generated from a product or service idea. NPOs must have funding. The essence of the mission plan is basically the same; relating the mission idea to its potential for attracting funding. Ironically, that's often the last concern of those starting nonprofits, and that sets the stage for an improvisational board culture.

Boards change every couple of years, and new people are sure to bring new ideas. Nature abhors a vacuum, so where there is no real plan, new boards are apt to go off into new directions. Unless the board is working a defined and enduring plan of some sort and new board members are appropriately briefed, board meetings may turn into brainstorming sessions, the board coming up with new approaches, dismissing previous ideas as lame and ineffective. The previous board's ideas may be discarded before having a chance to be developed to their fullest potential because they are not fully understood, or simply because they were someone else's ideas.

Regardless of what it's called, the board should have well-understood and permanent approaches to –

- developing a solid membership base,
- promoting faithful event and project participation, and
- creating a reliable revenue stream.

Evaluating the results in these areas is an ongoing task for each board. When a need for change and improvement is indicated, ideas can be refined and methods tweaked as needed. Through this process of consistent evaluation and improvement, a very powerful plan can eventually evolve.

This discussion will end here, since its purpose is not to provide guidance on how to write a mission plan. Its purpose is to convince you that money is a fundamentally pervasive issue. Whatever the project or activity, its impact on funding and potential for raising more money must be part of the consideration. The fortunes of your organization will rise or fall according to your willingness and ability to raise funds. Raising funds must therefore be an obsession of every board member.

Developing a Revenue Mix

Common sense teaches the naïveté of depending on one particular revenue stream for more than a quarter of the budget. Better to develop a diverse and sustainable mix of earned income, dues and donations to support routine activities, then use grants and contracts for special projects and new developments.

There is no *typical* revenue mix. What's right for you depends upon your particular attributes and activities, which probably have little in common with most other NPOs. Possible components are:

- Regular income – memberships, dues, annual appeals.
- Regular earned income – fee-for-service activities.
- Special ventures – merchandise sales, event tickets, royalties.
- Special events – annual meetings, membership outings.
- Major gifts.
- Capital campaigns – for buildings and equipment.
- Grants – corporate, foundation, government.
- Planned gifts and bequests.
- Endowment income.
- Investment income.

The Development Director

This is an extensive grocery list. Considering the scope of these options, collectively and individually, it is obvious that an intelligently designed and well managed fundraising operation is not realistically within the capabilities of a small all-volunteer board.

A development director is a person who works closely with the President and Board of Directors to develop and implement a comprehensive fundraising plan. Small NPOs that depend on contributed income should have a development director.

Even if your organization is not able to afford professional help, you should create this position and earnestly seek a volunteer to fill it. Since there are no formal educational programs designed to produce development directors, these skills are acquired through experience, often as an apprentice in a larger organization. People with this particular skill are therefore hard to find. However, your development director's job will be to create numerous, efficient and compelling opportunities for donors to support your organization, and to make the experience of giving satisfying and rewarding. This task is not fundamentally different than that of the sales manager of a for-profit business, whose job is to create numerous, efficient and compelling opportunities for customers to patronize the business, making the experience of buying satisfying and rewarding.

The important thing is that someone on your board or staff has the primary responsibility for the overall fundraising program.

Charity Begins at Home

A reluctant giver is usually also a reluctant asker.

As a part of your corporate culture, let every member of the board write a check for $25 at every board meeting. No more, and no less. Do this ritualistically and visibly. If you have quarterly meetings and six board members, this will provide $600 – probably enough to pay the expenses of your annual meeting. This will cost each one of you only $100. Anyone who can't afford that, or doesn't want to afford that, should decline the invitation to be nominated for a board position.

Fundraising must be an essential part of your board culture. Nobody on the board should think that raising money is someone else's responsibility. Hang this sign up wherever your board meets:

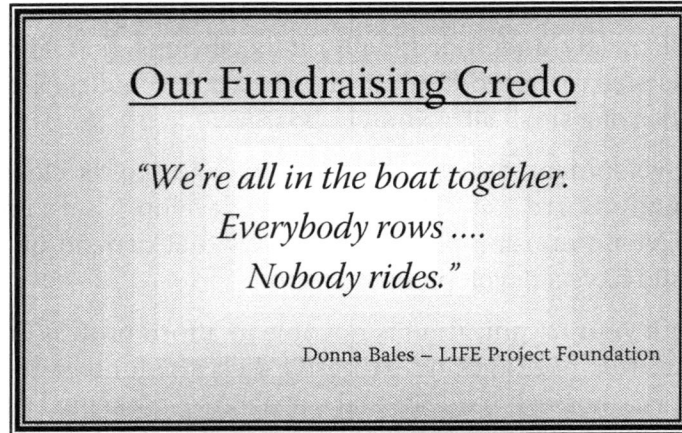

<u>Our Fundraising Credo</u>

"We're all in the boat together.
Everybody rows ....
Nobody rides."

Donna Bales – LIFE Project Foundation

It's a generally accepted doctrine that board members should be an organization's most cheerful givers. The usual rationale is that this sets an example for everyone else. That might be true to some extent, but there's probably also a huddle in most organizations who easily shrug that off, whispering to each other, "They want to be the big wheels; let them pay for the privilege!"

In other words, what's required by convention probably doesn't teach much by example. Moreover, acceptance of this presumption gives board members who are loath to row, an easy way to justify riding: *"I do my part by giving generously, thereby setting a good example."* Having decided that, they're comfortable leaving the real fundraising work to someone else.

The reality is this: if you're not giving, you won't dare ask someone else to give, or if your giving is penurious, you won't dare ask someone else to give generously. Yes, there are individuals who never give their organization a dime while serving on the board of directors, extenuating that with the assertion that their service to the organization is a suitable offering. They're not fooling anyone, probably not even themselves.

And speaking about fooling people, the records of contributions, showing who gave how much, should be visible to every board member. Absolute confidentiality makes it real easy for board members to play the role without actually giving much, or anything. It's a simple matter to provide a list of contributions received to date, beginning with the last board meeting. If confidentiality is otherwise deemed appropriate, pass these lists out at the meeting, review them, then collect them all and destroy them.

A small nonprofit organization that is hurting for funds usually has a board that isn't comfortable with fundraising, and isn't cutting the mustard in that essential responsibility. If you find yourself involved with this sort of board and you wish to avoid an unpleasant tenure, your choices are limited to two. You can –

- convince your colleagues to change their minds, or
- resign.

Delusions of Granteur

The *Giving USA Foundation* reports giving from four sources of contributions: individual (living) donors, bequests by deceased individuals, foundations and corporations.

According to Giving USA, charitable giving in 2005 from these sources amounted to $260-billion. Of this, about $7.5-billion was given as special disaster relief. The remainder reflects donors' commitments to other causes that mattered to them.

Individual giving is always the largest single source of donations. According to Giving USA and *The Foundation Center*, the overall distribution of giving for 2005 looked like this ...

- individual giving   76.5%
- charitable bequests   6.7%
- foundation grant-making   11.5%
- corporate donations   5.3%

The 85% that comes from individuals is easy money; it usually comes for the asking with no strings attached.

Grants are not easy money. Granters will make you jump through hoops to get their money (viz., grant applications), and will require a formal accounting of how it was or is being spent. You might even have to appear in a dog and pony show to pick up the check (viz., awards banquets) or report on all the great things you accomplished with their money.

Foundations and corporations account for only about 10% and 5% respectively of the available charitable funding. Author and fundraising guru Joan Flannagan says this:

"If you're only writing proposals for foundation and corporate grants, you're just chasing nickels and dimes."

If these percentages hold for your organization, grant seeking may not prove to be the best investment of your fundraising time and effort. The percentages clearly suggest that the fishing will be a lot better in the *"donors committed to causes that matter to them"* pond – your current membership, and the members you have yet to recruit.

If you're not comfortable with that, you're likely to engage in the sort of magical thinking that a grant will solve all your problems – *Delusions of Granteur.*

"Hello; May I Have Some Money?"

So just how do you get the money out of these committed individuals? Very simple; ask them for it. People will ordinarily give to you if:

- You ask them directly, person to person.
- You say specifically what the money is for.

"People," in this case, refers to individuals who have demonstrated a commitment to, or at least an interest in, your cause. A good starting point is your membership. Without any intervention, the "80/20 Rule" will become operative in your organization, with 80% of your financial support coming from 20% of your members.

Assume a small organization with dues of $25 and 160 dues-paying members. Most members think of the $25 as their annual donation, but a few (about two out of every ten) contribute more during the year, their total averaging about $100. The result is:

$$128 \times \$25 = \$ 3,200$$
$$32 \times \$100 = \underline{\ \ 3,200}$$
$$\text{Total} = \$ 6,400$$

These figures are not unrealistic. Without a strategy to develop individual giving, you will find that a small, but dedicated group is providing as much support as the entire rest of your membership. Suppose that by implementing a carefully thought out program, you get your whole membership more appropriately engaged, to the extent of reversing the 80/20 rule. Then the result could be:

$$32 \times \$25 = \$ \quad 800$$
$$128 \times \$100 = \underline{\quad 12,800}$$
$$\text{Total} = \$ \, 13,600$$

This isn't unrealistic either. The combined annual income of your 160 members is conservatively something like $6.9-million, so you're shooting for less than 0.2% (that's two-tenths of one percent). The $13,600 might still be small potatoes, but it's a lot better than $6,400. Thinking about the long term, you can accomplish a lot more over ten years with $136,000 than you could with only $64,000.

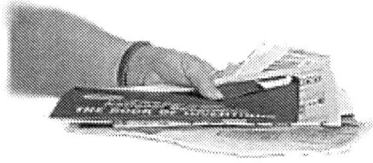

But you won't get the money unless you ask for it. You have to ask for it directly. Consider these two scenarios:

The ABC Foundation: You've got mail from the ABC Foundation, which you joined because you took an interest in it for some reason or another. The envelope contains a form letter appealing for support, a colorful brochure telling all the great things ABC does, a remittance envelope, and a sticker sheet full of fairly nice personalized address labels. You keep the address labels, thinking they'll come in handy for returning all those entry forms to Publisher's Clearing House. You're still somewhat interested in the organization, and agree that they do good, so you set the remittance envelope aside before throwing the rest of the mailing in the trash.

The XYZ Society: Your phone rings, and the caller identifies himself as Joe Dokes, a past President of the XYZ Society. You remember having met him once at an annual meeting. He's cordial but businesslike, and comes right to the point; XYZ has some great opportunities again this year, and he's seeking the financial support needed for your organization to do these things. He briefly describes a couple of these initiatives, and the good that is expected to result, then cuts to the chase. He says members are sending anywhere from $10 to $500, that most send about $100, and it would be really nice if you'd consider donating that amount this year. If you think you can do something for XYZ again this year, he'll send you a remittance envelope which will accept either your check or your credit card number.

Who's going to get your money; ABC or XYZ?

ABC's remittance envelope probably also eventually wound up at the landfill along with the rest of their mailing. What the heck; everybody knows that fewer than five out of every hundred respond to direct mail, so you discard the envelope feeling that you're in good company. But when

XYZ's envelope arrives a few days after Joe's call, a still small voice whispers that Joe will be disappointed in you if it doesn't come back as promised, accompanied by your check or credit card info.

Joe's postage-paid (a regular postage stamp, not a permit imprint) envelope has your name and other personal information already filled out for you, so all you have to do is enclose your check or enter your credit card information, then drop it in the mail. It has check-boxes for –

☐ $_____   ☐ $25   ☐ $50   ☑ $100   ☐ $250   ☐ $500   ☐ $_____

– with the "$100" box checked lightly with a lead pencil. That's a nice personal touch. Joe's reminding you of your conversation, but encouraging you to send whatever you think you can afford by erasing the check mark he penciled in, then checking the box of your choice.

Soliciting prospective donors directly in person has the greatest potential for success. Do that at annual meetings or other organizational events. However, when that isn't possible, a personal phone call is your next best choice. Direct mail marketing might seem like an easy and unobtrusive way to make your case but, as suggested above, the response rates are very low. With today's cheap long distance rates, and even free minutes on cellular phones, the per contact cost of telephoning can rival that of direct mail. But even if it doesn't, the higher response rate will provide a lower cost per contribution dollar; usually much lower.

Soliciting contributions is essentially sales work. There are few natural salesmen. However board members are usually personable, self-confident people, who can become successful solicitors with a bit of training and experience. A little role-playing practice is a good idea, rather than just expecting board members to start making cold calls without any rehearsal or practical experience. Following that, the first names on each person's calling list should be people they know and are comfortable talking to. If there are others who are just not cut out for this kind of work, better to face that fact and assign these board members to other fundraising tasks, such as doing the mailings and receiving the responses, than loose prospects through failed calls.

Give 'em What For

Embedded in the above two examples is another important secret for getting a "Yes." When asking for money, say why you're asking, explaining precisely what the money is needed for. ABC provided a form letter and color brochure clucking about all the good works they do. XYZ talked directly to the prospective donor about upcoming projects and other needs.

Discussing specific needs and challenges engages the donor by arousing a feeling of personal importance and direct personal involvement. Donors are often unmoved by nebulous philanthropic agendas, or opportunities to give for the greater good.

Consider the recent natural disasters, Hurricane Katrina ($3.27-billion) and the Indian Ocean Tsunami ($983-million). Private contributions broke all records, with donors actually seeking out charitable organizations and relief agencies to give their money to. A different example is the Foster Parents Plan, a child welfare charity that offers to designate a donor's money to a specific child somewhere in a needy part of the world, the donor supposedly becoming that child's personal sponsor. While there are several child welfare charities, this formula has worked great for the Foster Parents Plan for 70-years (total public support and revenue for 2006: $38-million).

Never Do Freebies

Whatever your religious persuasion, you've probably noticed that organized (or even disorganized) religion never passes up an opportunity to receive gifts. Everybody knows that's how it works, and none are offended by being asked for a donation during religious observances or other events.

Follow that example. Never overlook an opportunity to ask for support. The opportunities include –

- meetings – annual, special, board of committee
- special events – seminars, exhibits, workshops, projects
- all mailings – newsletters, notices

If you hear people joke (or complain) that you are always looking for a handout, you'll know you're doing it right, and they get it.

This does not necessarily mean that you should set a price or fee on everything.

Selling fundraising merchandise can raise sales tax and unrelated business income issues. Offering premiums for contributions technically requires that you credit the donor for the amount contributed, less the value of the item given in exchange. Low value merchandise can simply be offered to members without charge, but with strings attached – a handy contribution envelope. On average, this will actually return amounts larger than whatever price you would have put on the item were you to offer it for sale as a fundraiser.

As an alternative to charging admission to events, do as the churches do; let everyone in for free, but take up a free will offering. Do this in a highly visible and interactive way, not by simply setting up passive contribution cans.

Items ordinarily distributed for purposes other than fundraising, such as brochures, booklets and newsletters, should always contain a remittance envelope.

Never give anything away, or provide any service, without giving recipients an opportunity to respond with a generous contribution.

And So On ...

Americans are generous. According to *Independent Sector*, 70% of U.S. households contribute to various causes, giving away about 2% of their income each year. Money isn't hard to come by, but you have to ask.

Beyond that, success results from building strong, lasting relationships with donors and fundraising volunteers, when instead of focusing on the bottom line and immediate goals, you think about what donors want to accomplish with their money, and how that accords with your mission. Donors and volunteers should be respectfully and intimately engaged in what's going on within your organization, and on a consistent ongoing basis. Their continuing support can be ensured by your clearly communicating how important they are to your organization, and how much their generous contributions of time and money are appreciated.

There are hundreds of books about fundraising, and thousands of articles. But there aren't any secrets or magic formulas. Each organization must eventually find a mix of activities that works well for them.

Your discovery process is bound to include lots of learning experiences – disappointments and frustrations that teach you what doesn't work. But that's the entrepreneurial process – nothing ventured, nothing gained. Successes are almost always built over time, by those who have the faith to persevere.

8
Mustering Manpower

"La Garde meurt et ne se rend pas!."
— *Nicolas Chauvin (c. 1790)*

Mustering Manpower

On Volunteerism

Nicolas Chauvin was a soldier who served in the First Army of the French Republic and subsequently in La Grande Armee of Napoleon Bonaparte. He enlisted at age 18 and served honorably and well. Reputed with having authored the above motto, *"The Guard dies, it does not surrender!"* he was wounded seventeen times, resulting in his severe disfigurement and maiming.

For his loyalty and dedication, Napoleon personally presented Chauvin with the *Saber of Honor* and a pension of 200 francs. But Chauvin's distinguished record of service and his love and devotion for Napoleon, which had endured despite the great price he willingly paid, became a popular theme for mockery in later years. French society had moved on, high idealism and passionate nationalism then being considered passé.

N. Chauvin became the laughing stock of several popular Vaudeville plays, including the classic *La Cocarde Tricolore* (1831). As a result, the term "chauvinism" evolved, evoking images of an audaciously earnest dimwit valiantly devoted to a dubious cause.

So what does all this have to do with volunteer recruitment, assimilation and retention?

Volunteer Realities of Small NPOs

Much has already been written about the role of volunteerism in the nonprofit sector; how to find volunteers, how to manage them, and how to keep them. It's not the intention of this section to provide a digest or summary of all that. Instead, its scope will be limited to the realm of actual needs and practical solutions for small NPOs, as opposed to abstract, theoretical or idealized discussions applicable to the broad nonprofit universe.

With that in mind, it seemed like it might be refreshing to come up with a different name for people who are willing to give of their time and talent for what they feel are worthy causes. However, useful synonyms for the noun "volunteer" are hard to find. The only one, outside of the many with military connotations, was "chauvinist," which back in the day (before women's lib), was sometimes defined as "one who is indefatigably devoted to any group, attitude, or cause."

Indeed, every NPO has its chauvinists – often the founders, but otherwise people who are dedicated to doing whatever good is the organization's reason for being, often at the expense of what others value as more important personal priorities. As with the famous *Première Armée de la République Française,* important victories are never won without taking some casualties, and indeed these Chauvins of the small NPOs seldom escape unscathed, be the wounds more often to spirit rather than to the body. And then, like yet another monotonous rerun of *La Cocarde Tricolore,* comes derision. The chauvinists who serve small NPOs in positions of leadership had better be thick skinned, since the blame and ridicule resulting from inevitable disappointments often seems to come more generously than the praise and acclaim for successes.

So for the moment, let us speak of people who work for small NPOs without any pay as chauvinists, and attempt to restore this word to its most positive sense.

The Story of the Little Red Hen

There once was a little red hen who lived on a farm. The hen's friends were a little black dog, a big orange cat, and a little yellow goose. One day, the red hen found some grains of wheat. "We can make bread from this" she thought. The little red hen asked her friends, "Who will help me plant the wheat?"

"Not I" wagged the little black dog.
"Not I" purred the big orange cat.

"Not I" stretched the little yellow goose.

"Then I will do it myself." said the little red hen. And she planted the wheat without any help at all. She then asked her friends, "Who will help me cut the wheat?"

"Not I" barked the little black dog.
"Not I" meowed the big orange cat.
"Not I" fluttered the little yellow goose.

"Then I will do it myself." sighed the little red hen. And she cut the wheat without any help at all. The tired little red hen then asked, "Who will help me take the wheat to the mill and grind it into flour?"

"Not I" whined the little black dog.
"Not I" fussed the big orange cat.
"Not I" murmured the little yellow goose.

"Then I will do it myself." breathed the tired little red hen. So she took the wheat to the mill and ground it into flour without any help at all. The very, very tired little red hen finally asked, "Who will help me bake the bread?"

"Not I" growled the little black dog.
"Not I" screeched the big orange cat.
"Not I" hissed the little yellow goose.

"Then I will do it myself." muttered the very, very, very tired little red hen. And she baked the bread without any help at all. The hot, fresh bread smelled very good. The little red hen facetiously asked, "Now ... who will help me eat my bread?"

"I will!" yapped the little black dog enthusiastically.
"I will!" yodeled the big orange cat casually.
"I will!" trumpeted the little yellow goose excitedly.

"No, you won't! I will do it myself!" declared the little red hen. And she ate all the bread without any help at all.

The End

Where Little Red Hen Went Wrong

Small NPOs rarely have any paid staff. They're managed by volunteers and carry out their work with volunteers.

Volunteers are evidently not hard to find. According to Independent Sector's *Nonprofit Almanac – 2007*, almost a third of the U.S. population volunteers in the management and work of formal organizations. That's upwards of 89-million volunteers. As a class, men and women are equally likely to be found in volunteer roles, and the willingness to volunteer runs fairly constant through the various age groups.

Independent Sector places the estimated dollar value of volunteer time at $18.04 per hour (in 2005 dollars). With volunteers working an average 3½ to 4 hours per week, the total time given exceeds 17-billion hours, with a value exceeding $313-billion.

So where did Little Red Hen go wrong?

First, she didn't do anything to get dog, cat and goose engaged in her agenda. Four times she simply suggested they give her a hand, and each time the answer was, "Not I!" What if she'd said, "Hey gang … Look; free wheat! Let's take it and make us some nice hot bread! Umm … I can just smell the delicious vapors of those loaves baking in the oven already! Yum … hot bread with fresh butter and honey!"

Second, she didn't ask directly and personally. What if she'd said, "How 'bout it dog; you in? Could you go for some fresh, hot bread right out of the oven?" Chances are if she could have gotten dog onboard, cat and goose would have caved. Asking for help in the passive voice makes it easy for everyone to just sit around looking back and forth at each other, shrugging their shoulders and thinking up reasons why they're too busy to help out right now.

HR 101

The HR challenges for small NPOs are usually three; recruiting, managing and retaining manpower:

- For the board of directors and appointed staff positions.
- For regular day-to-day work projects.
- For special projects and events.

Recruiting volunteer help is different than hiring paid help in only one respect; volunteer help isn't compensated by receiving money for the work they perform. The process of recruiting volunteer help isn't otherwise different than seeking the right person for a paid position.

When you have a job to offer, treat it like a regular employment opportunity:

- Check your premises.
- Give it a job title and write a job description.
- Post it.
- Look for people who are qualified and will fit in.
- Use a job application and interview your prospects.
- Choose the best prospect and make them an offer.
- Provide a warm welcoming and a fair break-in.
- Bestow compensations appropriate to the job.

Check Your Premises

You're not a professional recruiter. You've just been roped into a task you really didn't want, and don't know how to do. Nobody else was up to the job either, but they all had enough pluck to say, "No!," or the guile to come up with an obviously lame excuse on short notice. So you're apt to begin with the self-defeating attitude that volunteers are hard to come by, that you'll be lucky to find anyone willing to take the job, let alone someone well qualified. In that mood, your *parti pris* might be to just get the monkey off your back. The criteria then become much less rigorous: "any warm body will do – blind, crippled or crazy; walking, creeping or crawling."

This is a good way to create bad situations. If the volunteer turns out to be an asset, that will be a wonderful stroke of luck. The chances are better that they won't be willing or able to take their job seriously. The organization will suffer and they will despair. After their unhappy experience, their ego defenses will motivate conversations with their friends and anyone else willing to listen, and most of what they'll have to say about you and your organization will not be good. To the extent that talk gets around, it'll be that much more difficult to find people willing to take a chance next time.

Dump that silly attitude. Start your search with high expectations, and the intention of finding a person who fills the bill. The word "volunteer" is a pay classification, not a job title. You are not offering pay because:

- Its good business; it enables you to use as much of your donated capital as possible for your mission or exempt purposes.

- You're offering a wonderful opportunity for people to give in other than financial ways; time is money.

- You're providing a great opportunity for someone to grow personally and vocationally, perhaps picking up skills they can take into their own work.

- You're making available a valuable resource for personal and collegial networking with highly capable people inside and outside of your organization.

The volunteer pay classification does not mean that the work is not essential or important. Not being in a position to pay for the work does not mean you can't expect to recruit a person who is highly capable and motivated. Nor does it mean you have no right set high standards and to be particular about whom you select for the opportunities you are able to offer.

Use a Job Title and Description

Every volunteer position can, and should, have a title.

Never use the word "volunteer" as a job title, or in the job title. A volunteer board member is a "Director." Someone to sweep the floors and mow the grass is the "Building and Grounds Keeper." One who answers the phone is a "Receptionist" or "Administrative Assistant."

Don't denigrate the job you have to offer by treating it as too mundane to name. Who can take pride in winning a job that isn't important enough even to have a name? If they get the job, how long will they keep it? In case someone asks your volunteer, "Exactly what do you do for the XYZ Society?" What sounds better? – "Durr, ahh … I sweep and mow and stuff." or "I'm the Building and Grounds Supervisor."

Provide a job description that communicates clearly and concisely what the responsibilities and tasks are, and the qualifications desired.

Describe what would constitute the ideal candidate and superior on-the-job performance. Here's an outline:

- Title of the position
- Where the job is
- Who's in charge (who the person will report to)
- General responsibilities - essential duties
- Who the person ordinarily works with
- Term of the job (how long)
- Qualifications (required skills and experience)

In writing job descriptions, focus on the job with respect to your organization's real needs. Rather than just writing a grocery list of tasks and responsibilities, indicate what the priorities are. Tasks are what the person will actually do. Qualifications are the skills, attributes, or credentials a person needs to perform the tasks. Outline the actual tasks and responsibilities definitively, and then decide what qualifications are actually needed. If credentials are considered necessary or appropriate for the job, say so. Otherwise avoid any suggestion that you'll value qualifications and previous experience not directly relevant to the position. References to personal attributes having no bearing on the ability to do the job, such as race, color, religion, age, sex, national origin or physical or mental disability are, of course, unacceptable.

Use specific language. For example, don't say "Computer literate"; say "Proficient with Microsoft Word, Excel, Adobe Acrobat." Don't say "Good communication skills" say "Ability to communicate business and financial information to the regular membership verbally and in writing." Don't say, "Handyman who likes outdoor work," say "Able to perform routine building maintenance tasks, including minor plumbing and electrical repairs. Maintains the grounds by mowing, trimming shrubs, weeding and managing the sprinkling system."

Committees should have job descriptions too (usually in lieu of job descriptions for individual committee members). For example, your bylaws probably authorize a nominating committee, whose purpose it is to find candidates for elected board positions and possibly appointed staff positions. The committee's job description will help its members understand what their title is, where they'll be meeting, the committee's purpose and its value to the organization, their individual duties and responsibilities, what qualifications they should bring to the committee, how much time will ordinarily be required and their term of service.

Job Postings

Volunteer opportunities must be equally available to all of your members. To make sure they are, announce them in your printed and email newsletters, on your web site, and at meetings. Jobs are sometimes coveted, and postings will bring applications.

More often they are not. Although postings may seldom bring applications, contention can arise when some members feel they were neglected or intentionally bypassed. This is especially apt to happen if the opportunities frequently go to the same people. That, in turn, is often the case because there is a small cadre of people who are very good about volunteering, and boards are typically not very good at recruiting.

Job posting is not the same thing as advertising. On occasion it will be appropriate to employ a more broadly based appeal to recruit volunteers. These will usually involve projects too large for your membership to handle without outside help, or activities specially intended for non-member participants, such as a town-wide Spring Cleaning Day, an Adopt-a-Trail program, or projects designed to acquaint the community's youth with the intangible rewards of civic engagement and public service.

Whatever the situation, offer the opportunities to your membership first.

Finding People for Your Board and Staff

To get people with special characteristics, skills and experience to fill positions of responsibility in your organization, use the *targeted recruitment* approach. By virtue of your job descriptions, you'll have a concise image of the kind of person needed for each position you're going to fill. You make a list of people who you think might fit the position you need to fill, and then ask them person-to-person to consider taking the job. For example, your nominating committee will become involved in this kind of activity when seeking candidates for upcoming officer elections.

Recruiting From the Inside

If you received any applications from job postings or word-of-mouth, you might be in luck. Otherwise, the search for prospective volunteers begins with your membership list. This can be an enjoyable exercise for a group who is familiar with the membership; your board, your nominating committee, or an informal gathering who have agreed to give you a hand. Print the list out and go through it name-by-name. Begin with a process of elimination:

- On the first pass, black out those whom you know would not be willing or able to volunteer – shut-ins, those living too far away, minors, and so on.

- Beginning again, of those remaining, scratch off those whom you know do not have the skills and experience desired, or who are otherwise not likely to be a good fit for this particular opportunity.

- On the third pass, there won't be many names left on the list. Mark those who have served before, or frequently volunteer, then go through the remaining names, adding the ones that seem to be the best prospects to a prioritized call list, along with the name of the person who will make the call.

- Elections for corporate offices are not handled like public elections. The usual practice involves a slate of candidates, one per elective office, offered by a nominating committee for election by the general membership. When more than one person is calling on prospective candidates for a single available position, avoid the embarrassment of duplicate nominees by making the calls in an orderly manner, according to your prioritized call list. Allow indecisive prospects a reasonable time to make up their mind, but set a clearly defined deadline – "May I phone you again this weekend to see what you've decided?" When you call again, if you receive anything other than a firm yes or no answer, say "I understand your uncertainties (or situation), and thank you for your consideration. May I note that you might be interested in considering the job again at some point in the future?"

- People who have volunteered before will usually be willing to serve again if they are able. After having exhausted your list of fresh prospects without success, it's time to call on upon this group. Make another prioritized call list and begin again. If your organization is typically healthy and happy, and people usually finish their volunteer terms feeling good about the experience and what they accomplished, you won't get very far into this list before hearing an enthusiastic "Yes."

Recruiting From the Outside

If you are not able to recruit needed volunteers from within your organization, it's time to go outside. At this point, provided your bylaws impose no seniority requirements (not usually a good idea) there's absolutely nothing objectionable about recruiting new members into leadership positions. People join nonprofit organizations for reasons of their own. An opportunity to serve in a leadership position is as good a reason as a chauvinist devotion to your mission. The situation is analogous to that of a regular for-profit business, where dogmatic adoration of the company's products and services is not an essential component of all the disciplines needed to make the company work.

Recruiting help from outside the organization will be more difficult, simply because you have no preexisting list of people with an interest in your organization. On the other hand, the field is wide open. Start a new list by thinking about –

- personal friends
- business/work colleagues (ask you boss for suggestions)
- people active in similar organizations
- people in organizations you serve
- people serving (or having served) on
  - city councils
  - township boards
  - zoning commissions
  - school boards
  - church boards
  - service clubs
  - chambers of commerce/visitor bureaus

In considering possibilities, broaden your thinking beyond people whom you feel might be especially keen on your mission. Other possibilities are people who are keenly interested in philanthropy or nonprofit governance, feel a calling to public service or civic engagement, or are retired, needing a venue for sharing their career expertise. Compiling this list will take more time and effort, but once you have it the procedure is the same.

The Application and Interview

When you find someone willing to be considered for the position, send them an *application packet*. This should include:

- A cover letter.
- The job description.
- The bylaws.

- A biographical information form .
- Your brochure.
- Any other literature deemed possibly of interest.

The biographical information request form should be designed only to capture contact information and facts reflecting the candidate's suitability for the position. A formal and invasive form that looks like job application will risk consternation and discouragement. The form should indicate your intention of publishing the information when presenting your candidates for election or appointment. A well-written resume can be accepted in lieu of your form; however the form should provide space for the prospect's signature, indicating their agreement to stand for election or appointment. An example of a biographical information form is provided on the *SfS* website.

Invite the prospect to your next board or committee meeting, for the purpose of getting to know you and your colleagues, to familiarize themselves further with your organization, and to be informally interviewed. Information missing from the candidate's biographical information can be obtained at this meeting. As a special courtesy, consider holding this meeting at a location convenient to your prospective volunteer.

This meeting should not have the feel of a formal interview or interrogation, although its purpose is to broaden each side's understanding of the other. If the candidate has any questions or reservations, this is the opportunity to answer such concerns. If during this meeting it becomes evident that the candidate might eventually find the position not comfortable for them, this is the best time to face up to that issue. Ego protection should be a careful concern in that case. After a thoughtful discussion of the requirements of the position and their personal interests and abilities, candidates may ask to be excused from further consideration, and that decision can be accepted gracefully. Hard-nosed evaluations resulting in unilaterally withdrawn nominations are guaranteed to produce enduring hard feelings.

The Transition Process

As mentioned above, it would be a very unusual occurrence for a committee-recommended nominee or appointee to ultimately be rejected. Smoothly and effectively easing one person out of a job and another person into it becomes possible when nominations and selections are made well in advance of the time the position formally changes hands, giving the two time to work together.

The practical implications involve continuity and reliability. When there is no real transition process, the risk is that *new brooms make clean sweeps*. Replacements are likely to change methods and procedures to those they are more familiar and comfortable with if the existing systems are not well understood. Lack of understanding can also lead to costly and embarrassing mistakes.

Learning the ropes is not merely a matter of teaching a new hand the nuts and bolts of the job, but also bringing them into the team with an understanding and appreciation of the organization's corporate culture. It is important for board and staff members to get along, and that's difficult when newly inducted people bring in baggage from past experiences, without accommodating the reality that organizations often have their own unique culture and ways of doing things, and all of them can be best.

As a final consideration, abruptly changing job-holders with no thought about transition issues will affect both the person leaving the job, and the one taking over in emotionally negative ways. For the person leaving the job, the message is that nobody cares much about what they know or think, or that people think their job was simple enough that even a chimpanzee could do it. The lack of an opportunity to share their knowledge and expertise with their replacement suggests that the work they were doing and their years of service wasn't really much appreciated. The person taking over will be similarly affected. If they get the feeling that most think the position isn't one that merits much concern, they might not be moved to engage it with energy and diligence. Or they might well be moved to conclude that the organization is obviously lame (amateurishly inconsiderate) when it comes to such matters, giving rise to some concern about the wisdom of their involvement.

A well-planned transition process says *Thank you!* to the outgoing job holder, and is the best way to cordially welcome and successfully break-in new help. The lack of any meaningful effort towards these ends is guaranteed to get things off to a bad start.

Finding People for Casual Activities

Broad-based recruitment methods are appropriate when you need people for jobs that do not involve decision-making or supervisory responsibilities. These include regular jobs, such as serving as a receptionist, tour guide or custodian, or jobs connected with special activities or events. Where you seek help and what you ask for depends upon your needs. Retired seniors are good prospects for regular jobs. Teenagers are usually a good choice for help with outdoor activities or children's events.

Your membership always has first dibs, so posting is mandatory. Announce the needs in your newsletters, email notification system, web site and by word-of-mouth.

Beyond that, advertising isn't likely to be very productive of prospective volunteers, but you may wish to employ free resources, such as community bulletin boards in retail stores, senior centers, churches, schools and city or township halls, as appropriate.

If your needs can be met by a group, other organizations will often be eager to participate. You might consider approaching groups such as:

- Other nonprofits – related or not.
- Church based senior or youth groups.
- Service clubs – Kiwanis, Rotary, Eagles, Elks, Moose.
- The local Sierra Club chapter.
- Boy scouts, girl scouts, FFA or 4H club.
- Martial arts academies.
- Corporate employee groups – labor unions.
- Police – fire fighters.
- Military groups.
- 12-step groups – AA, Alanon.
- Sheriff's departments and parole boards.
- Juvenile courts.

Whoa! Alcoholics, parolees and juvenile offenders?

We all suffer the pain of being imperfect, some of us getting tripped up while being more imperfect than usual. That doesn't necessarily mean we're bad, irresponsible, undependable, without any useful skills or undeserving of respect and opportunities. When bad things happen in the lives of good people, they're often sentenced to perform a number of hours of public service as an alternative to spending time behind bars. That can be a good incentive for volunteering. Depending on the work you have to offer, you might find opportunities to do two goods for the price of one.

Volunteers should always be identified using a simple application or registration form, and the time they contribute should also be documented. Filling out forms is not usually a task eagerly embraced by volunteers, so these requirements should be no more rigorous than absolutely necessary. Templates for simple forms suitable for these purposes are provided on the *SfS* website. The relevance of a minimal application form is readily understood by most people, so there is little resistance to providing such information. Filling out forms to document how people spent their time meets with less resistance when volunteers understand that for your organization's charitable purposes, their time is as valued as money donated. Both figure into the total good you are doing. You are not simply collecting data for administrative purposes. With this understanding, volunteers will usually be eager to record their contribution.

— ❧ —

Award and Conquer

Having started out with an anecdote about Napoleon, let us end with another. Napoleon is famous for uttering, *"Give me enough ribbons to place on the tunics of my soldiers and I can conquer the world!"* He was also big on medals, having commissioned more than 2,300 different awards during his reign.

The best way to show your appreciation for volunteers, whether board members, staff or casual workers, is to provide a richly rewarding overall experience. Some of the ways you can ensure that are –

- preparation – prepare the site or workspace and have needed supplies and materials available – don't waste volunteers' time by keeping them waiting

- cordiality – make introductions all around and provide a tour of the site or workplace – have refreshments, break and toilet facilities readily available and make sure you point them out

- benchmarks – be clear about the purpose of the activity and what's expected of them – explain the rules and how they'll be respected

- training and supervision – be sensitive about introducing people to the work, making sure they know what to do and how to do it – remain available to answer questions and help solve problems

- management – run things in a businesslike manner to demonstrate your appreciation of volunteers' time and skills – adhere to schedules, beginning and ending on time, allowing people to plan their day around your activity

- appreciation – praise jobs well done (a simply thank you often suffices) – publicly present certificates of appreciation, feature articles about accomplishments in your newsletters and, as appropriate, in news releases to the media.

To find out more about printing your own certificates, review Section 6, "Desktop Publishing." If you want to pass out medals, you can do that too. Lapel pins are nice, and can easily be procured online at very reasonable prices. For volunteers exiting board or staff positions, engraved presentation plaques are a thoughtful gesture, and are apt to subsequently be displayed with pride on mantles or in offices. They are also inexpensive and commonly available from a variety of online sources.

— ❧ —

The Secret of Long-Term Success

Burnout is just another word for *ingratitude*. Recognition fuels volunteer engines; they'll run for a while on fumes, but then they die. Once unhappy and disillusioned volunteers leave, it's always very difficult to get them back. What's even worse; negative word-of-mouth can easily undermine even the most diligent endeavors to attract quality replacements.

Nothing succeeds like success. A well-managed volunteer program is its own best recruiting and retention tool. A few good words by present and former participants is often all that's needed to bring new sign-ups.

Citing Napoleon one last time, he asserted "An army marches on its stomach." In a similar vein, one might say, "Volunteers are what makes small NPOs go."

— ❧ —

FriendsOfTheManitous.Org

Welcome!

Friends of the Manitous

Important Announcement

Ha quande lingues coalesce. Li grammatica de coalescent lingues. Li nov lingua franca va esse

Exciting Plan

Lorem ipsum dolor sit amet, consetetur sadipscing labore et dolore magna aliquyam erat, sed diam et ea rebum. Stet clita kasd gubergren, no sea ipsum dolor sit amet, consetetur sadipscing elitr, dolore magna aliquyam erat, sed diam voluptua rebum. Stet clita kasd gubergren.

Proud Accomplishment

No sea takimata sanctus est Lorem ipsum dolor sadipscing elitr, sed diam nonumy eirmod tempor sed diam voluptua. At vero eos et accusam et justo no sea takimata sanctus est Lorem ipsum dolor

Special Citation

Duis autem vel eum iriure dolor in hendrerit eu feugiat nulla facilisis at vero eros et accumsan et zzril delenit augue duis dolore te feugait nulla

Doing I.T. **9**

© 2007, FriendsOfTheManitous
All trademarks and registered trademarks appearing on

Al Gore did not invent the Internet;
neither did Bill Gates.

— 🌿 —

9
Doing I.T.

I.T. ("ahy-tee"): Information Technology

*The new information technology ...
Internet and email ... have
practically eliminated the physical
costs of communications.*
— Peter Drucker
Management Theorist

*The number one benefit of information technology
is that it empowers people to do what they want to
do. It lets people be creative. It lets people be
productive. It lets people learn things they didn't
think they could learn before, and so in a sense, it's
all about potential.*

— Steve Ballmer - CEO of Microsoft

An Internet presence is essential. A majority of U.S. households are now connected to the Internet, and over 198-million Americans are regular users. They're online doing business, enjoying entertainment, researching, shopping and communicating with each other. According to the U.S. Census Bureau, the most popular uses are:

- 88.3% – email
- 78.1% – information on products and services
- 67.4% – news, weather, sports
- 54.2% – purchasing products and services

And they're doing it conveniently and fast. Dial-up is out. Full-time high speed broadband connections now keep the majority of IT users within a mouse-click of whatever they need to do online. In fact, web surfing is almost as fast and convenient as working with information stored on the hard drive of one's own computer.

Every NPO, no matter how small, needs at least a bare-bones website. Most prospects, clients and interested third parties will check you out on the Web, and they'll expect to find at least a description of who you are, what you do, and how they can contact you. Members will expect to be able to email you and receive email from you, and they'll check your site for current information about what's going on.

The Internet is no El Dorado. Making your organization accessible to over a billion Internet users worldwide is not going to make you special. However, not being found on the Web will:

> *An information superhighway is being built in America, and those who have the requisite wheels will be transported to a dreamland of information sources. But those who lack the means will be left behind, consigned to look on while others access data that lead to contacts, jobs, power and, presumably, a better life.*
>
> *— Eli Noam, Columbia University Graduate School of Business*

━━ ✿ ━━

Instant Website – No More Excuses

If you don't happen to be very net savvy, don't let that discourage you. You can put a web site together for your organization, launch it and maintain it. You can handle its email. It won't be difficult, and won't take very long. This section will show you how.

Continue on, and you'll have an attractive, professional-looking, simple but fully extensible web site online within forty-eight hours, and for less than $50.

If that sounds too good to be true, it's only because you evidently haven't kept up to date. Not only can you have a web site for your organization online the day after tomorrow, the $50 will be your total cost for a whole year's service, including domain name registration and web hosting fees. Plus, you'll get a full-featured email server for your organization along with it.

But wait – there's more! Your web site will also have the capability of signing up new members, and receiving payments and contributions online.

Finally, *YOU* (or anyone else who is comfortable using a computer) can do it. You don't need any prior knowledge about web development, IT, web servers, protocols, or any of that. You won't need to learn FrontPage, Dreamweaver or any other expensive and complicated Web publishing program.

You'll work with your web pages using a simple text editor, preferably the NoteTab Pro program. If you can work with images in a program like PaintShop Pro or IrfanView, you'll be able to customize your pages with your organization's logo. Then you'll publish your site using CoreFTP Lite, the FTP utility that works something like Windows Explorer, letting you work with your files and folders on the remote web server just as if it was another hard drive on your own computer. If you have yet to download these software tools, do so now. Refer to Section 1 to find how.

All ready? Let's do I.T.!

The *SfS* Website Template

A template for a bare-bones web site is provided on the *SfS* website. It's simple, but nice looking and professionally done, and it's almost ready to go.

To get your site up and running, you'll do this:

1. choose a domain name for your organization
2. create an account with a hosting service
3. customize the pages for your own organization
4. upload your site to the web server
5. set up your email account(s)
6. set up a PayPal account
7. test your site, online form, PayPal link and email

Download the *SfS* Website Template

Download the website template from
http://www.solutionsforsecretaries.com/examples/9/sfswebsitetemplate.zip

Enter this URL in your browser's address box, and the download should begin automatically. When asked whether to open or save this file, choose *Save* and designate a location (such as "C:\temp").

1. Find the downloaded *sfswebsitetemplate.zip* file.
2. Right-click it and select *Extract Here*.
3. Click and drag the "OurSite.Org" folder to C:\.

The entire website is contained in the folder "OurSite.Org" It has seven pages and six sub-directories:

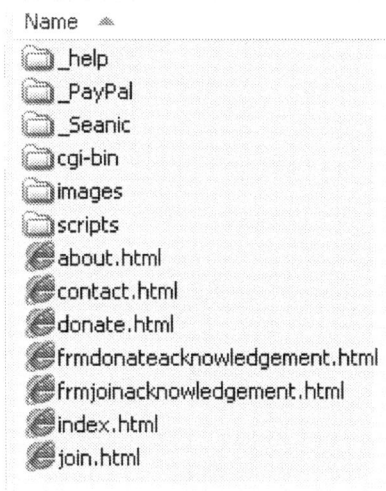

```
Name ▲
📁 _help
📁 _PayPal
📁 _Seanic
📁 cgi-bin
📁 images
📁 scripts
📄 about.html
📄 contact.html
📄 donate.html
📄 frmdonateacknowledgement.html
📄 frmjoinacknowledgement.html
📄 index.html
📄 join.html
```

- _help – contains auxiliary and readme files
- _PayPal – contains saved button code and a link to PayPal's site
- _Seanic – saved information about your hosting service
- cig-bin – contains the script and readme for your sign-up form
- images – contains images and graphics used on your pages
- scripts – contains style definitions and javascript for your pages
- about.html – information about your organization
- contact.html – your contact information
- donate.html – online payments and contributions
- frmdonateacknowledgement.html – a utility page
- frmjoinacknowledgement.html – a utility page
- index.html – your home page
- join.html – online membership sign-up form

Choose a Domain Name

Stations on the Internet are assigned numeric "IP addresses" (Internet Protocol). These are four-part arrays such as "192.168.0.1" or "192.168.0.254". To make things easier for humans to get this right, a system of domain names has evolved. For example, "disney.com" is easier to remember and enter than "199.181.132.250". When you enter a domain name in your browser's address box and click the *Go* button, your request is sent first to a DNS computer, also known as a "name server," which looks up the corresponding IP address, then passes it on. Your request will eventually reach a computer somewhere on the Internet having that unique IP address.

Your web site will be hosted from a computer known as a "web server," and will also have a specific IP address. You'll need to know what this is in order to enable a security feature in the program that services your online sign-up form, but otherwise you'd never need to know anything about IP addresses. Instead, you can define your own Internet address by choosing a domain name. That will be your address on the Internet, and your hosting service will take care of getting it into the DNS database. It'll then be your permanent Web address, and also the root of your email addresses.

The top-level domains are:

- commercial – yahoo.com, ups.com, google.com
- country – bmw.co.uk, daimler-benz-stiftung.de, toyota.co.jp
- educational – harvard.edu, stanford.edu, unl.edu
- government – ca.gov, nps.gov, whitehouse.gov
- military – army.mil, af.mil
- network – ameritech.net, att.net
- organizational – unitedway.org, redcross.org

You're free to use *.com*, *.net* or *.org*, but nonprofits should, and usually do, choose the *.org* domain.

The part of your domain name on the left side of the dot is called your "host name." You may choose anything that makes sense to you, ideally something that will be easy for your users to remember. The only rule is that what you choose must be different than any other host name in the .org domain. If, as an example, you are the "Pleasantville Community Partners," you might try "pcp.org". You'll no doubt find this is already in use, so consider alternatives; for example "pcpartners.org", "pleasantville.org", "pcpartners.org", "PleasantvillePartners.org" or even something as long as "PleasantvilleCommunityPartners.org" (domain names are not case-sensitive).

You must make your final decision when you create an account with the hosting service Seanic.net. However, you can see if the name you've chosen is available right now by going to –

http://www.seanic.net/system/whois?

> ❧ Note: when "domainname.org" appears in the following discussions, it is meant to be a placeholder for the domain name you'll select for your organization. Always substitute your actual domain name in place of "domainname.org".

Enter the host name you've chosen in the box, set the domain selector at ".org" and click *Check Domain*. You'll probably quickly discover that most common choices have already been registered by someone, so you might decide to take a time out to come up with a list of alternative choices. When you get a positive result for a domain name you like, click the *Click here to set up your new website …* link.

> ❧ Note: Before settling on a name that happens to be available in the ".org" domain, check out the same host name in the ".com" and ".net" domains. If there are any such sites, check them out to see if their content might be competitive or considered offensive to your prospective visitors., keeping in mind that they are likely to occasionally type "domainname.com", instead of "somainname.org." Think also about other likely errors. For example, Microsoft's "www.hotmail.com" provides the Web's most popular free email service. Kid's who mistakenly type "www.hotmale.com" in their browser's address bar will surely be embarrassed if Mom or Dad happens to be looking over their shoulder as that page appears on the screen!

Create a Hosting Account

There are lots of hosting services, with a variety of price structures. Seanic.net is recommended solely on the basis of price and performance, and several years of reliable service with several of my own web sites. (I have no formal or informal business connection to, or any other special arrangement with Seanic.net.)

Having clicked on the above link, you'll arrive at the Seanic sign-up page.

In the Domain Name form –

1. Your chosen domain name should appear in the *Domain Name** box.
2. Select *New Domain Registration*.

In the *Account Information* form –

3. Select *Standard Linux Hosting Plan (5,000 MB)*.
4. Enter a *Username*.
5. Enter a *Password*.
6. Open the "logon.txt" file in your "_Seanic" subfolder and record the username and password you entered. Save it.
7. Select *No* FrontPage 2000/2002 Extensions.
8. Under *Add-Ons/Extras*, check *None*.

In the *Contact Information* form –

9. Fill in the fields with your personal information. Seanic will send important setup information to the email address you provide here.

10. Click *Submit Account Registration* – a confirmation screen will appear showing the selections you have made and the information you entered.

    a. To make corrections or revisions, use your browser's *back* function to return to the previous form.

    b. If everything appears to be correct, touch [Ctrl+A] to select everything, then touch [Ctrl+C] to copy it to the clipboard.

    c. Open the "originalorder.txt" file in your "_Seanic" subfolder, the touch [Ctrl+V] to paste this information. Save it.

11. Click *Please Click to Continue* – the secure payment form appears.

In the WorldPay secure payment form –

12. Select the desired language and currency, then choose which credit card you wish to use.

13. Fill in your credit card information, then click *Make Payment*.

14. The payment confirmation screen appears. Touch [Ctrl+A], then [Ctrl+C].

15. Open the "paymentconfirmation.txt" file in your "_Seanic" subfolder, and then touch [Ctrl+V] to copy the payment confirmation. Save it.

16. All done!

Customizing the *SfS* Website Template

The website template provides seven application-ready HTML (HyperText Markup Language) pages:

- index.html – your home page
- about.html – information about your organization
- contact.html – your contact information
- join.html – online membership sign-up form
- donate.html – online payments and contributions
- frmacknowledgement.html – for response page
- frmdonateacknowledgement.html – PayPal response page

These need to be customized for your organization. The CGI (Common Gateway Interface) script that handles the form on the "join.html" page also needs to be configured for your new domain. Here's how:

Make NoteTab your default web page editor

Unless told otherwise, Windows will usually use its own text editor, Notepad, as the default text editor and web page editor. NoteTab makes it easy to change this:

1. Open NoteTab.
2. Click the *Utilities* clipbook at the bottom of the screen.
3. The clipbook opens at the left side of the screen.
4. Scroll down to *NoteTab Shortcuts* and click these three items:
   a. *Add Send To Shortcut.*
   b. *Add to Edit HTML file type.*
   c. *Add IE Default HTML Editor.*
5. Press the F4 key to dismiss the Utilities clipbook.

Force Internet Explorer to Allow JavaScript

Double-click the "join.html" file in your OurSite.Org folder. Internet Explorer will launch the page, but might pop up a warning about running scripts. This page uses a small JavaScript routine to prevent the form's *Submit* button from being inadvertently activated if the user touches the <Enter> key while filling in the form. Like most JavaScripts, this script is harmless. If confronted with this nuisance, your options are two. You may simply cancel the warning bar whenever it appears, or turn this annoyance off by doing this:

1. Click *Tools* on the IE menu bar.
2. Click *Internet Options*, and then click the *Advanced* tab.
3. Scroll down to the *Security* section.
4. Check *Allow active content to run in files on my computer*.
5. Click *Apply*, and *OK*.

Customizing your Home Page

Double-click the "index.html" file in your "OurSite.Org" folder. The home page template will open in a browser window.

1. Right-click the window and select *View Source*.

2. NoteTab should open, and the underlying html code for the page should appear. If word-wrap is on, toggle it off by clicking the "W" or pressing [Ctrl+W]. You should see line numbers at the left side of the document. If not, click *View* on the menu bar and check *Line Numbers*.

3. Scroll down to the bottom of the document. On Lines 89 thru 106 you will find step-by-step instructions that will tell you how to customize this page.

   ❧ Note: Page descriptions are for search engines. The description may be used by the search engine in its results pages. Create a description that will be meaningful when it appears as a search result, which usually means terse; short and to the point.

   ❧ Hint: The space provided for your logo is 180 pixels wide by 240 pixels high. Your image need not have this same aspect ratio, but should not be wider than 180 pixels. Resize it in IrfanView or PaintShop Pro if needed.

   ❧ Hint: You probably already have the copy needed for items 5 thru 9. Check your bylaws and other literature. These subjects are just suggestions. You may put anything on this page you think might be of interest to visitors, including images. In the interest of time, you may wish to stick with these items for now, and revise after inspiration strikes later on.

Customizing the Other Pages

Edit the other six pages in the same way, following the instructions provided at the bottom of the source code on each page.

Configuring the FormMail Script

Double-click the "readme.txt" file in the "cgi-bin" subfolder, which will open that document in NoteTab. Then from within NoteTab open the "FormMail.pl" file, also found in the cgi-bin subfolder.

There are four user-configurable variables in the "Define Variables" box (line 25 to 56), usually only one of which needs to be changed for your domain and host. These are:

- $mailprog – this tells the scrip where the mail handling program is on your web server computer. The default location is usually correct, so you won't need to change anything here

- @referers – this important line tells the script who is eligible to use it. Enter your domain name and IP address. Replace "scriptarchive.com" with your own domain name, and replace "209.196.21.3" with your own IP address. Requests coming from any other domain or IP address will be rejected. This very important feature prevents spammers from exploiting your form to dispatch their junk email through your mail server.

    ᰔ Note: to discover your IP address, refer to the set-up email received from Seanic. It will tell you that until your domain name propagates through all the name servers, you may access your site using a temporary address, such as "http://domainname.org.seanic11.net". To get the corresponding IP address, click *Start* on your desktop, then *Run ...* and in the *Open* box enter this (using the URL Seanic provided):

    ping –t domainname.org.seanic11.net

    The ping utility will fetch repeated responses from the web server, showing your domain name and IP address. Copy your IP address. Then press [Ctrl+C] to close the RUN window.

- @recipients – defines who is eligible to receive email responses from the script. This is another feature designed to frustrate spammers who will try to hijack your form. Left as is, only email addresses on your domain will be able to receive responses from the "join.html" form. Leave it at that.

- @valid_ENV – limits the kinds of information about the server that may be requested with form results, and is another means of frustrating would-be spammers. This may be left as is.

Having configured the @referers variable, click the *Save As* button on the NoteTab toolbar or press [Shift+Ctrl+S] and save "FormMail.pl" as "customfm.cgi".

ᰔ Note: Renaming the script eliminates attempted attacks by email spammers, who search the Web looking for pages with forms pointed to "formmail.pl".

FormMail is a versatile script. If at some point you wish to take advantage of some of its more advanced features, study the readme.txt file to learn more.

FTP Your Site to the Web Server

Having customized the site for your use, it is now ready to send to the Web server. (If you have yet to download and install Core FTP Lite, do that now.) To start the program, double-click the icon for Core FTP Lite which you'll find on your desktop.

1. Initial setup questions
   a. Default FTP client? – answer "Yes."
   b. Use "notepad.exe" to edit ascii files? – answer "No."
2. Site Manager form
   a. Site Name: domainname.org (or whatever you wish).
   b. Host/IP/URL: domainname.org (your domain name).
   c. Username: per your seanic signup (see your _Seanic folder).
   d. Password: per your seanic signup (see your _Seanic folder).
   e. Click the *Advanced* button, then select *Directory/Folder.*
      i. Use the browse button to find your "OurSite.Org" folder.
      ii. Click *OK.*
   f. Click *Connect.*

You will observe things happening in the *activity window* (just below the main toolbar). The contents of your "OurSite.Org" folder will appear in the *local list view window* on the left side of the screen, and the contents of your root directory on the web server will appear in the *remote list view window* on the right side, as shown below. You are now connected directly to the seanic web server. Click the *Disconnect* button (two red outward-pointing arrows) above the remote list view window, and answer "Yes" to the "Disconnect?" question.

Filename	Size	Date	Permissions
<..>			
cgi-bin		03/18/07 20:05	drwxr-xr-x
index.html	40	03/20/07 14:53	-rw-r--r--

❧ Note: If you receive a red "Can't establish connection -->" message in the transfer window, click the *Site Manager* button (blue up/down arrows) on the main toolbar and recheck the information you entered in Step 2 above. If trying this soon after receiving the setup email from seanic.net, your domain name might not yet have propagated through the DNS network; enter the temporary domain name provided in the seanic email (e.g., domainname.org.seanic33.net).

Click the *Connect* button (two blue inward-pointing arrows) above the remote list view window, to reconnect to the server.

1. Highlight the "index.html" file in the remote list view window and click the *Delete* button above this window (the button with the large "X").

2. Highlight the seven files and the "images" and "scripts" folders in the local list view window, as shown here, and then click the *Upload* button above this window (blue right-pointing arrow) to copy these files and folders to the web server.

3. Double-click the "cgi-bin" folder in both windows. Highlight the "customfm.cgi" file in the left window and click the *Upload* button to transfer a copy of this file to the cgi-bin directory on the server.

Filename
..
cgi-bin
images
scripts
_help
_PayPal
_Seanic
about.html
contact.html
donate.html
frmdonateacknowledgement.html
frmjoinacknowledgement.html
index.html
join.html

4. Right-click the "customfm.cgi" file in the remote list view window, and select *properties*. Check the boxes as indicated below to set the file permissions at "755".

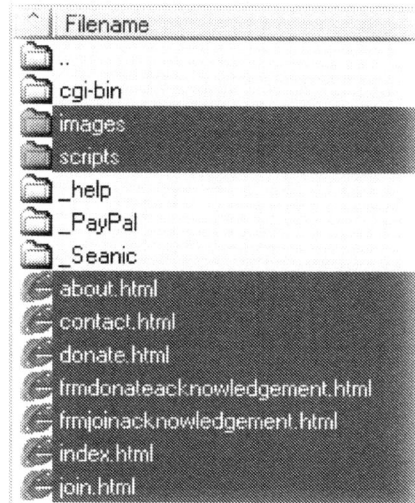

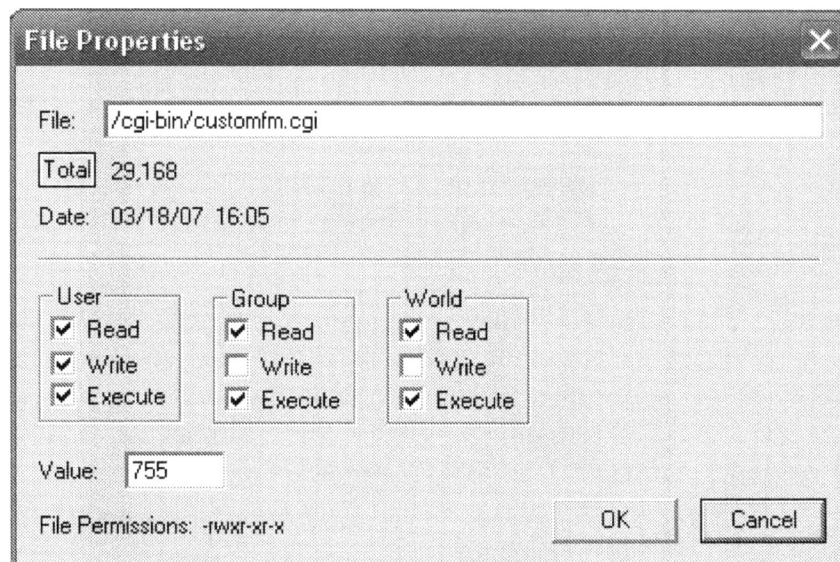

File Properties

File: /cgi-bin/customfm.cgi

[Total] 29,168

Date: 03/18/07 16:05

User	Group	World
☑ Read	☑ Read	☑ Read
☑ Write	☐ Write	☐ Write
☑ Execute	☑ Execute	☑ Execute

Value: 755

File Permissions: -rwxr-xr-x

[OK]   [Cancel]

5. To return to the next higher folder or directory in either window, click the *Up Directory* button above either window, or double-click the topmost folder..

6. Click the *Disconnect* button and close Core FTP Lite.

Set Up Your Email Server

To set up your email accounts, log on to your site's administrator's control panel using your web browser. Type this in the address bar of your browser (using your own domain name, of course):

http://www.domainname.org/admin/

1. Log on using your seanic username and password (the same ones you specified when setting up your hosting account.

2. Click *E-mail Manager*, and then click *E-mail Users*.

3. Click *Add New User*, and then fill in the *Add New Domain User* form.

   a. The "username" will be the first part of the user's email address and their logon username. For example, John Doe could be "jdoe", and John's email address will then be "jdoe@domainname.org". To retrieve his email, John will log in with a variant of his username; "jdoe%domainname.org".

   b. Enter the person's real name.

   c. Enter the password this person chose for their account. This will be used to retrieve their personal email from the server.

   d. Click *Add New User*. If you have more new accounts, continue to create them. Otherwise click *Cancel* to close the account setup form.

   e. Returning to the *User Manager – Domain Users* screen, you will see a list of all the accounts you have set up.

4. Click *E-mail Aliases*.

   a. Here you may arrange to have the mail server forward email sent to one address to an alternate email address. For example, if John Doe has a preexisting personal account, "jdoe@someother.net", his "jdoe@domainname.org" mail can be rerouted to "jdoe@someother.net".

   b. Your online form will send submitted responses to "webmaster@domainname.org" (using your actual domain name). There is no such address, although you could create a user called "webmaster" if you wanted to. Alternatively, you can just have any email received for this address sent to your personal email account. Simply enter "webmaster" in the first available *Email Address* box, then select your personal email address in the adjacent *Alias to User* box. Alternatively, you could have such mail forwarded to any email address outside of your domain by entering that address in the corresponding *or Forward to E-Mail* box.

    c. In the same manner, create a forwarding account for your PayPal messages, which will be sent to "payments@domainname.org" (using your actual domain name, of course). For the time being, have this address forwarded to your personal email account.

    d. The system has the capability of automatically replying to messages received. However, such canned responses are seldom useful or appreciated, so never check the *AutoReply* box.

    e. The system also has the capability of accepting any and all email addressed to your domain, even if no mailbox with that address exists. This is done by setting up an alias "default@domainname.org". This is not recommended, because it'll eventually turn your domain into a spam magnet, and you will receive lots of unwanted junk mail.

5. Click *Logout* to exit the administrator's control panel.

Set Up Your Desktop Email Program

    The illustrations on the following page show how to set up your email client to receive messages from your new personal email address. The examples refer to Outlook Express 6, but may be used as guidance for setting up any other email program. Please make note of these three important points:

- "yourname%domainname.org" is the logon for your email account (use the "%" character here instead of the "@" sign).

- Use the password associated with your personal email account, not the password for your hosting account.

- Because of the difficulty of policing thousands of users and the nuisance of email spammers, hosting services discourage the use of their servers to send user email. Therefore, use your regular outgoing SMTP mail server (the one provided by your regular internet service provider). Your organizational email will still be shown as originating from your organizational email account.

❧ Note: Encourage officers, directors and staff to create a domainname.org email account and use it for communications related to your organization's business and activities. Using private email accounts, especially free web-based accounts like hotmail, yahoo or gmail, will not project the professional and businesslike image you need to build for your organization.

❧ Hint: Setup instructions for other popular email clients are available online at http://www.seanic.net/support/mail.htm. Users who are not comfortable using an email client like Outlook, Outlook Express or Eudora can be directed to http://www.domainname.com/webmail/, your site's web based email client.

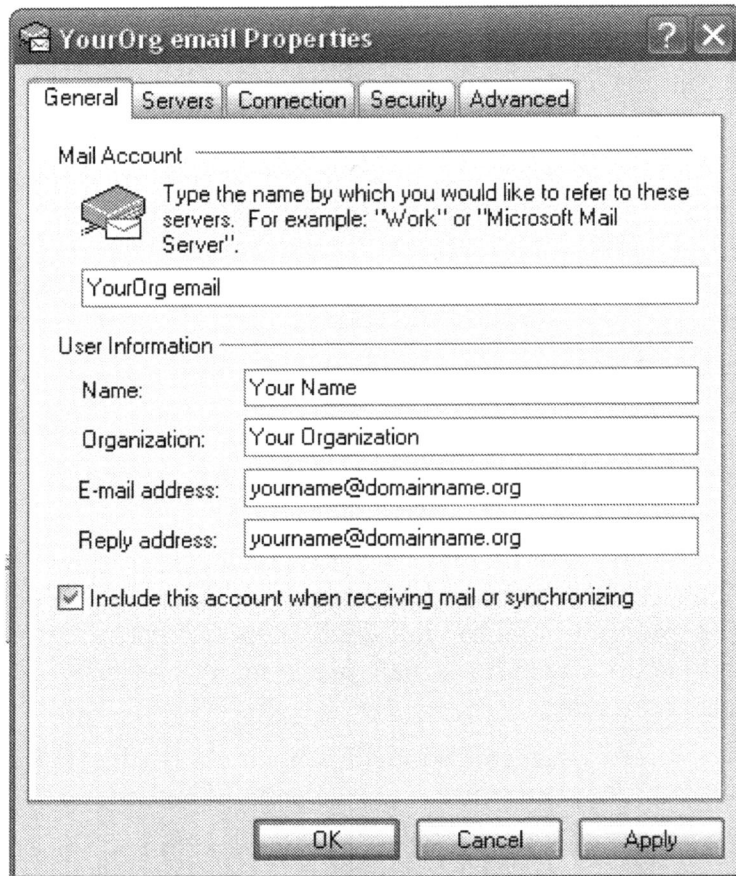

Set Up a PayPal Account

Your web site has the ability to receive payments and contributions online, using the PayPal payment processing system (a division of eBay). PayPal accounts are free. A small transaction fee will be deducted from each payment or donation.

A disadvantage is PayPal's requirement that that the account be linked to a real person, rather than an organizational entity. You can be that person, but when your term as Secretary expires and someone else takes over, it is very difficult to get PayPal to change the name on the account. For this reason, you might wish to use the name and address of your resident agent, rather than an elected or appointed director or staff person.

Money received by PayPal can be transferred directly to your organization's bank account; ordinarily your checking account. You will need your bank's routing number and your account number. To verify that the transfer system is properly set up, PayPal will attempt a couple of test transfers involving only a few cents each. You verify the setup by reporting the amounts of these test deposits back to PayPal. After that, you will be able to transfer funds in your PayPal account to your bank account. There is no charge for this service.

1. Go to http://www.paypal.com, and click the *Sign Up* link at the top of the page.

2. Select the country, if needed, then click the Start Now button in the *Premier Account* box. The *Create a PayPal Account* screen appears.

3. Fill in the form. Your email address and the password you choose will be used as your PayPal logon.

   a. Use "payments@domainname.org (using your domain name in place of "domainname") as the email address for this account, not your personal email address.

      ✤ Caution: This email address must exist, because PayPal will use it to send you a verification message. If necessary, return to Step 4.c. on the previous page and create the "payments@domainname.org" forwarding account.

   b. Open "logon.txt" in your _PayPal folder and record what you entered on this signup form.

4. Click the *I Agree. Create My Account* button at the bottom of the form. The email confirmation page appears.

5. At this point, PayPal will send a "Confirm Your Email Address" message to "payments@domainname.org", the address you provided as your contact email address. Open your email program, receive this message, and click on the *Click here to activate your account* link.

6. If you are not still logged in to PayPal, enter your password on the screen that appears. Otherwise the "Email Confirmed" page appears. Click *Continue*.

7. Your main account page appears. If you wish to do the set up for transfers to your bank account at this time, click the *Status: Unverified* link. The *Get Verified* page appears.

8. Click *Add Bank* button. The *Add a Bank Account* page appears. Fill out the form as directed, and then click *Continue*.

9. The "Confirm Your Bank Account" page appears.

10. If you have online access to your bank account, you can attempt the *Instant* confirmation method.

11. Otherwise select the *validating deposit* method and click *Continue*. The *Random Deposits* page appears explaining how that method works. After the random deposits appear in your bank account, log in to your PayPal account, click the *Confirm Bank Account* link and enter those amounts.

12. All done! Log out of PayPal.

Whenever anyone sends you money via PayPal, the system will send a message to the email address shown as the primary contact for your account. To move that money to your bank, log in to your PayPal account and click the *Withdraw* tab.

Testing Your Web Site

Enter your URL in your browser's address box to open your online home page. Click sequentially through the "About," "Contact," "Join," and "Donate" links at the bottom of the pages, inspecting each page for loading problems, missing images, dead links and any other visible problems.

Testing Your Form

Click the link to your "Join" page. Fill out the form, providing your personal email address, then click *Send*. The "Membership Sign-Up – Acknowledgement" page should appear.

⚜ Help: If an error message appears instead of the acknowledge page, either the "@referers" variable in the script was not correctly configured, the permissions were not correctly set, or the script was uploaded to the side in binary mode instead of ascii mode. Recheck the script configuration to make sure your domain name and IP address were correctly entered. Upload the script again, making sure that the *Auto Mode* button is clicked on the Core FTP toolbar. Check the properties of the server-side "customfm.cgi" file to verify that the permissions are set to "755".

If the acknowledgement page does not appear, review the source code of your "join.html" page, looking at your domain name as it appears on lines 58, 59, 60 and 61. Correct any errors.

Check your email. The information you entered in the form should have been emailed to "webmaster@domainname.org", which should have been forwarded to your personal mailbox.

⚜ Help: If the email does not appear, recheck your mail forwarding setup using your site's administrator control panel.

Testing Your PayPal Setup

Click to your "Donate" page. Click the *Donate* button. Your PayPal payment page should appear.

⚜ Help: Your "payments@domainname.org" remittance email address should show at the top of the page, and under the "Enter Payment Information" header. If not, edit the source of your "dontate.html" page to make sure your domain name is properly reflected on lines 55, 57 and 58.

1. Fill in the *Payment For* and *Price* boxes, entering "Dues" and "$10.00".

2. Click the *Continue* button at the bottom of the page. The *Billing Information* page appears.

3. Click the *Cancel and Return to Merchant* link at the bottom of the page. Your donation page reappears.

4. Users who complete the transaction are returned to the thank you page ("frmdonateacknowledgement.html") on your web site.

—— ⚜ ——

Towards a More Extensive Website

This completes the testing of your new site. You're probably surprised at having learned a lot more about web development than you ever expected to know, and feel good about accomplishing what you've achieved.

As it stands, your website will provide you with a credible presence on the Internet. Keep your information up to date, conscientiously answer your email, respond to membership information requests and gratefully acknowledge payments and donations. That would be sufficient.

But in time, you'll probably wish to add more content to your website. You can often create additional pages with the same look and feel quite easily simply by copying an existing page and changing the content in the body of the page. Adding links to your new page is easy – just use the links in the existing navigation bar as a guide, cutting and pasting to create another link that goes to your new page.

Any document you create in a word processor or as a desktop publishing project can be easily published to the Web by converting it to HTML or PDF format. HTML is preferred, because the file size is always much smaller and the document therefore downloads much faster. Use the Click-To-Convert program to create a very accurate HTML rendition of your original document. Many programs are now capable of creating PDF renditions.

Many people are afraid of hand coding, thinking that graphical web publishing tools like Microsoft FrontPage® will relieve them from the burden of having to learn anything about the coding of the pages they produce. Others belittle it as outdated and light weight – not capable of producing "kewl" content. Professional Web publishing tools are without question indispensable for large websites with lots of cross-linked content. But they are by no means easy to learn. For a small site, especially one built upon a good template, it's much easier to learn the few essentials one needs to know to manage the site manually, than it is to grasp the intricacies (and idiosyncrasies) of one of these highly capable products.

If you are not interested in getting into web publishing and development any further than you already have, consider recruiting a high school or college student as your organization's volunteer webmaster.

— ⚜ —

And the Answer Is ...

Are you still wondering just who did invent the Internet? If it wasn't Bill Gates or Al Gore, who was it?

The answer is, technically, the U.S. Government. The Internet was originally known as DARPANET; "DARPA" being an acronym for the Defense Department's "Defense Advanced Research Projects Agency." It was originally an attempt to securely link the Department with its supporting vendors and researchers, and was limited to rather quirky text-based communications provisions.

However, the Internet as we know it today was the invention of a young Englishman named Tim Berners-Lee, who in 1989, invented the World Wide Web, while working as a researcher at CERN, the European Particle Physics Laboratory. He wrote the first web client and server in 1990. Through his independent development of hyperlinks, a graphical user interface, and various supporting protocols, the Internet, which began as DARPANET in 1969, was changed almost overnight from a medium useful only to geeks and nerds, to the *information superhighway* we know it as today.

10
Conclusion

Failure is not an option!
NASA Slogan

— ✤ —

10
Conclusion

Helping Your Organization Continue to Thrive

This final section originally began with a discussion of the usual reasons small nonprofits fail. I deleted all that. It didn't seem a fitting topic for the conclusion of a book about making your organization look good.

Looking good, however, is only part of the game, and a top notch Secretary is only part of the team.

One of the keys to continuing success is *people*. The fortunes of your organization will rise and fall over the years according to its ability to recruit quality people for its volunteer board and staff. That doesn't necessarily mean influential people with experience and proven abilities. It can also mean people without impressive credentials, but who believe in the cause and are earnest about learning how to perform effectively in their role.

Another key is novelty and energy. Nothing stagnates like stagnation. Although change is inevitable, people remain generally averse to it. There's an old saying in retail, "If it's working, don't change it!" That's well worth keeping in mind, of course. But so is its flip side. When things aren't working anymore, it's time to embrace new ideas, and to do it with energy and enthusiasm.

The reluctance to try new things arises, perhaps, mainly from an abhorrence of error and failure. There's a wonderful song in the musical *"Chitty Chitty Bang Bang"* called *"The Roses of Success,"* which has these humorously inspiring lines –

For every big mistake you make be grateful! (Here, here!)
That mistake you'll never make again! (No sir!)
Every shiny dream that fades and dies,
generates the steam for two more tries!
(Oh) There's magic in the wake of a fiasco! (Correct!)
It gives you that chance to second guess! (Oh yes!)
Then up from the ashes, up from the ashes –
grow the roses of success!

A business person comes up with a great idea, makes a bundle and retires rich. People are in awe of that person's shrewdness. Nobody ever asks how many idiotic ideas preceded the one that worked.

The last man I worked for had lots of dumb ideas, some of which I was able to talk him out of, and others which he launched into with vigor, seemingly with the intention of seeing how much money he could squander before finally coming to his senses. He had lots of ideas. Most of them fizzled; a few didn't. He claimed to have started that business with only $1,500. He sold out twenty years later for $8.5-million and played for the rest of his life, spending lots of that money doing nice things for his old home town.

When it comes to your organization itself, "failure is not an option" might be an appropriate point of view. However, in the ordinary course of managing its affairs, keep in mind that human beings – you, your board and staff included – are all inherently fallible. You can't be right all of the time. Many of the things you try will prove fruitless, and may look rather silly after the fact.

And so a third key is to honor your humanity, upholding everyone's right to fallibility. You can't win successes if you're not willing to allow for failures. You'll never become a hero if you're afraid of looking like a fool.

— ❧ —

Additional Resources

Keep learning, and share what you know. A mind that is engaged and challenged stays healthy, inquisitive and creative, so this is good advice for everyone (and especially for seniors, who are apt to make up the majority on volunteer boards). There are lots of opportunities:

On the *SfS* Website

This book's supporting website, www.solutionsforsecretaries.com, has a forum where you can ask questions, provide answers to the questions others ask, and share your own unique ideas. Please do participate.

On the World Wide Web

There are thousands of websites offering all sorts of advice for nonprofit organizations. For example:

- *Independent Sector* is a leadership forum for charities, foundations, and corporate giving programs, committed to advancing the common good in America and around the world. See www.independentsector.org.

- *The National Council of Nonprofit Associations* (NCNA) is the network of state and regional nonprofit associations serving over 20,000 members across the country. NCNA links local organizations to a national audience through state associations and helps small and midsize nonprofits manage and lead more effectively, collaborate and exchange solutions, engage in critical policy issues affecting the sector, and achieve a greater impact in their communities. Visit www.ncna.org.

- *GuideStar's* mission is to improve philanthropy and nonprofit practice with information, serving more than 5-million users a year. In addition to serving as a central online source of information about specific organizations (including yours), GuideStar offers timely and relevant articles and reports of interest to nonprofit directors and managers. Find them at www.guidestar.org.

- *IRS* – the Internal Revenue Service offers a portal especially for nonprofits with a variety of definitive information on taxes and regulations, and immediate access to forms. These resources can be found at www.irs.gov/charities/.

- *Action Without Borders* aims to be a world-wide community networking resource. The website offers useful user-contributed information on a wide variety of topics, and the opportunity to add your information to its list of over 67,000 organizations. Go to www.idealist.org.

- *BoardSource* seeks to increase the effectiveness of nonprofit organizations by strengthening boards of directors offering consulting, helpful online articles, publications, tools, and a membership program. Visit www.boarsdource.org.

- *USA.gov for Nonprofits* provides official information and services from the U.S. government on grants, loans and other assistance, management and operations concerns and tax issues. The website is www.usa.gov

- *TechSoup.org* provides a range of technology services for nonprofits, including news and articles, discussion forums, and discounted and donated technology products. You'll find all this at www.techsoup.org

- *Nonprofit Good Practice Guide*, a project of the Dorothy A Johnson Center for Philanthropy and Nonprofit Leadership, offers newcomers and seasoned veterans information designed to help them manage their nonprofit organizations efficiently and effectively. Explore ten topic areas which provide articles, tips, glossaries and other resources at www.npgoodpractice.org

These are worth noting as "favorites," but by no means represent a complete list.

In Your Local Area

Workshops and seminars on topics of interest to nonprofit managers and directors are frequently offered throughout the year in most areas. These are usually offered by government, foundations affiliated with universities and colleges, or other nonprofits. Fees for these events are usually very reasonable if, indeed, there is any charge at all.

It's not always easy to be aware of these opportunities, since publicity is usually limited to website announcements and email notification lists. Towards getting connected to local notification lists, make sure your organization is registered with GuideStar.org and Idealist.org. Once you become an occasional participant in such events, notifications about future events will seem to have ways of finding you without much further effort.

While the subjects of these events are often of marginal utility, you're sure to discover that a more important value is networking. You'll invariably come away from every workshop or seminar with something worthwhile that usually isn't directly related to the purpose of the event; usually a new and potentially useful acquaintance or idea.

Your Future in Philanthropy

It has been said that every successful businessman goes through three stages: democracy, autocracy and philanthropy.

Philanthropy has been defined as "giving something or performing benevolent actions with no expectation of acknowledgement or reward." Other definitions are apt to mention altruism or selflessness. One could argue there is no such thing as either; that the definition quoted above becomes valid only with the insertion of the word *tangible* before the word *reward*. Do people ever do anything without expecting some sort of personal benefit?

Our culture engenders an appetite for tangible things, and as we grow up it trains us how to acquire them. Then we are valued according to how successfully we play that game. For most of us, the futility of that eventually becomes apparent, the game being a "no win" deal, since enough is never enough, and no matter how much is achieved, it never provides the promised security, happiness and contentment. Is it any wonder that the final stage for those who succeed best at this game is to give away what they've won?

Philanthropists readily affirm that the returns from employing their personal wealth and influence in philanthropic pursuits far exceed any satisfactions ever associated with its original acquisition. That opportunity is available to you too.

Few of us have enough money to fund a foundation. The wealth you can devote to philanthropic purposes probably won't consist of money. It'll consist of the knowledge and experience you've acquired over a lifetime, plus your personal time and energy ... the same things you used to exchange for tangible returns like wages, salaries, professional fees or profits, and the things those earnings could pay for. Now you'll be giving them away in return for intangible things better than anything money can buy.

In all times and all places there have always been and will always be needs that offer little or no profit potential and which, were it not for the nonprofit sector, would go unmet. There are needs in your community right now and, without doubt, at least several little NPO's in dire need of what you have to offer. Why restrict your interests to just one?

If you wish to continue in philanthropy, there is no limit to what you can personally achieve.

— ❧ —

Index

About the Author
Gene L Warner

For the past thirty years, Gene has worked as a self-trained, self-employed electronics engineer/entrepreneur. He is the founder of Warner Instruments, provider of special purpose temperature controls and alarm systems to industry under the well-known *FireRight Controls* brand name, since 1976.

Having finally given in to "semi-retirement," he turned his attention to volunteer work, serving during the past few years on boards and committees of small nonprofit organizations, and lending his experience as a practical and resourceful innovator to show how these small groups can more effectively leverage their limited financial and experiential resources.

Mr Warner lives with his wife and youngest daughter in Grand Haven, Michigan USA. The Warner's have four other adult children, all of whom have careers independent of the family business.

———— ❧ ————

BoysMind Books
PO Box 604
Grand Haven, MI 49417-0604 USA
www.boysmindbooks.com

www.ingramcontent.com/pod-product-compliance
Lightning Source LLC
Chambersburg PA
CBHW080908220326
41598CB00034B/5515